Polly Evans studied modern languages at Cambridge University before joining the editorial team at a leading London publisher. After four years she moved to Hong Kong where she worked as a journalist, before embarking on her epic journey around Spain. She now lives in London.

D0366438

IT'S NOT ABOUT THE TAPAS

Polly Evans

BANTAM BOOKS

LONDON · NEW YORK · TORONTO · SYDNEY · AUCKLAND

IT'S NOT ABOUT THE TAPAS
A BANTAM BOOK : 0 553 81556 3

First publication in Great Britain

PRINTING HISTORY
Bantam edition published 2003

5 7 9 10 8 6 4

Copyright © Polly Evans 2003

Map © Neil Gower 2003

The right of Polly Evans to be identified as the author of this work has been asserted in accordance with sections 77 and 78 of the Copyright Designs and Patents Act 1988.

Extract from *The Basque History of the World* by Mark Kurlansky published by Vintage. Used by permission of the Random House Group Limited.
Quote from *Tour de France, Tour de Souffrance* by Albert Londres © 1996 Le Serpent à Plumes.
Extracts from *Homage to Catalonia* by George Orwell (copyright © George Orwell 1937) by permission of Bill Hamilton as the Literary Executor of the Estate of the Late Sonia Brownell Orwell and Secker & Warburg Ltd.
Extract by Herbert R Southworth from *Guernica! Guernica! A Study of Journalism, Propaganda and History*, © 1977 The Regents of the University of California.
Extracts from *Barcelona* by Robert Hughes published by Harvill. Used by permission of The Random House Group Limited.
The Letters of Private Wheeler/ed. B H Liddell Hart, Windrush Press used by permission of The Orion Publishing Group Ltd.
Extract from *Dali, Un diari: 1919–1920*, published by Barcelona, Ediciones 62, 1994.
Extract from *Franco* © 1993 Paul Preston used by permission of HarperCollins Publishers Ltd. Copyright in the customised version vests in Bantam (UK), Luitingh (Holland), Goldmann (Germany).
Extract from *Life with Picasso* by Françoise Gilot and Carlton Lake used by permission of Time Warner Books UK.
Extracts from *South from Granada* by Gerald Brenan used by permission of Penguin Books copyright © Gerald Brenan 1963.
Quotations by Frederico García Lorca © Herederos de Federico García Lorca. All rights reserved. For information regarding rights and permissions, please contact lorca@artslaw.co.uk or William Peter Kosmas, Esq, 8 Franklin Square, London W14 9UU.
Extract from *The Story of Spain* by Mark Williams used by permission of Santana Books.

Every effort has been made to obtain the necessary permissions with reference to copyright material, and should there be any omissions in this respect we apologize and shall be pleased to make the appropriate acknowledgements in any future editions.

Set in 11/13pt Times New Roman by
Phoenix Typesetting, Burley-in-Wharfedale, West Yorkshire.

Bantam Books are published by Transworld Publishers,
61–63 Uxbridge Road, London W5 5SA,
a division of The Random House Group Ltd,
in Australia by Random House Australia (Pty) Ltd,
20 Alfred Street, Milsons Point, Sydney, NSW 2061, Australia,
and in New Zealand by Random House New Zealand Ltd,
18 Poland Road, Glenfield, Auckland 10, New Zealand
and in South Africa by Random House (Pty) Ltd,
Endulini, 5a Jubilee Road, Parktown 2193, South Africa.

Printed and bound in Great Britain by
Cox & Wyman Ltd, Reading, Berkshire.

Papers used by Transworld Publishers are natural, recyclable products made from wood grown in sustainable forests. The manufacturing processes conform to the environmental regulations of the country of origin.

914.6
E
05-05

To Mum and Dad

Acknowledgements

I'd like to thank Jane Gregory and Broo Doherty for their guidance, wisdom and good humour, Francesca Liversidge for teaching me pretty much everything I know about books, and everyone else at Transworld for teaching me the rest.

Thanks to Mum and Dad for the roof, food, drink and company, and Tim and Sophie for offering entirely opposing opinions on my first draft and so convincing me to call in the professionals.

Finally, thanks to Peter Record for encouraging me to take up writing in the first place and for listening sympathetically when I got cross with the computer.

Contents

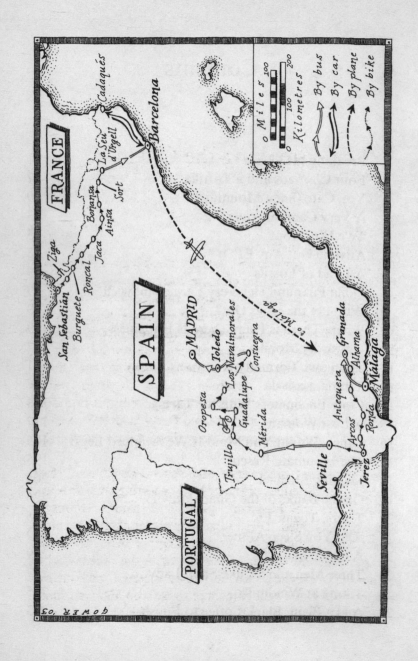

1

Breaking the Chain

I had to get out of Hong Kong.

The city was going crazy, and it was taking me down with it. The second economic crisis in four years was looming. The property boom had bust; the stock market was plummeting and brokers without bonuses were hurling themselves from high windows and making a nasty mess on the streets below. On the pavements, the hordes scurried, shoved and elbowed their way through the summer smog, screeching into their mobile phones in high-volume Cantonese like slowly strangled turkeys. Over the border in big, bad China, the superannuated Party leaders looked on bemused at their new dominion, at this petulant beast called capitalism.

In the market place, fruit and vegetables festered. Fish flipped over the edges of their plastic washing-up bowls and writhed on the blistering tarmac. Tensions simmered and tempers boiled. The stallholders settled their arguments with Chinese kitchen knives, the chopper being the Hong Konger's second-favourite weapon after the pointy end of an elbow, while the triads nervously fingered their tattoos and lopped off the little fingers of those who annoyed them.

In the alleyway beneath my flat, my neighbours tried to

improve their chances in these uncertain times by burning offerings on the bonfires of that summer's Hungry Ghost festival. The stock market could no longer be relied upon to provide riches so they turned to their ancestors instead. The smoke wisped its way past my windows and up to the spirit world carrying the charred remains of paper money, paper sports cars, paper Nike trainers, paper Big Macs and even paper Nokia 8310 phones, complete with paper batteries. Hong Kong is a material town, even in its spirit incarnation, and it doesn't do to antagonize the ghosts with last year's model.

Over in the office where I worked, tucked away among the antique shops of Hollywood Road, life was no less colourful. I was working as an editor on a weekly magazine. We covered the action-packed life of that non-stop, neon-flashing city; we tried to be incisive, quirky, offbeat, ahead of the curve. It didn't always work.

'This is the most fuckin', *godawful* PIECE OF SHIT that I have seen in ten years,' the publisher screamed at us one day, clutching that week's offering in his hand and shaking it violently as though he were trying to break its neck. The glass walls of his office shuddered; we editors looked sadly at our feet. Most of the men in our office were either gay or in therapy, in many cases both. They weren't afraid to find an outlet for their emotions, to clench their perfectly pert buttocks in indignation, to puff out their tightly T-shirted pecs, to squeal and stamp their cross little designer-shod feet. I was a straight woman; I couldn't afford a shrink. I dreamed of sitting, completely alone, under a solitary, leafy tree where nobody would raise their voice to so much as a whisper. One thing was clear: I needed a change of scene.

I decided to go to Spain. I knew the country and I spoke the language after a fashion, even if my attempts did make the locals laugh out loud. I'd even lived there for a while when, as a university student studying Spanish, I'd been required to spend a year abroad. I knew how to order a beer; I could even ask for different sizes depending on the level of alcoholic refuge the moment demanded. I vaguely understood the words on a menu. Spain would be a nice, restful destination, I thought. It would present nothing too difficult. It would be fun to go back – it was eight years since my last visit – and the fresh air and sunshine would do me good.

To ensure my recuperation, I'd even take some exercise. I wouldn't just visit Spain – I'd cycle round it. I set myself a target of a thousand miles and six weeks in which to cover them. I'd start at the top, in the chic beach resort of San Sebastián, then work my way east, over the Pyrenees and down to Barcelona where I'd strut along tree-lined boulevards with the beautiful people. Then I'd head south to Granada, and westwards across Andalusia to Seville, before heading up into Extremadura, Spain's wild west. I'd then pedal over to the historic capital of Toledo and finally end up in the modern hurly-burly of Madrid.

After six weeks of the cycling cure, I'd be lithe, fit, suntanned. If my tour took a few ups and downs, if I felt the need to let out the occasional primal scream, well, in Spain nobody would notice. They're used to craziness in Spain. In fact, they positively celebrate it. This is the land of the delusional Don Quixote, the obsessive Queen Joan the Mad, and the stark, staring Salvador Dalí. These are the people who have a festival during which merrymakers hurl lorry-loads of ripe tomatoes at each other, and another in which they run in the path of rabid bulls all in the name of fun. They drink whisky mixed with Fanta orange from choice.

Cycling in Spain would be a hassle-free adventure. The Spanish are meant to be fond of cycling: it ranks as the nation's second-favourite sport after football. They watch cycling, join cycling fan clubs, sponsor cycling and, yes, at the weekends they even go cycling. Spain, after all, is the land

13

of one of the most legendary cyclists the sport has ever seen, Miguel Induráin. In 1995, Induráin became the only person ever to have won the Tour de France five years in a row. The Spanish, used to scant glory on the world stage, went completely crazy. The press started to refer to Induráin as a god; the nation duly worshipped him. In the summer of 1995, an estimated *six million* Spaniards sat on the edge of their armchairs and bellowed encouragement at their television screens as the tall, lanky Navarrese pedalled through three long weeks of pain and glory. Thousands more actually travelled to France to see the great man pass before their very eyes. They gazed in awe as Big Mig's long, strong legs hammered up hill after hill; at 1.88 metres, he was ludicrously large for a cyclist. Hormone-high teenage girls screamed and reached out to touch him as he and his rippling quadriceps pedalled by.

When the Tour was over and they could safely abandon their TV sets, Big Mig's followers flocked to the cycle shops and kitted themselves out with shiny new bikes and resplendent Day-Glo Lycra outfits that never looked quite as good on paunchy computer programmers as they did on the pros. And on Sunday mornings, they took to the roads in their droves.

I wasn't exactly expecting the kind of reception that Miguel inspired – to be honest, teenage girls have never done it for me anyway – but I held out high hopes for the occasional friendly smile, an encouraging toot of the horn, cosy chats with new-found friends in rustic bars overseen by ruddy-faced, perpetually smiling barmen, ever ready with a refill of Rioja, a bowl of olives, a spicy slab of chorizo. My friend Sheena had a most exciting dream in which I had a wild and tempestuous fling with a bullfighter, a prospect I didn't dismiss out of hand. Romantic entanglements had been thin on the ground over the last year or so (I had had quite a steamy cyber affair with a policeman in New

Zealand, but after a while even he had to be downgraded from cyber lover to e-mail buddy) and bullfighters, let's face it, have very nice bottoms.

Only one small but vital ingredient for my recovery was missing: I didn't own a bicycle. And so I e-mailed Mr Chang, a bike builder over in Taipei – one of my Hong Kong friends had bought a number of bikes from him and Mr Chang promised to give me a good deal. Better still, he was travelling to Hong Kong on business and would hand-deliver my new acquisition to my door for no extra charge. He would build me, he said, a top-quality road bike, a truly cosmopolitan machine whose parts were sourced from the best manufacturers around the globe: a hand-made frame and Selle Italia saddle from Italy, clipless pedals from Germany, Shimano gearing from Japan, ultra-slim racing wheels from Taiwan. He'd fit a triple chain ring, enough to power me up the most gruesome of hills. The bike would be so light I could lift it with a single finger. It was to be a veritable lean, mean speed machine. A few weeks later, at 11.30 at night, the telephone rang. I was given a car registration number and told to bring the cash. Mr Chang and the bicycle were waiting in the alleyway downstairs.

Mr Chang beamed and nodded; his grey, thinning ponytail bobbed up and down. With his orange-patterned cycling jersey and yellow-tinted wraparound glasses, he looked as though he ought to have cycled all the way from Taipei rather than landed just an hour ago at the airport like everyone else. His accomplices rummaged around in the back of the van and produced wheels, then a frame. They gave a few practised turns of the spanner, and we all stood and gazed at the gleaming, pale-green bicycle before us. Beneath a dim orange street lamp I handed over a thick pile of banknotes. We nodded and smiled some more, then we shook hands and went our separate ways.

I handed in my notice at the magazine. I stoically survived

the tantrums and hysteria that broke out around me. Three more issues to go, then two, then one, before I would be blissfully alone, away from the whole crazy bunch of them, adrenalin pumping not because the deadline passed five hours ago and the incensed printer, facing a long night ahead, was about to take his chopper to the lot of us, but from the wild exhilaration of haring down mountain switch-backs, from whizzing carefree through olive groves and vineyards, concerned only with where my next beer might come from and what I might like for lunch. There'd be no more sandwiches gobbled on the run, no more congealed noodles delivered from the takeaway on the corner and scoffed in seconds flat with disposable wooden chopsticks and inadequate quantities of soy sauce squeezed out of ridiculous fish-shaped droppers; in a few days' time I'd be leisurely tackling plates piled high with tapas, hearty rabbit stews, slithers of perfectly cured ham – and drinking cold beer after cold beer in the recuperative sunshine of Spain.

2

Four Chorizos and a Tortilla

'Ah, you like to cycle,' muttered the airport security guard, spotting the helmet dangling by its strap from my hand luggage. He whispered secretively, breaking the unwritten rule of the uniform that dictates he should never be friendly, his eyes cast low as he fiddled with his night stick. And then I knew. This man too had another form, a different identity. On Sunday mornings, he shed the olive-green uniform, the heavy black boots, the power-toting gun and the belt full of bullets and dressed up in figure-hugging, bright yellow Lycra – and went out *in public*.

It was disappointing, however, to find that the Spanish enthusiasm for cycling hadn't extended to the taxi drivers of Madrid's Barajas Airport. Perhaps these guys were out plastic shrink-wrapping their cabs' back seats as Induráin chugged to the top of *col* after *col*. Wherever they were, they clearly weren't bonding with bikes.

'No,' the taxi driver pronounced, directing a reproachful glare towards my shiny green bicycle. With his whiskers set and bristling, he bundled a well-groomed couple with manageable wheelie suitcases into his car instead.

'No,' said the next. '*That*' – an accusing stab of the finger – 'won't fit.'

'No way, José,' said a third – or something like that.

Things weren't getting off to a very relaxing start. I begged, I pleaded and I cajoled. I had a go at anger and indignation. I tried lying through my teeth: 'It fitted perfectly well in the taxi I took yesterday.' Nothing worked. In the end, I reverted to type, and just stood around getting in the way.

When enough of a bottleneck had been created outside the arrivals hall, a kindly policewoman took the matter in hand. She took aside the next cab with a roof rack and told him he was to take me away from there with no further ado. Perhaps she was a closet Lycra case too.

The driver was a stout character, with a spiky little moustache. He shook his head with some vigour.

'No,' he said, glaring at the bothersome bike. 'It won't fit.'

How about the roof rack, I suggested. The driver puffed his cheeks, let out a mighty sigh that sent his facial hair a-quiver, and grudgingly set to with the ropes.

'I don't like it,' he grumbled some minutes later when the bicycle was fixed firmly and securely to the rack. 'I have to warn you, I think it will fall off.' He gave a much-practised shrug.

'Well, perhaps we could chance it,' I ventured. And off we went, all the way to the city's Chamartín train station, listening out anxiously for telltale scrapes and thuds as we wended our way through the traffic.

My bicycle never did fall off the taxi's roof, so I was still wheeling it when I arrived in San Sebastián some hours later. It was early evening. The sun was shining, the weather was perfectly warm, the birds were singing in the trees and the elegant people of San Sebastián were out strolling in that calm, leisurely way I hoped soon to emulate.

I had a few things to do in San Sebastián. I needed to find a bike shop to fix my gears which I'd destroyed before leaving home in one of my very rare attempts at bicycle maintenance. That episode had ended, I'm ashamed to say, in a not-very-self-controlled fit of temper in which I shouted at the bike and called it names. I also had to eat lots of tapas, and that would take some time, so I checked into a hotel for a couple of nights. Unfortunately, it turned out to be San Sebastián's annual film festival that week, so all the desirable hotels were fully booked. I checked into an undesirable one instead, which featured among other things a rubber mattress cover, bed sheets with holes, and a yellowing piece of paper pinned to the wall which demanded, in wavering block capitals that suggested a hand that doesn't hold a biro very often, SILENCE AFTER 11PM. ANY DISTURBANCES AFTER THIS HOUR WILL BE DEALT WITH BY THE POLICE. I thought it quite delightful.

It was not, however, the kind of place in which to spend many minutes freshening up. This suited me well, as freshening up on arrival at a hotel in a new town is something I've never been able to fathom. When I arrive in a brand-new destination I'm beside myself with anticipation. In the taxi from the airport, I have to exercise every restraint to stop myself from telling the driver to drive faster . . . yes, it's desperate, no I can't wait. I'm dying to get out into the streets, to check out everything all at once, to eat from each and every one of those amazing-looking roadside stalls whose food would, in reality, strike me dead with a single bite, to get horribly lost because I'm too excited to stop and look at the map. Finally, eventually, we arrive at the hotel; I bite my lip through the entire, laborious checking-in process, and then somebody says brightly, 'Let's all go to our rooms and freshen up, and meet back in reception in, oooh, let's say an hour from now, shall we?'

An hour? How dirty did they get during that three-hour flight in that pristine, sterilized cabin? What are they going to do for *a whole hour*? Cellophane wraps? Deep pore cleansing? Full-body exfoliation? The gruesome-sounding

Power Peel? It's all I can manage to dump my bags on the bed, take a thirty-second comfort stop and, on occasions of extreme self-control, a cursory wash of the hands before all the exuberance fuelled by unknown adventures surges inside me. I can't contain myself; I have to rush into the street and stride around energetically until the adrenalin supplies are sapped and I collapse, exhausted, to regain my composure with a cold beer in the sun. But then patience has never been my strong point.

It didn't take me long, then, to discover that San Sebastián is a wonderful place. It has an old-fashioned charm – a broad promenade and wrought-iron balustrades along the beach-front, and an atmospheric maze of pedestrianized streets making up the old quarter. Despite its antiquated style, San Sebastián is still the most chic beach resort in Spain. The town elders were either very wise or very slow, and they never installed those games arcades and fast-food joints that have turned other formerly fashionable locations into neon-flashing infernos. And so the beach remains much the same as it must have been a hundred years ago. Close your eyes, and it's easy to envisage the elegant ladies of bygone times emerging from changing huts in those voluminous black swimsuits (think Judi Dench in *Mrs Brown*) that assured the wearer's propriety. Open your eyes, of course, and it's not like that at all. This is a European beach resort, where acre upon acre of ample flesh bursts forth from frighteningly tiny bikini bottoms. The Spanish, let's face it, have never been great ones for the pale, starved image of heroin chic. That would involve forsaking chorizo.

In the old quarter, I made straight for the tapas for which San Sebastián is famous. There are various stories about the origins of tapas. Some people say that once, a long, long time ago, one of the kings of Spain was becoming concerned about drunkenness among his subjects. In an attempt to keep them sober, he ordered bartenders to serve little snacks with their drinks. Others have it that eighteenth-century innkeepers, who would rush out with refreshments for their customers as they stopped to change horses, found that flies would get to the wine before the patrons had a chance to drink it. So they took to covering the glass with a little piece of bread or cheese – the word 'tapa' literally translates as a cover or lid.

But frankly, who cares? However they started, tapas have become a culinary institution that's imitated across the globe, from California to Canberra. The problem is that when you eat tapas outside Spain, they're never quite the same. International-style tapas restaurants linger unsettlingly in the fashionable parts of town: they're chic, expensive, and not like a real *tasca*, or tapas bar, at all. A Spanish *tasca* is an egalitarian institution: futures traders vie with farmers for the last marinated anchovy – but then the bartender brings another plateful and the problem is solved. The Spanish like to drink for hours on end – it's perfectly common to start with a tipple at breakfast time, and the bars often don't close until dawn – but they don't like to get drunk. And so they snack.

If you want to eat tapas, San Sebastián is the place to be. The old quarter of town is packed with *tascas* that are heaving with hungry customers every night of the week. After about seven p.m. their counters are covered with plate after plate of tapas (or, as they're known in Basque, *pintxos*) of every persuasion: little rounds of bread topped with *bacalao* (salted cod), cheese, ham or chorizo, eggs with mayonnaise, squares of potato omelette. The array is such that it can almost be overwhelming for the uninitiated. For those who need a little help, here's an eight-step guide to eating your fill with tapas.

1. Stroll the streets for quite a while working up an appetite and looking as beautiful as you can manage.
2. Select the most crowded, smokiest *tasca*. It is very important that the bar has a messy floor. In Spain this is considered a sign of a popular establishment and not an indication that the cleaner has just walked out in a huff.
3. Order your drink and ask the bartender for a plate.
4. Deliberate.
5. Consider the fact that the tortilla looks good . . . but then the *croqueta* might be nice instead . . . or perhaps a slice of ham or a hunk of sausage.
6. Pile the plate with all four.
7. Don't gobble or drink too fast. Remember, you've got to keep this up for several hours yet.
8. When you've finished, remember above all else to chuck your paper napkin on the floor as a courtesy to the establishment.

Any self-respecting Spaniard will pay up at the end, having returned to the bar a couple of times for refills. If your Spanish is shaky, however, and you don't know how to say three pickled herrings, two marinated eels and a small slice of tripe, you might find it easier to stick the plate under the bartender's nose while it still has food on it, so he can tot up the bill before it's too late and the whole lot has disappeared down your gullet.

But the elegant San Sebastián waterfront also has a darker side, for this is the heart of Basqueland. It can be a little tortuous trying to figure out exactly where the Basque country is. You might be forgiven for thinking that the Spanish region known as the 'País Vasco' is the land of the Basques. But it's not, or at least not all of it. The so-called

Basque Country consists of only three of the seven Basque provinces – Guipúzcoa, Vizcaya and Alava. A further three are in France. The seventh, Navarre, was declared an autonomous region all by itself in the Spanish Constitution of 1978. The Navarrese speak Basque and look Basque, although, apparently, only a minority of them actually consider themselves Basque (or, indeed, Spanish) and prefer to be known simply as Navarrese. Confusing? Absolutely.

The Basque nationalists claim that here on the sophisticated San Sebastián beachfront, in the prison overlooking the water, Franco's guards shot 21,780 Basques in the eight years that followed the Civil War. Franco hated the Basques. They resisted him during the Civil War; he called in the German planes that bombed Guernica, killing in a single afternoon nearly seventeen hundred people in a town with a population of seven thousand. The Basques had fought throughout history to keep a level of autonomy, to rule by their traditional legal code, the *fueros*; Franco insisted on a united Spain ruled by one man – himself. He outlawed the *euskera* language, the very essence of Basqueness, and persecuted those who defied him.

Nowadays, San Sebastián is known for its frequent confrontations between ETA supporters and the police – and sadly it's ETA, the Basque liberation movement, that most people think of when you mention the Basque country. Set up in 1959, while Franco still ruled Spain with a vice-like grip, ETA was originally an intellectual, cultural movement whose most violent activity was to enliven walls and monuments with graffiti. It didn't take long for its tactics to change. In 1961 its members derailed their first train. In June 1968 two *etarras* killed their first policeman when he stopped their car for a spot check; two months later the group carried out its first planned assassination of a hated San Sebastián police captain. Franco died in 1975 and Spain became a democracy but the *etarras* are still outraged by their lack of autonomy and what they consider to be state persecution. The violence continues; to date, they've killed more than eight hundred people.

That first night in San Sebastián, I had just put my first forkful of tortilla in my mouth when an almighty bang rang out in the street outside as the police, dressed in helmets and ski masks to hide their identities for fear of terrorist reprisals, fired off blanks to break up an ETA demonstration outside.

'*Hostia puta!*' screamed the bargirl, clapping her hands over her mouth and rushing to the door, past which terrified tourists were careering at a sprint. Her fellow bar-dwellers leapt to their feet, spilling their beer, and craned to see through the windows. I struggled with the urge to hurl myself under the stout wooden table and huddle on the floor with three weeks' worth of used paper napkins and fluff-encrusted hunks of chorizo. Call me a coward, but I'm just not used to gunfire in the street on a Monday night.

A few more reports rang out. We shuddered collectively, gasped, muttered profanities. And then, within seconds, it was all over. The pedestrians outside let out a little chuckle, feeling foolish about their over-reaction, and went back to strolling elegantly once more. The bar-dwellers returned to their beer.

'Oh my God! What's happened? What's going on? What was that noise?' I quavered.

'Bah. It's nothing,' said the bargirl, rapidly regaining her composure.

Nothing? In the roads surrounding the old quarter, police vans sat bumper to bumper, their blue lights flashing, while groups of helmeted, gun-toting reinforcements stood around looking mean – and their guns were *huge*. Let Arnie get his hands on one of those and he could annihilate the entire universe in minutes. And, while I knew my fight-or-flight receptors were over-sensitive right now, well – wasn't that *normal* when people started shooting at each other in the street?

The people of San Sebastián seemed not to think so. After the initial excitement, they seemed not to notice that their pretty, cobbled streets had been taken over by swarms of very fierce-looking armed men, and continued eating their anchovies and sipping their beer as if nothing were amiss. These people weren't just cool. They were going on refrigerated. Feeling positively hot-blooded after only one day in Spain, I scurried back to the safety of my rubber-sheeted bed.

There were no corpses or blood stains littering the street the next morning, which I took to be a good sign. It might, however, just be a question of time. I had woken early, leapt eagerly from the rubber sheet, showered in the grungy communal bathroom without catching any skin diseases that I knew of yet, then shoe-horned myself into my tightest, brightest Lycra and hurled myself fearlessly into the roads of San Sebastián in search of the bike shop the hostel owner had recommended.

The problem was, I wasn't really very good at riding my bike. I still considered clipping my cleated shoes in and out of the pedals without falling off to be a magnificent feat of timing and co-ordination. And, well, didn't those speeding Vespas seem to be going frighteningly fast? Did the driver have to turn his head so carelessly to the side to smooch with the girlfriend clinging on to him from behind? Is that spotty teenager with a bum fluff chin really old enough to ride a moped? Shouldn't he be wearing a helmet? And put out his cigarette? And . . . bloody hell! *He's coming straight at me!* I flung the handlebars to the side and veered precariously into the opposite carriageway. And then I remembered: in Spain, they drive on the right.

Finding the bike shop wasn't easy. I managed to get swept

up onto a dual carriageway and had to clippety-clop back on the hard shoulder in my bike shoes – the kind that snap very nicely into your pedals, but transform the simple act of walking into a whole new sport. But it was worth the search. Should the Pope ever find they're short of a saint in heaven, or that the Virgin is in need of a little extra company, I'll come right forward and propose Javi from the Jaia bike shop in San Sebastián. Javi examined my muddled, botched gears and resisted looking at me with horror and disparagement. He just tinkered and tested, tinkered and tested, and tinkered and tested some more.

'These gears have half-notches,' he explained patiently. 'They work like this . . . click . . . you see . . . click . . . and again . . . click. Now you try . . . there you go, that's right . . . click . . . try it once more . . . click . . .'

And, without a flicker of an accusatory glare: 'You might find the brakes more effective if you closed this little lever here. It brings the brake pads within three light years of the wheel. They work better that way . . . click . . . you see? Click . . . and again . . . click . . . now you try . . . click.' You see, that way you might stand more than a snowball's chance in hell of actually keeping all three of your brain cells inside your thick skull instead of sprayed over the tarmac of Spain, he might have quite reasonably added – but, being charming, didn't.

He even gave me a special valve so that I could pump up the tyres using the air machine at a petrol station instead of tiring out my inadequate little arms. And when the tinkering and teaching were all over, he charged me one euro for the valve.

Javi even suggested a test run for my first day in the saddle, a short, simple ride from San Sebastián, over the hill to Orio, and westwards to the scenic fishing village of Getaria. It was a delightful little route, he said, featuring quiet country lanes and glorious ocean views. This road, as it happens, is the first snippet of the course of the Clásica San Sebastián road race, one of the most prestigious one-day races on the pro cycling calendar. It was the first race Texan golden boy Lancc Armstrong rode in after turning professional in 1992. That day, the rain came down in buckets and soon turned to freezing sleet; Armstrong came in dead last – although nearly half the field didn't finish at all – and the Spanish crowd jeered him as he crossed the line.

Looking at the Clásica course profile, the first ascent – the only hill I had to climb that day on my own severely curtailed route – is shown as little more than a pimple. It seemed closer to a full-blown boil in the flesh. An old man drove by in his van.

'*Ánimo! Ánimo!*' Come on! he called out, winding down his window and thumping the side of the van with much gusto and the occasional guffaw as I gasped and groaned, my face becoming pinker with every revolution. I got off and walked. This cycling business was turning out to be a little more difficult than I'd thought. My sleek, ultra-light road bike didn't seem to be carving up the hills quite as single-handedly as I had anticipated; it was beginning to look as though my legs were going to have to play a rather more active role than I had hoped.

I never made it to the pretty little fishing village on the coast. At Orio, I turned round and headed home. The pros do the whole of the 227-kilometre course in not much over five hours; I did about a tenth of that distance and, if you count my rather leisurely lunch on a hilltop overlooking the ocean, my time wasn't far different. There seemed to be some room for improvement as far as my cycling was concerned. My legs were burning, my lungs were wheezing, my brain was crying out for a cold beer on the beach – and my tour didn't even start till tomorrow.

3

You Call *That* a Mountain?

Ninety-one kilometres didn't seem a terribly long way when I planned my route, the maps spread across the entire floor space of my tiny Hong Kong flat, but then I had a glass of wine in my hand and anything would have seemed like a good idea. Perhaps it was the wine's fault; perhaps it was the overexcitement that comes before an adventure, but in my planning I made one significant oversight: I forgot that the Pyrenees has mountains. I forgot to consider that cycling ninety-one kilometres through the Pyrenees might be rather more taxing than cycling, say, ninety-one kilometres through Holland. I forgot that, while the cycling pros might do two hundred-odd kilometres a day in the mountains during the Tour de France, I am not a cycling pro, nor anything approaching. And I forgot that on the first day it's a good idea to take it easy.

On the other hand, maybe my early demise was due to eating the wrong stuff. As I sat on San Sebastián's La Concha beach in the low, early-morning sun, watching the men with their tank-like machines clear scraps of rubbish from the deserted, deep-yellow sand, I chomped my way through a chocolate pastry and a strong, sweet coffee and remembered the wise words of my athlete friend, Laura.

'Whatever you do,' Laura warned in tones that threatened doom and damnation, 'don't eat sugar.'

Sugar would do terrible things to my blood glucose levels. My energy would soar gloriously for one brief and giddy moment, then plummet to hideous, uncharted depths leaving me a burnt-out wreck. Laura should know about endurance because she's one of those truly insane people who think it's fun to run through snake-infested jungles and desolate mountain ranges for days on end – and she doesn't take medication to cure the compulsion. She once found herself competing in an Ironman race *by accident*. (An Ironman consists of a 3.8-kilometre swim, followed by a 180-kilometre bike ride, and then you top it all off by running a marathon. Not the kind of thing I've ever found myself doing intentionally, let alone by accident, but I suppose life's full of surprises.) I was secretly quite pleased, anyway, that Laura's guilt-provoking little voice crept up on me only when I had very nearly finished my breakfast. By that time the harm was no doubt done so I scoffed the lot and called it good. And then I got on my bike.

It was only now that I discovered that riding with laden panniers is not at all the same as pedalling along with just a puncture repair kit and a mobile phone. I had exercised every austerity with my packing. On top of my two sets of very tiny Lycra bike kit, I had allowed myself just one set of clothes. But somehow, the accessories piled up. The tube of travel wash was indispensable. And, while I might be able to manage for six weeks without a change of clothes, rinsing them out in the sink and, on some unfortunate occasions when my laundry logistics went awry, wearing them again damp, I didn't think it would be advisable, or indeed pleasant, to go without the Eve Lom cleansing cream and accompanying muslin cloth, nor the Aveda hydrating lotion, nor indeed a small pot of nail varnish and a tube of cuticle cream in case the going really got tough and I felt the need to soothe my nerves by painting my toenails.

In an attempt to prevent myself from carrying too much, I had steered away from the conventional double panniers and gone instead for the single bag that sits on top of a rack above the back wheel, and a small front handlebar bag. Packed so full that every extension bulged, my rack pack wasn't the most aerodynamic of accessories. The weight, positioned high off the ground, threw off my balance and, until I was used to it, turned riding into a precarious affair that would have been much improved by a set of stabilizers. I wobbled so unnervingly and made progress so slowly that, by the time I reached Hernani, ten kilometres south of San Sebastián, nearly an hour had passed. If I kept going at this rate, I calculated, it would be another ten hours before I arrived at my bed for the night. From deep within me, the tiniest sensation of doom began to claw its way into my consciousness.

Hernani might seem a boring suburb best known for its cider, but one particular cider mill in the village has a valiant past. The owner of the mill, Juan Manuel Larburu, provided a vital link in Operation Comet, the Second World War resistance movement that smuggled Allied pilots shot down in northern Europe across occupied France, over the Pyrenees and to the British Consulate in Bilbao. His mill was a safe house and rest stop where pilots slept and refuelled before continuing their hazardous journeys.

There was only one part of the French–Spanish border where crossing was feasible. This was the tiny section on the western coast, in the Basque country, which was governed by occupied – as opposed to Vichy – France. The Basques were having a particularly rough ride under Franco, who had banned their language and dashed their hopes for self-rule. Seeing the war in Europe as an extension of their own battle against right-wing dictatorship, many of them were prepared to face the dangers involved in working for the Allied resistance movement. This was a risky endeavour even in Spain because, although the country was supposed to be neutral, Franco was in practice an ally of Hitler. (The two men only met once after which Hitler commented to Mussolini, 'I would rather have three or four teeth pulled than have to meet that man again.')

The pilots would travel by train through France to St Jean-de-Luz on the French side of the border. From there, they would be led by Basque peasants and smugglers who knew every rock and root of the hills along creeks and tiny paths, over the mountain and into Spain. Once at the British consulate in Bilbao, they'd head to Gibraltar or Lisbon, and from there back to England.

Larburu, the Hernani cider miller, was unfortunately less lucky than most of the fliers he helped. He was turned over to the Gestapo in March 1944 and never seen again.

I didn't stop in Hernani for rest and cider as my countrymen had done before me. Instead, I upped the pace. Gratifyingly, I knocked off the next few villages in something approaching a respectable time and even managed to avoid being eaten by any of the very large, fiercely barking dogs that rural Spaniards insist on keeping instead of locking their doors. The city suburbs with their lorry-choked roads and surrounding factories receded into the distance; quiet lanes shaded by leafy trees took their place. The panic started to subside; after a couple of hours, I was even beginning to muster up a quiet confidence. Then the first mountain hit.

Looking at the map now, it's little more than a hillock. At a mere 695 metres, it's remarkably audacious of the Puerto de Usateguieta to call itself a *puerto*, or mountain pass, at all. In the Tour de France, let's face it, they polish off six or seven passes a day in the mountain stages, and I don't suppose they'd even count this. But I didn't know what a lamentable little pimple this hill was at the time because this was before I'd learnt to read the map, before I'd worked out that the word *puerto* meant pain, before I'd realized that those pairs of chevrons on the wiggly lines of the map indicated the severity of the gradient and the figures between them the height of the summit.

The hill went up and up. I climbed and climbed and climbed some more. Up and round and round and up and up and round I went. The time ticked laboriously by; minutes turned to hours, and still no summit. Up and round and up and round and up and round again. Christ, my luggage weighed a tonne. What on earth had I put in there? Was there anything I could do without, something I could hurl over the precipice to lighten my load? Might startle the sheep though, and that would be unkind. I climbed and climbed some more. My legs were really starting to hurt now; the higher I went, the lower my confidence sunk. It's incredible, I thought; this mountain is going on for ever. Where on earth is the top? Will there be snow soon?

Oh to have trained a little harder, to have garnered just a zillionth of Induráin's famous powers of endurance! Whatever the pain, his marvellous legs would patiently power on up. But my legs weren't, well, quite as *big* as Mig's. Where I was grimacing and groaning, Miguel's face would be totally inexpressive as he carefully studied the legs of his opponents, reading the minute give-away signs on their veins and muscles that told him when they were tired, when it was time to attack.

Attack! God, I was using every drop of energy just to stay on the bike at all. How on earth did he do it? His coach reckoned his trump card was precisely that Mig was Big: 'The secret's in the length of his build,' he said. 'His legs provide more power than other riders can generate.' Others say his success lay in his temperament (stoical, placid, imperturbable, said the Spanish; boring, said the French). Some of his opponents even put Induráin's presence on the podium down to otherworldly reasons: 'He's an extraterrestrial,' said former world champion Gianno Bugno after the 1992 Tour. 'He's superhuman,' said another world champion and Tour-winner-in-waiting Lance Armstrong three years later.

The hill went up and up some more. I was no longer enjoying myself. I was thoroughly fed up. I hated cycling. Loathed it. *Detested* it. Things soon became so bad that even thinking about Induráin's legs failed to make me feel better. Why did nobody tell me that this was going to hurt so much? What on earth had possessed me to desert that nice comfortable Hong Kong office, with its gratifying twizzly foam-padded chair, which, for Christ's sake, they gave me a nice cheque at the end of each month for sitting comfortably in? Where had I gone wrong? I must have been losing my mind. I had traded in a comfy chair (it had a reclining function as well if you fiddled with the knob under the seat, I now recalled) and free, unlimited use of the coffee machine – *and* the water dispenser – for *this*. God, my bottom hurt.

It started to rain. I stopped and put on my rain jacket. The rain eased off; then I was too hot. I ate a peach for strength. It had been squashed in my pannier and gone rather pulpy. I'd only cycled thirty-something kilometres and my legs felt as if they might not have another revolution left in them. The bike sighed and moaned beneath me. The panniers were dead weights. And the abominable thought kept recurring: I had to keep this up for the next six weeks.

I tried to lift my spirits by playing little tricks with my mind. Find ten things to be grateful for, I told myself. I tried my best, and ferreted around in the dingiest recesses of my mind for the cheerfulness that had once lived there quite openly. One – I have not yet been gobbled up by a hungry dog. Two – I still have one rather squashed, rapidly fermenting peach and a couple of Jordan's breakfast bars in my panniers. Then I got stuck. I couldn't think of anything else. My formerly bright and blithe disposition had, in the short space of a morning, been overpowered by this rather small, insignificant hill.

The drizzle set in again. I put on my rain jacket once more. And I pedalled and pedalled up and round and round and up and up and up. The wobbles moved from my legs to my chin. What on earth have I taken on, I quavered, fighting hard to keep back the tears of self-pity. I'm supposed to be enjoying myself, I whined. And on the very first morning, things are so bad that I'm about to cry.

When, eventually, I reached the top my legs were so worn out that it took three attempts just to wrench my cleats from the pedals. There were two options. The first was to cycle back down the hill and take the next flight home. But then people would know that I'd failed. The second was to clatter weakly into the restaurant just in front of me and have a spot of lunch.

It was hardly the best meal of my trip. There was nothing wrong with the restaurant. Had it not been enveloped by a drizzly black cloud, it might even have had a pretty view. There was nothing wrong with the rabbit stew. But by now I was an emotional wreck. The fear had set in. My confidence had dived. I was convinced I'd taken on more than I could manage.

Oh, to have lived a couple of hundred years earlier! Then I could have applied for a spa cure instead. I could have just lain on my back, stared at the ceiling, and sipped weakly from a cup of sulphurous water from time to time. You'd soon get used to the taste – wouldn't you? I've always thought it would be marvellous to be a lady of centuries past. Any glimmer of a problem, of a sticky situation, you could just take a nice big breath and the restrictions of your corset would send you into a very feminine faint. By the time everyone had finished rushing around wafting smelling salts, they'd have forgotten all about whatever awful thing you had done and you could retire weakly to your bedroom with a headache. As it was, I was a child of the post-feminist age; I was meant to be able to hold on to a husband, a high-paying job *and* my sanity. I'd failed at all three. And there I was thinking that pedalling over an enormous great mountain range would make up for my shortcomings, allow me to salvage something from the mess. Certifiable lunatic! It was already killing me – and I was still less than halfway through the very first day.

'Dessert? We've homemade *flan*,' coerced the waitress with a well-practised twinkle that probably worked better on bored male lorry drivers than on female cyclists on the verge of hysteria.

'Ah, no, no, I really can't. Must push on,' I resisted. The waitress looked concerned. Who was this creature in the unsightly tight clothes who didn't drink wine with her lunch and then turned down Pepa's perfectly good homemade *flan*? No wonder she was so pale and skinny. Looked like she needed a good few litres of olive oil to fatten her up.

The two lorry drivers at the next table poured themselves another glass of red wine, settled back and stretched out their legs.

'Not a good day for cycling,' the fatter of the two called over, dragging deeply on his Ducados.

Tell me about it, *señor*.

I pushed on through the Navarre countryside, through attractive stone villages, apple orchards, and magnificent, lush, green countryside, only slightly marred by the rain. These villages have something of a spooky past: in the early seventeenth century there was a severe outbreak of witchery round here. In 1608, in Zugarramurdi, just a few kilometres northeast of the road I cycled along now, a young girl named María de Ximildegui claimed to have attended witches' covens. She denounced another local girl, 22-year-old María de Jureteguía, who denied everything – but Ximildegui's stories were so convincing and ripe with detail that she was believed. Jureteguía realized that her only way to escape the flames, for these were the days when they burned witches, was to confess, beg for mercy and in turn denounce her 'fellow witches' – and so she told the authorities that she had been led into witchcraft by her 52-year-old aunt, María Chipía Barrenechea. A whole string of confessions resulted until, in the end, ten witches in that one remote village had confessed to a spree of hideous spells and tricks over a number of years, including killing children and sucking their blood. The following year, the Inquisition came to town and arrested four of the supposed witches. Jureteguía told the Inquisitors that her aunt had made her guard a flock of toads and had shrunk her to a size so tiny that she could pass through cracks in walls. Others described sexual orgies in which they had sex both with the devil and with each other, as well as the killing of children and the eating of corpses. At the Auto da Fe of Logroño in 1610, twenty witches were denounced. Nine confessed; the other eleven were burnt at the stake. By the following March, the Inquisition had discovered in the tiny village of Zugarramurdi 158 witches among a population of 390; a further 124 were under suspicion. In all, 1,590 confirmed witches and 1,300 suspects were found in Navarre.

But these girls were long gone; their demise no longer concerned me. Still struggling against the urge to just give up and weep, I battled on through the rain. I spent so little time admiring the scenery that I can now recall only the occasional snapshot of the villages in which those Navarrese witches were denounced and burned four centuries ago: a narrow, cobbled village street flanked by tall stone houses; in the fields around them the ever-present chiming of cow bells, or horse bells, or goat bells, for the people in this part of the world attach bells to all animals, whose movements together create a soft, rounded harmony that echoes gently round the hills. In the days that followed, I'd stop the bike, admire the views, and take a photograph or two. I'd even, astonishingly enough, learn to enjoy the ascents up the mountain passes with their slow, rhythmic pace, the reward of the panorama from the summit and the hair-raising descents that followed. On this first day, though, I enjoyed none of these things. I spent most of the day trying not to cry. I was wrought with anxiety and exhaustion and concerned only that I might never reach my destination at all.

I eventually arrived in Ziga eight hours after I'd set off. It seemed to me the loveliest village in the world. For though Ziga is not the place to go if you're after a lively night out or a cosmopolitan dining experience, or indeed if you want to buy anything groovier than a kilo of potatoes, for anyone convalescing from a recent bout of hysteria its peace, quiet and tinkling cow bells are just the medicine.

There's only a handful of houses, and the trends of modern architecture don't seem to have made their way over the mountains. In these Navarrese villages, even the new houses are built in traditional style: three or four storeys, with shutters and balconies on the upper levels, overflowing with pink and red flowers. The people of Ziga – all forty or so of them – seem to take their village's good looks seriously if the floral adornments are anything to go by, although nobody had thought to remove the dead, disembowelled cat that lay surrounded by its own viscera in the middle of the street. It looked as though it had been there for some days. The houses' ground floor windows are tiny, the floors are stone and the doors are vast wooden portals. This is where the animals would traditionally live – their fermenting manure apparently kept the house warm – and, in many of the houses in Ziga, seemed still to be doing so if the trumpeting and braying coming from within was any guide. On the other hand, Ziga didn't seem like the kind of place likely to boast a very large gene pool, so the noise could simply have been dinnertime conversation.

The house I stayed in, though, wasn't offering shelter to oxen but to paying guests and thirsty villagers in berets. Hats are very important to Spaniards, especially the old ones. Their obsession with headwear goes back even beyond the old men of Ziga's considerable lifetimes. During the eighteenth century, when Carlos III ordered that wide-brimmed hats had to be replaced with the French-style tricorn, such severe riots broke out that the king had to flee Madrid and the minister who had drawn up the decree had to leave the country altogether.

The beret itself came in vogue among the Basques during the First Carlist War in the 1830s. The most famously valiant of the Carlist generals was a local man named Tomás Zumalacárregui. With his fine Basque nose and strong Basque chin, he rose to be something of nineteenth-century poster boy, and his dashing red, tasselled beret made the headgear all the rage. These hills are not given to fickle changes in fashion and the people have been wearing their berets proudly ever since.

I'm not sure if a cycling helmet counts as a dashing item of headwear; mine certainly conveyed no style whatsoever when I stumbled self-pityingly up to the house, which belonged to the family of lodgings known in Spain as *casas rurales*, or country houses. Like bed and breakfasts in Britain, these are private houses whose owners let out a couple of rooms or more.

Skirting round the dead cat, I stumbled to a halt outside the *casa rural*'s heavy wooden doors, where Merche, the proprietress, was exchanging vital tidbits of gossip with her neighbour. I peeled my battered body from the bike. I had said I'd arrive between two and four in the afternoon; it was now half-past five.

'I'm so sorry to arrive so late,' I started. Merche looked confused. *Late?* What on earth could this strange, uptight, time-obsessed northerner be on about? She arrived within a week of when she said she would, didn't she? Surely then, she's perfectly on time.

'The journey took me a little longer than I'd thought,' I explained. 'It nearly killed me.'

'Really? Where did you come from?'

'Oh,' I told her smugly, 'I've come all the way from San Sebastián.'

'Ah,' said Merche, narrowing her eyes and looking at me unimpressed. This wimp needs to toughen up, said the look in her eye.

Merche marched across the flagstone ground floor and up a wooden staircase that had been polished with great dedication over a number of years, giving its steps a rich, smooth patina. I limped along behind. My room, at the top of the house, had wooden beams, pale green painted shutters, a large double bed with a carved wooden frame and a vast, soft sofa. The en suite bathroom looked brand new. Outside the window lay the village's sixteenth-century church with its booming bronze bells and, beyond, an idyllic rural scene of rolling, green hills. It may have been late September but in this part of Spain there's enough rain to keep the grass an intense shade of emerald even through the summer.

It was from these hills that Wellington's troops finally pushed Napoleon over the border and back into France during the Peninsular War. One of the more curious elements of warfare in those days was the way women accompanied the troops: it was common for regiments on foreign service to take a certain number of soldiers' wives with them, and if their husbands were killed in battle the women would frequently remarry another soldier in the regiment. I wondered how those women had managed on their endless journeys, and how many of them had succumbed to

40

girly tears. Perhaps women were made of sterner stuff in those days.

I ran the bath, climbed into the soothing hot water, screamed with pleasure and then clapped my hand over my mouth lest anyone hear me and wonder what I was doing having so much fun in the bathroom all alone. Then, wrapped up in fluffy, white towels (an attempt to fool myself that I'd just been through a spa treatment and not eight hours of butt-busting agony), I laid my maps out across the bed and rewrote my route, this time without any form of alcoholic assistance. I'd been thinking I'd cycle all the way over to Figueres, near the east coast, where Salvador Dalí built his extraordinary museum to house his work, before heading down to Barcelona. Ludicrous thought! Only now did I realize that it was a whole week out of my way. The Dalí museum was relegated to a day trip from Barcelona and, new route established, I made my way down to the shop and asked Merche to recommend me a nice big bottle of local wine. I explained to her that the alcohol would make my legs feel a lot better.

'Really?' She looked rather perked up by the idea. 'Is wine good for the muscles?'

'Well, not exactly,' I had to admit. 'But it's a very good anaesthetic.'

Eager for its effects, I hastened back to my room and my comfy sofa, and glugged down several glasses in a shamefully small number of minutes.

There aren't any restaurants in Ziga so supper was served at home. There was no menu; the dishes on offer were reeled off in a thick Navarrese accent by a swarthy man with the characteristic Basque nose and sizeable earlobes (in Basque, you insult a foreigner by calling him a stumpy ear) whom I took to be Merche's husband. There was only one other table, taken by a grumpy-looking middle-aged couple who spoke only Basque, or *euskera*. Conversation was not an

41

option: *euskera* is known to be preposterously difficult and to bear no relation whatsoever to any other language on earth. I smiled at them weakly, downed my camomile tea and opted for an early night.

I slept badly. I had a vivid and disturbing dream in which someone took all the screws out of my bike so that when I tried to ride it, it fell to pieces and became a heap of scrap metal. It doesn't take a psychoanalyst's couch to work that one out.

4

A Very Cantankerous Pig

'Must be at least a hundred kilometres to Burguete.' Merche's husband shook his head and rubbed his chin in a manner that seemed to help him with the delivery of bad news. 'And there's two tunnels on the way. One of them's at least five kilometres long. You don't want to be going through those on a bike.'

I never did work out where he got his information from. He seemed a kindly enough man, not a person given to deliberately misleading distressed tourists. Maybe the morning tipple was playing games with his memory. Maybe living in a village with only fifteen houses addles the brain. Or maybe he just hadn't been out a lot lately. Whatever the reason, he didn't have the first idea what he was talking about. It was a mere eighty-five kilometres to Burguete, my next destination, and there wasn't a tunnel to be seen. According to the cyclist I met at the top of the first pass of the day, there never had been.

'Do you come here often?' I asked him as we arrived gasping and gulping at more or less the same moment at the brow of the hill. I was feeling rather pleased with myself: this mountain had seemed easier than yesterday's and I had pedalled all the way to the top without crying once.

43

Between wheezes, he explained it was the third time he'd climbed that particular hill, that he lived in one of the villages in the valley below, and please could he have a drink from one of my water bottles. I gave him the bottle and we collapsed in our respective little heaps at a respectable distance from one another. A few hundred metres away, a herd of mountain horses galloped across the green, green pasture, their long blond manes and tails flowing in the breeze, the bells around their necks chiming with that soft resonance that makes one think at best of healthy mountain hikes, and at worst of *Heidi* films on rainy Sunday afternoons. Really, I thought, they were rather beautiful. If pretty horses like those kept cantering across my path, I could learn to loathe the mountains a little less.

When we'd regained our composure sufficiently to speak in full sentences, I asked him about the road to Burguete and its looming tunnels.

'Tunnels? What tunnels?' he asked, astonished. 'I've cycled that road a hundred times and there aren't any tunnels.' But what neither Merche's husband nor my new acquaintance thought to inform me was that I might be delayed by close encounters of a beastly kind.

Navarre, it would seem, is big on pigs. It's big, in fact, on very big pigs. I passed several vast, porky creatures in the course of the morning; fortunately, they were far more concerned with rooting around in mud for their elevenses than with giving chase to a bike. This type of behaviour, I was soon to learn, is a sign of maturity in a pig. Younger pigs are much more easily distracted from their nosh.

At about lunchtime, I happened upon four small, pink piglets with wonderful, gravity-defying, curly-wurly tails. They were in the middle of a happy family outing, snuffling out acorns on the roadside. (Acorn-snuffling, I understand, is the porcine equivalent of a family picnic.) Playing the role of chaperon and snuffling instructress was Mother Pig.

44

She was large and brutish, with a cantankerous demeanour, a magnificently turned-up snout, and huge, pendulous udders.

As I lumbered round the corner, their family outing took a turn for the worse. At the first glimpse of my skinny green racing bike and hulking bundles of luggage, the four little piggies took fright. They squealed and snorted and galloped off down the road as fast as their tiny trotters would carry them. Mother Pig stopped munching, paused for a moment to swallow her acorns, then slowly and thoughtfully raised her great, grumpy head and glared at me with awesome ferocity. Despite her bulk, she looked like the kind of pig who might, in exceptionally provoking circumstances such as when someone interrupted her lunch, have a sprightly charge in her.

Finding deep within me a small reserve of speed myself, I set off down the road in the piglets' wake. With their pink little tails bouncing like springs behind them, they galloped four abreast across the width of the lane, their trotters going clippety-clop, their squawks of consternation echoing round the valley. They were certainly pretty; unfortunately they were also brainless and wouldn't let me pass.

After I'd unwittingly herded the piglets along the road for about a kilometre, I began to worry. What if we went so far that they lost their bearings and were never reunited with Mother Pig again? How would they feed themselves? Can small, pink piglets survive on roadside acorns alone? Or, deprived of the milk from those great, distended udders, would they just shrivel and die, ending their days as dried-up little pork scratchings under the acorn trees of Navarre? I got off my bike and tried to edge my way slowly past. If I wasn't actually riding the bike, I thought, perhaps they wouldn't notice.

My plan might even have worked, had a mighty rumpus not broken out behind me the moment my feet touched the ground. With a thunderous stampede of hooves and much disgruntled snorting and grunting, Mother Pig came lumbering round the corner at a canter, herded by two very lively-looking pig dogs. Which would get me first? It was a tense time indeed.

One of the dogs came straight for me. Quaking, I forced myself to stand my ground, to look the dog bravely in the eye, to pretend that I wasn't afraid. Dogs, like lions, are apparently more likely to eat you if you run away. It seemed to work; the dog lost interest and went back to duty. He rounded up Mother Pig once more, and the rambunctious threesome thundered ahead. I gave them a healthy start before starting to cycle again, but I'm happy to report that I did catch up enough to see all five pigs reunited and herded safely back to their farm.

But if you thought the four little piglets lived happily ever after in curly-tailed, acorn-snuffling bliss, I'm afraid to say you were probably wrong. Almost certainly, those four little piggies went to market – and then they probably had their legs slung over the counter of a smoky bar full of hungry, ham-loving Spaniards.

The Spanish are very enthusiastic about eating pork. Apparently it all goes back to the Reconquest, the somewhat protracted struggle of the Christians to wrestle Spain back from the Moors after they invaded and occupied the country at the beginning of the eighth century. As the Christians slowly (we're talking eight hundred years) and bloodily worked their way down through the peninsula from their northern territories, it became increasingly unfashionable to be Muslim or Jewish in Spain.

In 1492, the Catholic Monarchs, Fernando and Isabel, finally marched into Granada, the last Moorish stronghold. Having dispensed with the Moorish king Boabdil, Fernando and Isabel declared that all Jews in Spain must either convert to Christianity or face exile. Ten years later, the Muslims were given the same ultimatum. In one year, three hundred thousand Muslims converted to Christianity; those suspected of secretly celebrating their old religions were subjected to zealous questioning at the hands of the Inquisition.

Moors and Jews didn't eat pork. Christians did. Publicly stuffing yourself with sausage and ham was considered rather a good way to prove your loyalty to your new faith and so save yourself from a toasty demise. The *conversos*, or converts, would therefore take to the streets on their respective Sabbaths, Friday and Saturday, and openly eat pork in the hope of saving their bacon. Sadly for them, it didn't always work.

It's admittedly hard to find nice things to say about the burning of heretics, but if a fear of the fire was really the thing that inspired the Spanish to do delicious things with pork, well, at least some good came of it. Pork meat isn't usually eaten uncured in Spain, except in the form of suckling pigs and pork chops. More often you'll see it as sausages – such as chorizo, *salchichón* or *morcillas*, those delicious black blood sausages that turn the stomachs of the faint of heart – or as the ever-present leg of ham.

There are principally two kinds of ham. The more common one is *serrano*, which comes from white-coated pigs like those whose family picnic I so rudely interrupted. Traditionally, *serrano* ham came from mountainous areas, the sierra, where the colder air was good for curing meat. These days, though, when the curing room can be cooled at the flick of a switch, pigs can be reared just about anywhere.

The real prize pig, though, is the *ibérico* variety. This is a black-haired beast native to Spain; apparently it's a descendant of the wild boar. From the ham connoisseur's point of view, though, the important thing isn't the colour of the pig's bristles, nor the fact that its ancestors had ferocious tusks, but the way its fat is marbled through its muscles making its meat particularly succulent. Whether or not an *ibérico* pig reaches the zenith of the piggy world and is classified *ibérico de bellota* – acorn-fed – depends on how greedy a fat pig it is. After weaning, the pigs are fed on fodder and cereals before being let loose to guzzle acorns. If they manage to eat enough to double their pre-acorn-snuffling weight on acorns alone, they are considered acorn-fed. If they need extra fodder to fatten them up, they become a mere *ibérico*. Exercise, in the form of squealing down lanes in the path of bicycles and yapping dogs, is bad for fattening and very poor behaviour in a pig.

Did Miguel Induráin have such problems with dogs, hogs and other animals when he cycled through these mountains, I wondered. Induráin, after all, was more or less a local boy. He grew up on the outskirts of Pamplona, just a few kilometres to the south-west, and they say the reason he became such a great cyclist and strong climber was that he spent his formative years blasting up and down these same hills that I was pedalling through now.

In 1996 his friends came too; that was the year the Tour de France came to Spain. The *peloton* powered over the Pyrenees and down this very road on its way to Pamplona in recognition of the Señor's cycling achievements. It was to be a hero's homecoming. Spaniards lined the road for more than a hundred kilometres, crazy with excitement, brandishing cardboard cut-outs of Big Mig dressed in his favourite shade of yellow. In Villava, the village just outside Pamplona where Induráin's family lived, not another ounce of chorizo-fattened flesh could be squeezed into the streets, onto the pavements, or the overhead balconies. They wore yellow T-shirts and caps predicting the sixth victory of Villava's most famous son; everywhere were posters, fans and stickers proclaiming the glorious sixth coming. Over these very hills

– the Alto de Erro, the Alto de Mezkiritz – the demi-gods pedalled alongside their leader.

Except that Induráin wasn't the leader that year. He had already given hints that he was getting a little browned off with schlepping up and down hills, a predicament I could well relate to. 'You've given a great performance for the people, for the fans,' he told a French journalist, 'but in the evening, when you're alone, or in the morning, when you get up and think things over, you ask yourself, really, what have I done? You have climbed a mountain and then you've come down it. First you went up it and then you came down. Nothing else.'

Poor Big Mig. As the crowds palpitated on the streets of his home village, he was far from putting on one of the spectacular breakaway shows of his past. The first cyclist sped down the street. It was not Induráin. Another group approached, the people craned their necks, stood on tip-toe to catch a glimpse of their idol – but he was not among them. The minutes dragged by; the band struck up a *charanga* to drown out the question on everyone's lips: where on earth is He? Finally, Induráin spun into Villava nine minutes behind the stage leader. The people went crazy anyway – but the dream was over. Induráin came eleventh in the Tour that year. Six months later, at the age of thirty-two, he retired. He went back to his little farm a mile away from the village where he grew up, back to his wife and son. A man of few words, the ultimate introvert, he declared his intention to live a simple life and fade into obscurity. He's even given up watching his diet: these days he's Even Bigger Mig – and the expansion has all been widthways.

If the Tour de France cyclists were sweaty and uncomfortable as they pedalled along this stretch of road that I cycled on now between Zubiri and Burguete, they could have consoled themselves with the thought that they, at least, could take a shower in the evening and enjoy a fresh change of clothes in the morning. This is more than can be said for many of their fellow travellers who have hiked in their droves along this same route over the centuries, for this road is also part of the Camino de Santiago.

The Santiago pilgrimage started up in a rather sticky time for Christians. Back in the ninth century, most of Spain was ruled by the Moors, who had invaded from Muslim Africa. St James, after whom the pilgrimage is named (Santiago means St James in Spanish) was of course long dead. Legend has it that some eight hundred years earlier he had come to Spain to preach the gospel; after that he went back to Jerusalem where Herod unkindly chopped off his head. Following his execution, his decapitated remains were apparently shipped back to Spain by two disciples and a boat crewed by angels. The disciples buried the bits in a field, built a shrine, and after a while died themselves. Before too long, everyone had forgotten all about St James.

Come the ninth century, though, the Muslims ruled vast tracts of Iberia and the Christians were badly in need of a little spin doctoring. When a lowly shepherd saw stars falling on a hillside and discovered there the bones of St James, the Christian king Alfonso the Chaste lost no time in scoring a marketing point for Christianity and built a church and a monastery on the spot. The place was named Santiago de Compostela, St James of the Field of Stars. The pilgrims came and prayed; St James answered their petitions by galloping down from the Milky Way on a fierce white charger and hacking to death thousands of nasty Moorish infidels. Ever since, Christians have flocked to Santiago de Compostela to seek St James's blessing.

Back in the early days, the pilgrims' religious fervour heavily outweighed their ablutionary concerns – we're talking one hair shirt and no tubes of travel wash. The failure to wash used to be considered a great Christian virtue, as bath houses were an institution much favoured by the Moors. (During the Spanish Inquisition, a common denouncement was, 'The accused is known to take baths.') Such was the travellers' spiritual devotion, and so powerful their stench, that in the end the cathedral authorities at Santiago found it necessary to build the biggest incense burner in the world – it's the height of a grown man and takes eight sturdy friars to swing it – to mask their fetid bodily odours after many weeks of walking.

But whatever the pilgrims' shortcomings in the field of personal hygiene, the Camino has attracted big names through the ages. Charlemagne, Dante and Chaucer all made the journey. More recently, so did actress-turned-spiritual guru Shirley MacLaine. As might be expected, Shirley had rather more otherworldly communications than most along the way. She discovered the meaning of the cosmos, the secrets of ancient civilizations and the true path to higher love, as well as insights into several of her own past lives: she was once the gypsy lover of Charlemagne and, going back earlier, was one of the earliest, androgynous human beings of mythical Atlanta.

I wasn't following the Camino, though. I was going in the opposite direction, towards France, which might explain why I had no visions revealing whom I had slept with in centuries past. This was a shame, as I might have had some fun. But along the road I passed a number of modern-day pilgrims in tasteful tones of Goretex with their scallop shells – the centuries-old pilgrims' emblem – strapped to their rucksacks. They raised their walking sticks in pilgrimish greeting, I waved cheerily back (today I wasn't even faking my good humour; on the contrary I was feeling rather smug) and cycled on towards Burguete, my stop for the night.

Burguete lies high in the mountains, just a few kilometres from the pilgrimage's major border crossing to France. It's yet another pretty and spotless mountain village surrounded by green hills and grazing horses. Other than being a strategic point on the Camino de Santiago, the first stop over the border from France and just up the street from the ancient Roncesvalles monastery, Burguete's claim to fame is that Ernest Hemingway used to like to come here – maybe when the excitement of watching men in tiny, shiny trousers and pink silk tights sticking spears into bulls down in Pamplona got too much for him, for Hemingway was fond of the bulls.

He wrote about the village in his books. It's to Burguete that the characters of *The Sun Also Rises* come for a few days' trout fishing in the River Irati before heading off to the wild japes of the San Fermín festival down in Pamplona. They trundle into the village on a dusty bus surrounded by old Basque men with berets and wine skins (this being a novel by Hemingway, Jake and Bill, the two characters involved, drink copious quantities), and speak to each other in that extraordinary aberration of the English language that people used in the 1920s. Apparently people back then really did say things like 'what ho' and 'awfully swell' and it wasn't all just one huge joke on the part of the period's writers.

It would be safe to say that Burguete has not hurled itself headlong into the twenty-first century. Things now are almost exactly the same as the way Hemingway describes them. The stream and the crossroads that Bill and Jake drunkenly clatter over are still there. There's still only one proper street, and that takes the expression 'main road' to new levels of diminution. There is also one small shop, where I bought enough local chocolate and home made almond cookies to keep me in high spirits on mountain passes for days to come.

Jake and Bill stayed in an inn on the one and only street. They found it awfully pricey at twelve pesetas a night but forgave the establishment because limitless wine was included. I reckoned it was probably the place with the green painted doors and the patterned smoked glass windows, on the left hand side as you head in the Roncesvalles direction. It didn't look as though it had changed a lot since the 1920s either.

I decided against spending the night in such a place just in case the bathroom facilities had been updated with the same regularity as the décor. I stayed instead in another *casa rural*, this time the house of a couple with two small children.

'We leave the door open till midnight,' Doña Victoria, the wife, beamed at me. And they did – wide open. That their two toddlers might waddle out and meet their maker under the wheels of a passing car wasn't a concern as there weren't any.

'Are you coming in or out, Juanito?' Victoria asked her three-year-old who was loitering around the doorway. 'Ah, OK, out you go, you go and play outside.' And Juanito and his toy car toddled off to sit on the pavement outside.

I arrived in rather better shape than I had done the previous afternoon and managed a whole half-hour before heading off in search of alcoholic sustenance. The restaurant I'd pinpointed for dinner – quite by chance, I'd read a recommendation for it that morning in the local paper – didn't start serving till eight-thirty, so I went into a bar just next door to the church that Hemingway mentions to pass the time. I wondered where Hemingway himself would have gone for his evening whisky or six, or his couple of bottles of Fundador. It's well documented that he liked a little lubrication, but I couldn't find anywhere in modern-day Burguete that would be worthy of Papa's patronage. The bar I ended up in was a grubby little place filled with mountain men with copious facial hair – which led to an interesting question. What is it about mountain dwellers and bushy beards? Is it some kind of evolutionary development to keep one's cheeks warm at altitude? Or is it just a very long way to the nearest shop to replace one's razor? I pondered the matter while I drank my beer, read the paper, and tried to stave off the hunger pangs till the late, late hour when the Spaniards deem it respectable to dine.

Soon, one of the hairy-chinned mountain men sauntered over for a chat, to check out the fresh meat that had inadvertently stumbled into this grotty watering hole that had not seen a new face since the days when Julio Iglesias was sexy. His name was Martín (pronounced Mar*teen*) and he was a builder, specializing in roofing. He probably wasn't doing a roaring trade in a village that had only built five new houses since Hemingway's day, but no doubt those five roofs were constructed with love and care. Martín asked what brought me to Burguete; I explained my journey, how I'd battled over the mountains from San Sebastián, how I would be heading to Barcelona and then down south.

'*Dios mío*, your thighs must be very strong,' he commented, ogling them shamelessly. 'And you are all alone? You have no husband?'

'Well, no,' I confessed. 'You see, the muscular, intelligent, witty, rich sex god that I was intending to collar as a life partner hasn't shown up yet. I'm holding out hope, though. I've got several years left in my ovaries before all my eggs shrivel up and die and even then, there are still loads of girl babies for sale in China.'

That'll teach him to stare at my legs.

5

Two Old Trout

High up on a tiny mountain road seems a strange place to broadcast one's deepest thoughts, let alone the grisly details of one's matrimonial disputes. The villagers of the Roncal Valley clearly think otherwise: graffiti, spray-painted across the tarmac, is a big feature of the area. I wondered why anyone would climb to two thousand metres to pen – or paint – platitudes: 'Money creates hatred' . . . 'The law's the same for everyone' . . . 'You pay, we hunt.'

More exciting than these banalities, though, were the lines that seemed to make up a conversation or, better yet, a domestic spat. Personally, I mused to myself, I have always favoured a resoundingly slammed door and a high-volume shriek over hiking up a two-thousand-metre mountain with a can of spray paint to vent my anger. By the time you'd tramped up that high, let's face it, the endorphins might have taken over and you wouldn't feel cross any more – and how tediously healthy that would be. On the other hand, it occurred to me, perhaps my behavioural preferences bore some relation to the no-show of the muscular, intelligent, witty, rich sex god. I made a mental note to dwell on that one later, at some point in the future when my legs didn't hurt so much.

'Money betrays,' proclaimed wobbly, white letters writ large across the tarmac of one hill. Ruminating on that one, I pedalled on a little. 'It's not a betrayal when you've already been warned,' came the reply fifty metres or so further up. And then the final line in that peculiar conversation, 'Nobody likes being locked out of his own home.'

What was the story behind that little exchange, I wondered. I pushed on up the hill and imagined it something like this: *Mountain Man marries Mountain Woman. They're cousins but nobody cares because this is the mountains and there aren't many people to go round. A cousin, after all, is better than a goat. They settle down in a mountain house. They don't have much, but their pigs and their sheep, living in the room downstairs, keep them in ham, homemade cheese that Mountain Woman churns in a large vat in her mountain kitchen, and woolly pullies that Mountain Woman spins and knits herself. And so they live quite contentedly – until Pedro the Pilgrim arrives in town. Pedro is rich and he is worldly. He's from Madrid, where he's made a fast euro selling bullfighting posters to tourists. Pedro has a genuine Goretex rain jacket. He has shaved his facial hair. Mountain Woman swoons. Never before has she seen the silky-soft flesh of a grown man's cheek.*

Pedro the Pilgrim tells Mountain Woman of the world beyond the mountains. He tells her of busy streets filled with bars and restaurants, and fashionable ladies who buy their sweaters in shops.

'If you like,' he says, 'I can take you there in my 1988-model Seat.'

Mountain Woman feels a warm glow inside. She's never been shopping before, but she's heard it's just the ticket after a hard day's churning at the urn.

'Either you give me enough money for a sweater from a shop, or I'm going to Madrid with Pedro the Pilgrim,'

Mountain Woman tells Mountain Man. 'Don't say you haven't been warned.'

Mountain Man doesn't have that much money in the tin. He's so upset that he takes his tractor out for a long and reckless drive. When he arrives home the doors to his mountain house are locked. They've never been locked before; Mountain Man didn't even know they owned a key. And Mountain Woman has gone.

Well, at least it took my mind off the hill.

It was a tremendous day of blue skies, slow, steady climbs and magnificent descents. As I cycled out of Burguete early that morning, scarcely a soul was about. The air was crisp and cold – the temperatures had dropped not far above freezing during the night – but it was already getting warmer, the sun climbing in the clear, deep-blue sky. As I turned left at Hemingway's famous crossroads, the perfect silence, the utter stillness was broken only by the horses in the field who cantered to the fence, whinnied in greeting, tossed their heads, and snorted clouds of steamy, hot air from their nostrils. They were telling me, in horse language, that today was going to be fantastic.

I pedalled along the mountain roads, the deep-green pastures punctuated by the occasional white, oblong house. These houses stood all alone, scattered one by one across the mountainside. Did anyone still live there, I wondered. Were these tiny blocks the homes of farmers' families, whose children set off at daybreak for the long trek to school? As I came round one corner, I found a small herd of horses trotting six abreast along the road in front of me. Two of them were foals and one of the mares was clearly expecting further patters of tiny hooves sometime soon.

At the top of the second pass of the morning, I sat down and cracked open my celebratory banana. Really, I thought, this cycling game wasn't so bad after all. Gazing at the panoramic views out over the Pyrenees, the mountains rising majestically for as far as the eye could see, I was on top of the world – and I'd arrived there entirely under my own steam. The warm glow of self-satisfaction began to creep through me.

In Hong Kong, I considered, it was Friday afternoon – the magazine's deadline day. Here I was, flying all alone on my bicycle through some of the most amazing scenery in the world, the silence broken only by the occasional whinny of a mountain horse or the quiet click of my gear change. Over in the office in Hong Kong, on the other hand, it was six o'clock, and the volume would be rising. The magazine's final proofs should have been finished – but they probably weren't. The production manager would be trying to placate the printer ('Put the chopper down. Put the chopper down. Place the chopper on the floor and raise your hands above your head . . .'); the managing editor would be trying to marry tactical attempts to speak soothingly to the production manager ('Yes darling, of course darling, any minute now darling') with encouraging his staff to get a bloody move on; the publisher would be glaring menacingly at the proofs as they emerged nervously from the printer, striking out insufficiently snappy headlines with his thick, red, felt-tip pen and screaming, 'Fuck me, who the fuck took that *fuckin' terrible photo* . . . Well tell him he's FUCKING FIRED.' Should I ring them right now on my mobile phone from high on a mountain pass and tell them what a wonderful, peaceful time I'm having? No, perhaps not.

I climbed back on my bike for the wildly exuberant, hair-raising descent. The endorphins rushed through my body (so *this* was that mysterious state, the exercise high) as I set off down the other side of the hill at terrifying, exhilarating speed, the wind rushing against my face, roaring in my ears.

'I'm free, *I'm free,* YIPPEEEEEEEE,' I cried at the top of

my lungs to nobody in particular as I hurtled down into the valley below.

Tonight's bed was in the home of a certain Doña Alicia in Roncal, a rather gloomy, tight-knit village in the easternmost valley of the Navarrese Pyrenees. Doña Alicia liked to collect, and seemed to have been indulging her habit for some years. Not a square metre of her hall wall remained untouched by a decorative pot or a painted plate. They were overshadowed only marginally by the vast, hairy, black boar's head that leered out at everyone who entered. Its mouth was slightly open, baring two menacing fangs. I never quite dared ask Doña Alicia if she'd shot the beast herself, or perhaps strangled it with her bare hands; if so, she was clearly a woman to be reckoned with.

This collecting fixation probably wasn't Doña Alicia's fault; it was almost certainly in her genes. Collecting seems to have been a weakness of Spaniards across the ages, from the highest echelons of society down, and some of Doña Alicia's forebears collected far stranger things than plates. King Felipe II, who ruled Spain in the second half of the sixteenth century, is known to history as a rather spartan, severe man who tried to stamp out Protestantism and Islam in a particularly heated manner. 'If my son were to oppose the Catholic church, I myself would carry the faggots to burn him,' Felipe declared.

He was also, however, very big on collecting. On top of the regular books and paintings (this is the lucky man who, curiously for one so tediously pious, slept with Bosch's wondrously sinful *The Garden of Earthly Delights* hanging over his bed), Felipe also ran a prodigious line in pickled body parts: he gathered 103 severed heads, including that of St Laurence, and an extensive collection of arms, legs, fingers and toes. These, apparently, were religious relics and not charred infidel remains hot from the bonfire.

Felipe's father, Carlos I, had been similarly afflicted, though, to look on the bright side, his hobbies didn't involve formaldehyde. Carlos, a self-indulgent glutton, abdicated in 1556 and retired to a monastery where, almost toothless and plagued by gout, he dedicated himself to his vast collection of clocks which he tinkered with obsessively in an attempt to get them to chime in unison.

'How could I possibly have hoped to unite all my dominions when I cannot make these clocks strike the hour together?' poor old Carlos is said to have despaired, and then, I suppose, he guzzled another beer and a plate of anchovies, for this was how he liked to pass the time.

Carlos, who enjoyed his nosh, would have been disappointed with Roncal. The village is famous for its cheese; its culinary prowess, however, doesn't extend to its restaurants. I could only find one place to eat and that was in the dingy-looking dining room of the village's one and only hostel. It didn't start serving till nine so I warded off my hunger with a small bottle of local cider: Navarre is apple-growing country and the local brew is meant to be good. This one was dry and cloudy and full of sediment, and I have never felt the need to sample it since.

At 9.02 I arrived at the restaurant. It didn't seem to be a very popular establishment – maybe there was a really fabulous place tucked away up a street I hadn't discovered, and the hungry people of Roncal had all gone there for their supper. Whatever the reason, the place was still in darkness when I arrived. The staff looked a little unsettled to see a customer at all, but turned on the lights willingly enough. It was, they said, possible to eat here. The tables were even laid for dinner, though the knives and forks were placed the wrong way round. It was a bad omen.

The choices on the menu were few. The fish salad consisted of a medley of ingredients conveniently sourced from tins: tinned sweetcorn, tinned mussels, tinned asparagus, tinned tuna and tinned beans. It was huge and unwieldy. My inability to finish it, combined with the pressure of being the only diner in the restaurant, produced an uncomfortable sense of performance anxiety. I'd made little headway with the salad when my second course arrived: two rather-too-enthusiastically fried eggs and a few slices of chorizo, all swimming in a pool of brown-tinted oil. I was just debating how to smuggle the lot into my napkin and hide it under the table next door when the waitress's beady eye was distracted by the unexpected arrival of a middle-aged couple. It was a booming night for the restaurant in Roncal.

My fellow diners made a dour pair. She was bony with tight, pinched cheeks; he was stooped and chastened, the result, no doubt, of many years of browbeating. She ordered the fish, he ordered the pork, and the waitress and her notepad tottered off to the kitchen.

'You should have ordered the fish like I did,' the sour-faced woman hissed at the henpecked man.

'But I don't want fish. I want pork chops.'

'Yes, but it would have been better to order the fish. It's local.'

'But I don't feel like fish. I feel like pork.'

The conversation carried on in this vein for quite a while. In the end, they lapsed into a disgruntled silence, which suited them rather better. Some minutes later, the celebrated fish and the offending pork chop arrived. The man slumped, crestfallen. He waited for the waitress to leave before daring to open his mouth.

'It's too big. I asked for a small one.'

'Well, I told you you should have gone for the fish like I did.'

'But I didn't want the fish. I wanted the pork chop, but now it's too big.'

The humourless hag didn't deign to reply. Instead, she raised her knife and fork theatrically and, with a triumphant, gloating, told-you-so smile and a smug little shake of her heavily hairpinned head, she attacked the fish. Alas, it had been somewhat too vigorously fried and was swimming in a slippery pool of oil. At the first strike from her fork, the hard old trout flew off the plate, hovered for a few deliciously exciting seconds in mid-air, then shot under the chair of a neighbouring table, slammed headlong into a week-old, grime-encrusted chip, and skidded to a halt.

'Oh fuck,' said the miserable woman. It was the most intelligent thing she'd said all night.

6

Anyone Got Any EPO?

Unless you're a cyclist, you probably think honking is fun. Quite why cyclists have adopted the term to mean that nasty, wuzzy-headed, on-the-verge-of-collapse feeling you get when you've spent more calories than you've put in the bank, I don't know. Happily, I didn't go all the way. I just had the cycling equivalent of a bit of a fumble.

'It's a windy day. No good for cycling,' muttered Doña Alicia's husband as I loaded my bike ready to leave in the morning. Really, the Spanish were turning out to be a pessimistic lot. What had happened to their famous *alegría*? When was anyone going to tell me that it was a fabulous day for cycling, that my route was full of wonderful, exhilarating descents rather than horribly arduous climbs? Is your breakfast wine tumbler half full or half empty, *señor*?

At the top of the first pass I broke the First Rule of Laura and snacked on chocolate. Neurosis and paranoia weren't on the list of symptoms that she'd threatened me with, but it was none the less at this point that they kicked in. What would I do, I wondered as I gazed at the endless, green hilltops stretched out at my feet, if a big, black, brutish wild boar, rather like the one on Doña Alicia's hall wall but a little bit more lively and with its body still attached, took a fancy to my chocolate? My slightly addled mind harked back to a book I'd been reading called *Spain's Wildlife*. 'The males have razor-sharp, nine-inch tusks to repel attackers,' writes author Eric Robins. To support this intimidating description, there's then a photograph of an unhappy-looking cameraman shinning his way inexpertly up a tree trunk as an angry wild boar charges at him from beneath. For this photograph to be in existence, there must of course have been two cameramen. Quite what the second was doing taking pictures while his friend was on the verge of being savaged by a raging beast with nine-inch tusks, I don't know. Perhaps they didn't stay friends for long.

As I dwelt upon the wildlife possibilities, I realized that I hadn't passed another person or, indeed, a car for at least the last hour. I was high up a mountain, on a tiny, unpopular road, in an area known for its menacing beasts. Help would not be fast at hand in the case of an unfriendly approach. It was at this point that I remembered reading somewhere that there were meant to be one or two rather large brown bears still roaming about somewhere in the Spanish Pyrenees. An adult brown bear grows to more than two metres tall and weighs in at around 250 kilograms; in a sprightly mood, he can run at up to fifty kilometres an hour. My top speed on my bike at this point was forty-eight kilometres an hour and that was when I was going downhill; I weighed fifty-five kilograms. The odds wouldn't be on my side if I had to tussle with a bear.

A few hundred years ago, these mountains would have been perilous spots for reasons quite apart from the boars and the bears. For this part of the Pyrenees, close to the French border, was the domain of smugglers and the guards who hunted them down. For many centuries, the mountain dwellers moved freely through the hills; before proper roads were built across the valleys, villagers in the Spanish Pyrenees found their French neighbours over the hill easier to reach than their compatriots many hours' climb away. The animals grazed and roamed at will – the sheep weren't good on political boundaries – and the people made ends meet by trading oils, fruit, salt and tools from Spain, and mules, cattle and textiles from France.

When the pesky authorities started passing laws about such things, the wily mountain folk were having none of it. They knew every creek, every crack in the earth over those hills, and they defiantly carried on as before. Their trade with their French neighbours, they said, was the only way they could survive. Without it they would starve. And so, almost every family in every village became involved in contraband.

The nineteenth-century queen Isabel II once received a request for a royal pardon for the inhabitants of one Pyrenean village, Aisa, just a few kilometres from my route. The whole village, it turned out, was implicated in a crime: they had stolen a consignment of goods from a government store, goods which the guards had confiscated from them a few days earlier. The problem, wrote the local priest to the queen, was that not one family in the village was innocent: twelve men had been arrested and the rest had fled over the border to France. There was not one man left in the village to till the land, to tend the herds, to provide for the women and children. Unless their menfolk were granted a reprieve, the women and children from the village would surely starve. The queen read the priest's letter – very slowly. It took her three years to grant the reprieve – by which time, presumably, the women had either starved or found themselves some new men.

And so these Pyrenean villages became the land of legend. The smugglers were gallant knights, taking from the rich taxman for the good of the poor. They even became the heroes of poetry: in 1783, the French poet Frédéric Soutras brought out his epic work 'The Last Smuggler' about a man

65

called Brice from the Spanish village of Estensan. The illegitimate child of a teenage mother, Brice took up arms against authority in his teens, the poem relates. He was a great seducer, a wonderful lover, a veritable Don Juan. He shot three guards all in the name of justice – and finally died in hiding in the hills.

Despite the title of the poem, Brice wasn't the last smuggler, of course. There have been many, many more since him. Just below the mountain pass on which I nibbled my chocolate and worried about bears lies the village of Echo. Here, in the nineteenth century, lived a certain Pedro Brun. Brun was tall, rugged and muscular; again and again he risked his life to cross the mountains and trade in the contraband goods that would keep his people alive. Valiantly he defied the laws of a draconian government far, far away. The poor, downtrodden villagers adored him; the authorities did not.

News of Brun's exploits travelled far and wide until, eventually, they reached the court of Queen Isabel far across the arid plains of the *meseta*, in Madrid. Isabel was not amused. She wanted Brun's handsome head, and her orders were proclaimed across the land. When the news reached Brun himself, he didn't so much as raise a manly eyebrow. He simply saddled his horse and rode straight to the royal palace.

'You wanted my head?' he asked the queen as he knelt before her. 'Well, here you have it, and my body as well.'

The queen swooned. Legend has it that this was because she was overcome by the selfless offer of the man who knelt before her though, with a little imagination, one could surmise that Brun wouldn't have taken a bath for a while and it could have been his virile mountain odour that knocked her out. Anyway, a little wafting of smelling salts later the queen came to. Brun explained to her how his people depended on contraband for their very survival; Queen Isabel took pity and pardoned him.

Today, with our united Europe, there's no need for smugglers. The Pyreneans seem rather sad about it. 'You used to hide a little bottle of Pernod in your clothes and nervously smile at the customs official,' a border town woman tells Mark Kurlansky in his book *The Basque History of the World*. 'Now it's not any fun at all to go across.' The old rugged heroes are probably sitting at home in their slippers, telling tales of daring deeds past and suffering from that twenty-first-century male self-esteem syndrome they talk about in self-help columns while their wives nag them to go and get a nice job in the factory or at least help out with the dishes.

Oh well, to hell with them. This is the twenty-first century. Forget girl power (*so* nineties) – this is the age of butt-kicking babes, of girls with guns. I'm meant to be able to wrestle bears all on my own – *and* keep my frosted-pink manicure intact.

I finished the last of my chocolate and set off down the other side of the mountain. Almost immediately, the next hill wound its way up to a second summit and down again to Echo, Pedro Brun's home village, and then the road began to climb again. Oh, bloody hell. Just how much of a superwoman was I meant to be? My perfectly waxed legs were beginning to *hurt*. If I was a *real* butt-kicking babe, I wouldn't be riding this dumb bike. Action heroines don't pedal. They speed along in slick convertibles like the girls in *Charlie's Angels* or fly from the rooftops between kung-fu kicks like Michelle Yeoh in *Crouching Tiger, Hidden Dragon*. In *The Matrix,* they travel instantaneously into whole new dimensions – *and* get to wear tight black PVC outfits. I bet they don't have to rinse them out in the hotel room sink with travel wash between shoots either. One thing was clear: somewhere, somehow, I had gone horribly wrong.

The road was interminable. I stopped for a break to stretch my groaning back; within five minutes of climbing back on the bike I was just as uncomfortable as before. I had only twenty kilometres to go to Jaca, my stop for the night, but I'd had more than enough. A cursory check of my body parts came up with the following diagnoses: my back was aching. My left shoulder was agony. My right buttock was tight and sore; both knees groaned with every rotation. If I really put my mind to it, I thought I could detect a slightly sore throat and the beginnings of a mouth ulcer. In the last four days I'd spent twenty-six hours in the saddle. I was knackered.

I stopped for a sandwich and a Coke. Sugar and caffeine, I thought, might just carry me through the last few kilometres. Of course, if I were a real cyclist, I'd stick a caffeine suppository up my bottom like the pros do. Or, better yet, I'd jab a nice big syringe full of amphetamines straight into my stomach muscle.

Doping has been rife in professional cycling for years. 'Under the mud our flesh is white as a sheet . . . our eyes are swimming, and every night we dance like St Vitus instead of sleeping,' cyclist Henri Pélissier told a journalist, Albert Londres, in 1924, the year after he won the Tour de France. Insiders always knew drug-taking went on, but the true extent was only revealed to the wider world with the scandalous unravelling of the Tour of 1998. A couple of days before the start of the race, a bespectacled Belgian named Willy Voet was stopped by customs officers near the Belgian–French border; he was carrying enough dope to spin the wheels of every team in the Tour. Voet was a *soigneur* – the guy who takes care of massage, food bags and vitamins – for Festina, one of the race's highest-rated teams. Over the days that followed riders' hotel rooms were raided, arrests were made, and some of the world's top names in cycling were stripped naked in police cells. A cold, rubber-gloved policeman's finger went where stimulating suppositories had gone before.

The Tour de France, whose cyclists had enjoyed the adulation of the world, looked fit to crumble. Riders, caught up in their own whimsical little world – 'Planet Tour' as one sports writer called it – were outraged at the indignity of actually being expected to obey the law like everyone else. Like petulant tricyclists, they sat down on the tarmac, ripped off their race numbers, and refused to pedal.

The dirt being dished in this case was not amphetamines, which are easily detected in urine tests and so tend not to be used in the bigger, dope-controlled races. The scandal of the 1998 Tour was the widespread use of EPO. EPO (erithro-poietin) is a naturally occurring hormone that stimulates the body to produce red blood cells. The more red blood cells you have, the more oxygen your blood can carry. The more oxygen your blood can carry, the longer and harder you can pedal before reaching your lactate threshold – that's that horrible moment when your legs burn and you start gasping for breath. At this point, your body is in oxygen debt, and the muscles are producing more damaging lactic acid than your blood can flush away. If you're sprinting a hundred metres, obviously the fatigue from lactic acid build-up won't damage your performance too critically as you're only on the run for a few seconds; if you've got to keep on pedalling up and down mountains seven hours a day for a three-week race, though, you're going to want all the oxygen you can get.

Many athletes, caught up in their own little universe of contracts and point scoring, didn't even see taking EPO or other performance-enhancing hormones as doping. Ever since they were teenagers, they had been cocooned from the real world, cosseted from reality; only their cycling results mattered. And so, when everyone else was taking cortisone, EPO and growth hormones, they did too. If the drugs weren't picked up in tests, they didn't exist.

The problem for the authorities is that the athletes and

soigneurs have always been one step ahead of the tests. Tests for amphetamines were only brought in after the British rider, Tom Simpson, died on the slopes of Mont Ventoux during the 1967 Tour. The temperatures reached forty degrees that day; Simpson was near delirium. On the final stretch of the mountain, he fell for the first time. Onlookers rushed to help him; 'Put me back on my bike,' Simpson rasped. Two kilometres later he collapsed again – but this time there was no going back. The autopsy confirmed the presence of amphetamines and alcohol in his blood. Combined with the searing heat and the extraordinary levels of exertion the climb had demanded, they had created a lethal cocktail.

Drug controls became more stringent as the years went by but the pros just developed increasingly creative ways to get round them. Willy Voet, in his book *Breaking the Chain*, describes how he used to insert a condom into the doped rider's anus and then use a syringe to fill it with clean urine. A tube with a small cork in the end was then run out from the condom and covered in carpet pile or short hair to make it invisible. If a charged-up rider came in and found his name on the list for random drugs testing, he would go to the team car to change his clothes and have this contraption fitted. Voet claims to have used this system for three years without ever having a rider caught.

Paul Kimmage, the first ex-pro to 'spit in the soup' by writing a book, *Rough Ride*, about drugs and pro cycling, tells of unusually cheerful riders at the start of those races that are known in the trade as the 'Grands Prix des Chaudières' or Chargers' Grands Prix. Amphetamines have to be taken two hours or so before the finish to give the most effective kick; as most races lasted six or seven hours, riders had to carry the charge with them and great japes were had at the start line as they checked their colleagues' pockets for syringes – and frequently found them. Voet tells how riders would cut in half the tube of a syringe containing a small amount of amphetamine and sew it into the inside of their jersey, level with the stomach. At the right moment, injecting the drug was a simple operation.

When the dope testers started checking haematocrit levels (which indicate your ratio of red cells and therefore show whether you're stuffed to the gills with EPO), the cyclists and their *soigneurs* were, as usual, ahead of the game. Willy Voet reckons that by the 1998 Tour de France about two-thirds of riders had their own testing machines. If one of Voet's riders was called for random testing when his haematocrit level was unnaturally high, Voet would simply stick him with a ready-prepared sodium drip to dilute the blood just enough to pass the test. The transfusion only took a few minutes and was easily done while the doctors waited for the rider to come from his room.

When the Festina affair came to trial, Voet told the court that drug-taking was rife among all the teams. He pointed out that, even after six years of using performance-enhancing drugs, the Festina riders still weren't standing on the podium, so the opposition, surely, must have been taking them too.

When they brought in better testing for EPO, the drugs machine just moved on one step further and invented hormonal cocktails that the scientists had no effective test for. If the authorities are going to charge athletes with illegal drug abuse, they actually have to find them in possession. Everyone hoped that, after the terrible Tour of '98, professional cycling would clean up its act. It hasn't. In the Giro d'Italia 2001, four hundred police officers swooped on the hotel rooms of all twenty teams. They found enough drugs to keep the whole of Colombia in gold medallions: caffeine and corticoids, human growth hormone and testosterone, insulin, the asthma drug-cum-stimulant salbutamol, as well as used syringes. Italy's bright young star, Dario Frigo, who

71

was at that point placed second in the race, was sacked by his team after illegal drugs were found in his hotel room; Marco Pantani, who ironically won the infamous 1998 Tour, was also found guilty of doping. Other high-profile names were placed under investigation.

Unfortunately, I had no caffeine suppositories or amphetamine shots; I had not been on a course of EPO. I pedalled on painfully slowly. My body was jelly; my brain was goo. They say that cycling is a sport for both legs and head: even when your legs are gone, if you use your head you can still succeed. But my head was finished too. All the blood glucose that was supposed to be in my brain had been diverted to my worn-out thighs. I was beginning to feel woozy, light-headed and beset by negative thoughts. So this, then, was the onset of the famous bonk.

With every corner, every brow of a hill, I willed Jaca's jumble of sand-coloured buildings to appear – and again and again, I found nothing more than endless stretches of dry, flat land and the derelict wrecks of settlements long deserted. This part of Spain is littered with abandoned villages. Their huddled, tumbledown buildings have no roofs and their dusky stone walls have fallen into disrepair, the green grass of this fertile region sprouting unheeded where spotless stone floors once lay. These houses have known no inhabitants for some forty years, since the 'economic miracle' of the 1960s. This was when the country folk, tired of the privations of the post-war period and the 'hungry years' of the fifties, were lured to secure factory jobs in urban areas. They packed in their crops and their donkeys, packed up their belongings, and packed into the rapidly overcrowding cities in their droves. In just a couple of decades, countless small villages and hamlets lost their entire populations as the young and able-bodied moved to the towns, and the few elderly who remained passed on to better places still.

When, eventually, I did arrive in Jaca, my mind was so addled that it took half an hour to find the hotel. I smiled dolefully at the receptionist.

'Is it possible to stay here for two nights?' I asked.

'No problem.'

Thank you God. With two nights' rest here, I could take tomorrow off, lie in bed late and then idle away the hours with the newspaper, a coffee, then perhaps a beer and a tapa or two to revive my flagging limbs. This was not, thank goodness, the Tour de France.

Jaca is a bit of a tourist centre in season. The active crowds of Spain come here for their holidays, taking time out from behind their desks to hike up mountains, hurl themselves down canyons, and risk life and limb on white-water rafts. The town with its pretty cobbled streets and glorious, towering cathedral is full of almost-funky outdoor clothing stores and souvenir shops selling gaudy T-shirts and tacky ceramic olive dishes. Unfortunately, the season is summer, and we were now well into autumn. The outdoor enthusiasts with their lithe, fit bodies and suntanned smiles were back behind their city desks and out-of-season OAPs had taken their place.

It was this latter type of tourist that had taken up residence in my hotel. It was not just the guests who had been around a while, though. Outside the dining room hung a framed, photocopied excerpt about the establishment from Hilaire Belloc's essay 'The Pyrenees' – and he wrote it in 1909, which says something for the place's age. 'At Jaca,' wrote Mr Belloc, 'you will find the Hotel Mur, which I have called the kindest little hotel in Europe, and certainly the cleanest in Spain. You will leave Jaca early after spending there your second night.'

The hotel was still clean. The chambermaids were so keen to keep it so that they bounded into my room with their buckets and dusters the next morning while I was still tucked up asleep.

'*Hombre!*' said the one with the mop as she bustled through the door and saw a strange, person-shaped lump in the bed.

'Aaagggghhh,' I replied.

'There's someone *in bed*!' Señora Mop hissed to Señora Buckets who was hovering with her Harpic in the corridor outside.

'Uh,' I confirmed.

I finally allowed them in an hour or so later when I went off for a wander round town; when I came back, they were still in there mopping away fastidiously. And yes, the people were kind. When I eventually dragged myself out of bed and stumbled down to breakfast, they'd cleared away and were sweeping up the dining room.

'Not to worry,' said the waitress with an untroubled beam. 'It's not too late.'

She then vanished and reappeared moments later with a steaming cup of coffee and a sugary bun. The real downer of the Hotel Mur was the rubber sheet on the bed. And the fact that the bedside lights didn't work. And the fact that you had to pay a fifteen-euro deposit for the TV remote control in case you did a runner with it. And the other clientele.

I was the youngest guest of the Hotel Mur by at least thirty years. Every other room in the place was filled by the two parties of geriatrics who were having a bit of a knees-up on their once-a-year village pensioners' outing.

'Are they all together?' I whispered to the receptionist. 'There must be a hundred of them!'

She grinned conspiratorially. 'Not far off. There's one lot of forty-nine from some village near Zaragoza, and another group of forty-five from somewhere up north. They're hell.

Keep mislaying things, losing their room keys, locking themselves out. One old dear got stuck in the bathroom yesterday. It was an hour before anyone noticed she was missing.'

Holiday packages for pensioners are popular in Spain since they are government-sponsored. The idea's that the fluctuations of the tourist trade are eased by the off-season visitors. As an additional bonus, the old folk get a cheap holiday – and, of course, the programme helps to secure the 'grey vote' for the government in the next election. Except that none of them are grey – or the women aren't at least. The trend in Spain, however, is not for blue rinses. The colours here are different. They have yellow rinses, red rinses, orange rinses and brown rinses. When a large group sits together, the result is a lovely blend of autumnal tones.

Perhaps these old women dye their hair such colours to offset the rather gloomy appearance of their clothes. Did nobody tell them that black's not in this year? That the fashion gurus want us to wear bright colours instead? Here is a whole generation of women to whom it means nothing that brown is the new black, or that grey is the new brown that was the new black last year. Or that pink stripes are the new grey that was the new brown that was once, a very long time ago, the new black. (Before that, it was OK to wear black, but that was back when Pepe and Manuel were still alive so their wives weren't wearing black but blue.)

Imagine what it must be like when Spanish widows chat over a plate of chorizo about what to pack for their holidays.

'So, María Remedios, what are you taking to wear in Jaca?'

'Well, María Jesús, I couldn't quite decide but I think I've finally settled on the black dress with short sleeves, and my black cardigan in case it gets chilly in the evenings.'

'Ah . . . so which black dress exactly is that?'

'You know, dear, the one with the pleated black skirt and very generous black waistband that I had to have taken out last year after I consumed my two thousandth litre of olive oil.'

'Oh, the big black one you bought at José's All Black shop?'

'No, no, dear, not *that* big black one. You know, the one I got at Black Widows in 1983, the spring after Manuel passed on.' The two women lapse into silence for a moment while they complete a series of flurried signs of the cross.

'And what about your shoes?'

'Well, I was thinking perhaps the black ones.'

'Oh, you mean the ones you bought at One Foot In The Grave the summer Carmen's Antonio had that affair with Marta from the post office and caught the clap?'

The pensioners at Hotel Mur sat together and chatted a lot – in the dining room, in the lounge, in the reception, pretty much anywhere as long as they didn't have to sit alone – and they gossiped incessantly and boomingly, in the way that deaf people talk to others similarly afflicted. If they had to leave the hotel, they did so in a pack. On the first night, I watched as their two buses pulled up outside the door and the guide shepherded them, still chattering, into their seats. There was no inter-*pueblo* rivalry between these two tribes. But I belonged to neither of them – thank heavens. I made good my escape from Hilaire Belloc's kindly hotel, found an outdoor table at a tapas bar under the cathedral walls, and tucked into mushrooms, prawns, olives and beer.

The next morning, I took my relaxation seriously, determined to build up not just my energy levels, but my fat reserves too. After my shamefully late breakfast, I pottered round Jaca's five or so streets for a couple of happy hours, poking in shops full of rubbish, a bookshop, and the odd sports-clothing store. I had a coffee and a large slice of apple tart in the sun, ambled a little more, touched up my carbohydrate stores with a beer and a cheese and ham toasty, and read the paper on a café terrace.

Then I hit upon the problem with spending an entire day in Jaca: there is only so much time you can bear to spend e-mailing from the cyber café surrounded by overexcited kids on the Playstation. You can only browse in a limited number of shops selling rock-climbing ropes. There are only so many times you can wander round the same five streets before the Guardia Civil start to give you shifty looks.

'Excuse me, *señorita*,' they seemed about to say, 'but this is the sixth time you've strolled down this boring little street, peered into that tacky shop window and read the hackneyed jokes painted on the tasteless ceramic olive jars. And it's siesta-time, *señorita*. Decent people don't wander the streets during the siesta. Hadn't you better go back to your hotel?'

The hours slowly, slowly ticked by. I read my book a little, then strolled some more. I tried desperately to spin the evening out till at least eight thirty when I could respectably eat dinner. Filling these dead hours between when I wanted to eat (about seven o'clock) and when the Spanish restaurateurs deemed it appropriate (anything after nine) was turning into something of a daily ritual. I took refuge in my hotel room and watched *Lois y Clark: Las Nuevas Aventuras de Superman,* which was on TV every evening and to which I was becoming fast addicted. Today, Jimmy's father had shown up. Jimmy (whose name Lois *y* Clark pronounced 'Cheemee') is a young guy at the newspaper where they work – and his father turned out to be a terrible crook. It was only in the nick of time that Clark was able to change into his Superman outfit and save the world. It was exciting stuff.

Finally I gave in and ate anyway: stewed rabbit with mountain mushrooms. It was tasty but fiddly, with little meat and much spitting of bones. I was suddenly desperate to leave. How prescient Mr Belloc was in his comment that his readers would leave at the crack of dawn on day two. Perhaps he too had spent a few hours too many wandering the cobbled streets and poking around shops full of 1909-style outdoor clothes: woollen knee socks and garters, practical tweed jackets to keep off the chill. And, let's face it, poor Mr Belloc wouldn't even have had the option of checking his e-mail at Ciber Centro.

7

A Load of Fossils

Some might call it cheating. I call it a stroke of genius. The problem was that I was faced with an unexpected deadline. I needed to be in Barcelona by Sunday, as my parents had just announced that they were coming to check that I was really alive, that I hadn't been abducted by a hairy-chinned mountain man, that both my legs hadn't dropped off from the effort of climbing mountain passes.

My mother had been nervous about the trip from the start – where was I going to stay? Had I booked my hotels ahead? How many pairs of knickers had I packed? What if I found myself an object of attraction to a vast, almost-extinct, 250-kilo brown bear? I tried to pacify her. I would take my mobile phone, I said, and she could call me whenever she liked. She did. I would be crawling up and round, round and up some endless hill, or sitting smugly on the top of the mountain, surveying the conquered pinnacles at my feet, when a high-pitched 'blippety-blippety bleep bleep . . . blippety-blippety bleep bleep' would emanate from my handlebar bag and everything would start to shake. No, these weren't the shudderings of a gradually shifting mountain, nor seismic shock waves emanating from deep within their Pyrenean core. This was my mother on the telephone.

Today was Wednesday. If I rolled my next two days' routes, which were short ones anyway, into one, and took a bus over the tedious flats of central Catalonia, I'd get to Barcelona on time. Would a hundred kilometres in one day over mountains be too much, I wondered. And then I had the brainwave. A rude, four-letter word to the purer kind of athlete, perhaps, but a beautiful sound to me.

'Please,' I said to my new friend the hotel receptionist, casting a furtive glance around me to make sure nobody would hear, 'could you order me a *taxi*?'

The first thirty kilometres were going to be tiresome anyway. They followed a dull, flat highway, replete with thundering lorries and whooshing cars. It was so much more agreeable to travel them in the back of an air-conditioned car. The taxi driver was an affable fellow and much intrigued by my journey. I told him I was heading today to Ainsa.

'Ainsa?' he gulped. 'But to get to Ainsa you have to go over the Cotefablo pass.' I checked my map. Sure enough, there was a pass called Cotefablo about ten kilometres from Biescas, where I'd asked him to drop me.

'That's right,' I said cheerfully.

'*Madre!*' said the taxi driver. 'That's a top-grade hill. When they have races round here they sometimes make them climb Cotefablo, but it's only for the grade one cyclists.'

I was beginning to feel a little uneasy. What exactly was a grade one cyclist, anyway? Whoever they were, I had a nasty feeling they might not include my name in their number. We rounded a bend in the road.

'Ha! There it is! That's Cotefablo over there.'

The taxi driver waved his arms eagerly towards the right, showing scant regard for normal conventions that dictate you drive with your hands on the steering wheel. I looked over and let out a little yelp. Cotefablo was towering and resplendent, its high, distant peak shrouded in mist. It was a very big mountain indeed. I began nervously to count my bananas.

'Oh, don't worry,' said the taxi driver, who seemed to be rather enjoying himself. 'The road doesn't go all the way to the top. You'll only need to climb about two-thirds of it. And Cotefablo's not half as high as the passes you'll have to climb over the next few days on the way to Sort.'

We arrived, thankfully, at Biescas before he could say any more. I indulged in a little positive thinking, rationed my bananas and began to pedal slowly and steadily. Clearly I was going to have to keep this up for some time. After a while, I stopped for my first banana, then pedalled slowly some more and – here's the funny thing – arrived ten minutes later, rather effortlessly, at the top. Grade one indeed!

The beautiful thing was that after the Cotefablo summit, it was all downhill. I hurtled headlong, gathering speeds I had hitherto only dreamed of. I careered and I cruised; I even managed to let go of the brakes enough to stop my hands cramping. I wasn't as a general rule very good at going down hills. It was a small comfort to know that I wasn't alone – Gianno Bugno, once world champion, was apparently so disconcerted by belting down mountains that he had to hum Mozart to calm his nerves. He had good reason to be scared, though. The pros reach quite terrifying speeds on the descents and they scorch along so close to one another that if one of them takes a tumble they can all go flying, sometimes with tragic results. In the 1995 Tour de France, former Olympic champion Fabio Casartelli died descending the Pyrenean Col de Portet d'Aspet at high speed. He crashed and slid across a vicious camber before smashing his head against a concrete post. He wasn't the first person to perish on a Tour descent. In 1935, the Spaniard Francesco Cepeda died after plunging down a ravine on the Col du Galabier in the Alps; in 1957, radio reporter Alex Virot and his motorcyclist driver, Rene Wagner, were killed when they fell into a ravine and died during the Barcelona-Ax-les-Thermes stage.

Fortunately, nothing so grisly happened to me. The most dramatic result of my increased speed was that my contact lens popped out of my eye and stuck to my sunglasses. But whatever the state of my lenses, I was obviously getting better at mountains. I positively flew through villages and valleys, spun round the switchbacks angling my dangerously laden bike racily into the corners, and let out high-volume whoops of joy each time I came round a bend alive. I became so fuelled on adrenalin, so excited by my own infallibility, so high on my new-found cycling prowess, that I began to sing – out loud. I even made up my own lyrics: 'I'm nearly there, oh yeah / Oh yeah, I'm nearly there / Nearly there, nearly there / Oh yeah, oh yeah,' I bellowed from the depths of my lungs, to no easily identifiable tune.

'Watch out, Kylie, I'm coming,' I shrieked as I tore round the last bend and along the final stretch of road. And so it was that, rather pleased with myself, I arrived in Ainsa in time for lunch.

Ainsa is a big tourist attraction in an area that doesn't have many. Its fortifications go back to the eleventh century and there's a pretty seventeenth-century church with big, clanging, bronze bells. The town has been beautifully and sympathetically restored. The cobbled streets are so clean it's unsettling. The stone houses have wrought-iron balconies and perfectly blooming begonias. But here's the thing: the old quarter of Ainsa has no soul. It feels like an empty shell. Nobody seems to actually *live* in those pretty little houses; there's no feeling that anybody gives a damn about the clean, cobbled streets or the pert, pink flowers. Down the hill, in the less desirable new town, it's a different story. The streets were teeming. But even in the early evening, when the whole of Spain takes to the streets for its daily *paseo*, the old quarter of Ainsa was as dead as the eleventh-century knights who once fired arrows from its ramparts. Once the tour buses had packed up and gone home, the place was horribly, eerily empty.

I arrived at the hostel where I'd booked a room. The door was locked. To be fair, though, it was lunchtime and, thinking the owners were probably off somewhere eating, I went to have a spot of lunch myself. As I settled into an outdoor table in the elegantly restored Plaza Mayor, the waitress wrinkled her nose. My chain had just come off so my fingernails were black and oily, and I probably didn't smell at my freshest, but there was no need for nose-wrinkling, at least not while I was watching. I tried to ask the way to the washroom. She didn't even let me get the words out before saying rather pointedly, 'It's upstairs.'

The food was good but overpriced. I went for a 'Pyrenean Platter', a tourist dish if ever there was one. It consisted of two kinds of chop, sausage, ham, mushrooms, potatoes and salad. They charged extra for the bread and for the bottled water that the waitress brought when I'd specifically asked for tap.

Still, I felt more kindly towards the world with a full stomach, and headed back to the hostel. The door was now open, but nobody was to be seen, so I put my head round and shouted my most winning rendition of '*Hola*.' A door quietly clicked shut at the end of the corridor. I imagined I'd disturbed a guest mid-siesta so, thinking the owners must still be eating lunch, settled down on the step outside and started to read my book. After a minute or two the bedroom door opened again and the cleaner emerged. Clearly she'd thought I'd gone away. No such luck: I pounced and told her I'd booked a room.

'Well, I wouldn't know anything about that,' she said grumpily. 'You'll have to talk to Rosa.'

'And where will I find Rosa?'

'Oh, you can't talk to her now. She'll be having her lunch. You'll just have to wait.' And with that, she was off.

'Will you be seeing Rosa?' I asked her rapidly retreating back with just a glimmer of hope in my voice.

'Not likely. I'm going for *my* lunch now. I've not eaten yet.' And that was the last I saw of her.

'May your siesta be plagued by terrible nightmares,' I muttered after her, and for good measure cursed her to the unpleasant fate of washing other people's dirty bedlinen for the rest of time. Sitting back on the hard, stone step, I pulled my phone from my bag and called the hostel's number many times. Nobody answered. And so I sat, increasingly irritated, for more than an hour. Eventually, on about my tenth attempt, an old man answered the phone. I explained that I had booked a room and was waiting outside.

'Oh,' he said. 'I'm just upstairs. I've been watching you sitting there for ages. I wondered what you were doing.'

Other than stupid hoteliers, miserable cleaners and offensive waitresses, the town was populated entirely by tourists, most of whom were pensioners. It was obviously a big week out for the rinse brigade. To add a little variety, there was also a busload of bored, fractious teenagers and their fraught-looking teacher. They were unpleasant children but I had to sympathize. Ainsa is hardly a top destination for a school trip.

I went to the museum.

'Open,' said the sign on the door.

'We're closed,' said the woman at the desk. 'But if you want, you can look at the fossil collection. It's one euro fifty.'

I declined. There were plenty of perfectly good fossils eating ice creams in the town square and I could look at them for free.

Climbing the church belfry only cost sixty cents, but it was nearly the death of me. I perched on a precariously steep and narrow staircase to photograph the impressive bronze bells at just the moment they chose to chime. Having nearly tumbled in fright down the staircase to meet a messy end, I went off the belfry.

The church itself was free. If the thought of actually keeping your cash in your pocket unsettled you, though, you could put a euro in a slot and listen to a scratchy, five-minute tape recording of a Gregorian chant. Fortunately for me, one of my fellow tourists had already done the deed so I didn't feel obliged and, instead, made my way down to the crypt. It featured attractive old Islamic pillars and arches: after the Christians had overthrown the Moors and sent them packing back to Africa, they built a good many churches on the sites of mosques. I was to learn more about the Christian church-building mania a few weeks later when my by then firmer and tauter legs had pedalled me into Seville. For now, though, I could only remark that the arches were pretty.

The next stop on the tourist route was the Museo de Oficios y Artes Tradicionales, a traditional arts and crafts museum. It cost two euros fifty to walk through the door and, as far as I could fathom from the promotional literature combined with a sneaky peek through the window, comprised a collection of wooden implements and spinning wheels. Perhaps I am a terrible philistine. I accept that I don't know my spinning wheels. But I reckon that once you've seen one spinning wheel (and I saw plenty on my very own school trips all those years ago) you've seen them all. I kept my euros and headed down the hill to the modern part of the town where I indulged in such quotidian, twenty-first-century activities as buying today's newspaper and tomorrow's bananas.

On the way, I passed a huddle of increasingly desperate teenagers waiting disconsolately by their school bus. Neither the teacher nor the driver was anywhere in sight. The kids had obviously been ready to go home to their skateboards and computer games hours ago. They must have tired of the delights of fossils and spinning wheels before their time was up and had been forced to seek out their own ways of killing time; in this case, seeing who could create the most damage by hurling rocks at a now-battered signpost. They were still at it when I walked back, though I'm happy to say the signpost was resolutely holding its own.

I liked the new part of town very much better than the old. It was buzzing with people, all of whom were friendly and polite. I poked quite happily around the outdoor sports shop.

'Can I help you, *señorita*?' asked the delightfully well-proportioned man at the counter.

It was a shame I couldn't prolong our conversation by buying anything from him as I couldn't carry another thing in my panniers. I returned to the old town reluctantly and drank an overpriced beer in the empty Plaza Mayor. The weather came out in sympathy with my mood: a light drizzle set in and I was forced back to my hostel to watch *Lois y Clark* and sit out the long wait till dinner.

On the dot of nine o'clock I headed to the only restaurant that had a reasonable menu posted on the door. It was the only place in the old part of town that actually had people in it, which gave me high hopes, though I subsequently learned that its popularity was due only to the fact that Real Madrid was playing football on the telly. The Spanish enthusiasm for football surpasses even their fondness for eating entrails, and Real Madrid is one of the teams that most inflames the spectators' passions. Unfortunately for both players and fans, this season they were doing remarkably poorly, and on this particular evening they gave a suitably gloomy performance against Las Palmas. The barstool-footballers of Ainsa were taking Madrid's failure to heart and the mood in the place was grim.

'May I have a table for dinner?' I asked the man behind

the bar. His eyes were glued to the television screen; Real Madrid was going in for a tackle.

'We're not serving food,' he grunted without making eye contact, as if dinner were a ridiculous request to make of a restaurant, and on an important day like today of all days. In the end, he rustled up a plate of cold, fatty chorizo and threw it down on a table in the bar area amid the strangely bestial sounds of men engrossed in the beautiful game. I bolted my food and bought a big bottle of comforting Rioja – to take away. I slunk back to my room and the company of my TV remote control, and clandestinely guzzled my wine from the bathroom water glass. It was 9.55, and time for the most pressing appointment of my day: the weather report. Such things are important when you spend your days battling with the great outdoors.

8

Doña Pilar and Her Very Large Sandwich

'Buh-duh-buh-duh-buh-duh-buh,' bumped my bike over the immaculate, litter-free cobbles of Ainsa's Plaza Mayor, the cryogenically frozen heart of that characterless town. I had risen early, eager to leave, and had managed to rustle up a coffee and croissant in the only bar showing the slightest sign of life. The barman was buried deep in his newspaper.

'Er, excuse me, could I have a black coffee and one of those?' I asked, pointing to the pastries.

'*Madre de Dios!* Where did you spring from?' said the barman, astonished at the sight of a fellow human being, and a strangely dressed one at that.

Certainly, nobody else was to be seen in Ainsa that morning – the hostel owner, for one, had crawled back under his rock – for the tour buses had yet to despatch that day's victims for their visits to the over-rated fossil collection and the over-priced spinning wheel display.

'K-k-k-k-k-k-k-k-k-k-k,' clattered my wheels over the unmade-up surface, for the first thirty kilometres of the road I took out of Ainsa were being dug up. 'BAH-BAH-BAH-BAH-BAH-BAH,' blared the jackhammers and

'Vrooooooooom,' boomed the JCBs in the place of the gentle tapping woodpeckers and the whinnying wild horses of the days before. Workmen with hard yellow hats and leering grins stood in for snorting pigs and cavorting sheep.

The roads of this part of northern Aragón have seen more demolition over the last century than is perhaps reasonable for a road to expect, for the pastures of Aragón provided the site for one of the bloodier fronts of the Spanish Civil War. It was not far from here that George Orwell was injured – he was shot through the neck by a stray bullet – while fighting against the Fascists. Bundled into an ambulance, he was sent to the hospital at Barbastro, about fifty kilometres south of Ainsa.

'What a journey!' writes Orwell in his subsequent book about the conflict, *Homage to Catalonia*. 'It used to be said that in this war you got well if you were wounded in the extremities, but always died of a wound in the abdomen. I now realized why. No one who was liable to bleed internally could have survived those miles of jolting over metal roads that had been smashed to pieces by heavy lorries and never repaired since the war began. Bang, bump, wallop!'

It was around these hills that the Trotskyite militia unit with which Orwell was fighting, the POUM, tried to wrestle back land from Franco's Nationalist forces. They were a raggedy bunch as Orwell describes them, with threadbare, louse-ridden uniforms, decades-old weapons that didn't work, practically no training, and marching skills that showed 'far less cohesion than a flock of sheep'. Alongside them limped a number of dogs, enlisted as mascots. 'One wretched brute that marched with us had had POUM branded on it in huge letters and slunk along as though conscious that there was something wrong with its appearance,' Orwell wrote. And so the men and boys, for many of them were only fifteen or sixteen years old, sat seemingly endlessly in their trenches, fighting the cold, the lice – 'the human louse somewhat resembles a tiny lobster, and he lives chiefly in your trousers' – and the rats. These last were huge, bloated creatures, some of them the size of cats, to whom Orwell formed an understandable objection when they ran over his body as he lay down at night. (Orwell's horror of the rodents in the Aragonese trenches is said to have inspired Room 101 in *Nineteen Eighty-Four,* the torture room that contained for each person their worst imaginable fear which, for protagonist Winston Smith, was rats.) At times Orwell's militia abandoned their faulty, outdated weapons and fought the war with a megaphone instead. They tried to break the spirit of the Fascists whose trenches lay just a few hundred metres away: 'Buttered toast! We're just sitting down to buttered toast over here! Lovely slices of buttered toast!' the megaphone man would bellow across the hills.

Buttered toast, indeed! Perhaps I've lived a too-luxurious life – I come, after all, from the post-rationing generation – but I fancied something more than plain buttered toast for my mid-morning break, which I took to ward off any further frisky moments like the one that had nearly broken my spirit on the way into Jaca. I stopped in a small village and ate a very large cheese and tomato sandwich in a down-at-heel café. A group of old men stood around the bar, their heads in a cloud of smoke, a carpet of cigarette butts at their feet, and discussed the issues of the day.

'*Buenos días,* Jesús.'

'*Qué tal,* Ángel.'

'So, what happened to you this morning? You weren't at Gabriel's for the eight a.m. tipple.'

'Mislaid my flat cap, *hombre*! Couldn't leave the house.'

'*Qué coño!*'

They dragged on their Ducados, puffed and wheezed a little, and then took a slurp of frighteningly cheap wine.

'So we'll see you at the park bench for the three p.m. sit-and-stare session?'

91

'Oh yes, that's always a good one. I'll try to be there.' A long pause. More wheezing.

'And Ignacio's getting a few of us together to sit and do nothing in the square at about five-thirty. I think we'll probably go straight there from the post-siesta tipple at Aurelio's.'

Or words to that effect.

Back in the saddle, I trekked up the 1,500-metre Coll de Fades. The staccato machine-gun fire of decades past and the present-day battering of jackhammers receded into the distance as I came out of the war zone and into the peace of the mountains.

For an hour or so, I cycled along a high ridge road. I was on top of the world, looking down over spectacular views of endless mountains dressed in rich autumn colours. Then, winding down the switchbacks on the other side, I passed tiny villages of sand-coloured houses perched precariously on the edge of a cliff, or sitting in solitary glory on the crest of a hill. These villages comprised only ten or fifteen houses, from whose windows must have stretched uninterrupted mountain tops for as far as the eye could see. Over each clump of houses towered the ubiquitous church steeple.

Maybe it was scenes like these that inspired Goya to paint his famous renditions of the countryside and its peasants. Francisco de Goya was Aragonese; he was born in the south of the province, near Zaragoza, in 1746, and is reckoned to be by far Spain's greatest painter of that period. Goya lived most of his adult life in Madrid, but a Spaniard's loyalty belongs to his *pueblo,* his home town, first and to king and country second. From Madrid, Goya used to write letters to his friend Martín Zapater in Zaragoza begging him to send the Aragonese chocolate and nougat that he craved from home.

Goya's works included not only formal portraiture of

kings, queens and dukes – for he was a court painter to
Carlos III and Carlos IV – but, as he grew older, an
increasing collection of paintings that showed his affinity for
the common people. Goya, after all, was a commoner
himself. He wasn't originally called Francisco de Goya; he
was born plain old Goya, but added the 'de' in later life to
try to prove that he was not the ruddy-faced country
bumpkin everyone thought he was, but came from noble
stock. He struggled to make his name in the early years. He
was an impetuous, argumentative, arrogant young upstart
from the provinces: he had to wait till he was forty before he
was appointed King's Painter, and longer still to acquire
the coveted position of Royal Chamber Painter. Looking at
his likenesses of the monarchs of that time, it's a wonder ho
wanted the job, as painting their portraits must have been a
business fraught with the risk of causing offence. Both
Carlos III and Carlos IV were quite staggeringly unsightly.
Goya's portraits of the former show a gangly posture, a
bulbous great nose, a non-existent chin, and a goofy, imbe-
cilic grin, while the latter boasted a bloated body, a round,
red face with puffy cheeks, and expressionless, vacant blue
eyes. And, presumably, these were *favourable* likenesses.
They seemed to make the royals happy, at any rate. One
famous sitter who wasn't so pleased was the Duke of
Wellington, who had garnered considerable favour in the
Spanish court after he'd driven the French from Spain in
the Peninsular Wars. Goya depicted Wellington as cold,
disdainful and proud. The Duke was offended to the soles
of his Wellington boots and, rumour has it, the two men
nearly came to blows right there in the artist's studio. It's
lucky for Goya that they didn't. Goya was nearly seventy,
deaf and infirm; Wellington, on the other hand, was rather
good at fighting.

Despite the risks, Goya's status as court painter pleased
him. He was a social climber and a poser, so concerned with

appearances that he bought an English-made, gilded two-wheel carriage – one of only four in the city – which he loved to take for spins around Madrid. He only changed it for a four-wheeled carriage after a series of accidents, one of which nearly killed another man. Even then, he was much troubled when his brother's family came to stay and he was obliged to buy a pair of tamer mules for them to drive around with – what if people were to think that he had been forced to downgrade in this demeaning way, and that the mules were for his own use? The horror!

More famously, Goya managed to embark on an affair with Spain's most desirable lady, the Duchess of Alba, who was so glamorous that she wore a new pair of shoes every day. (This was a time when female feet were considered particularly alluring, for women had only just broken the social taboo that demanded their toes be kept hidden under voluminous hooped petticoats.) But we'll talk more about the Duchess of Alba and the unfortunate fate of her feet when we go down south, to the steamy estates of Sanlúcar de Barrameda where this Aragonese country boy courted his society girl in the shade of the sherry vineyards.

That night I stayed in a very tiny village called Bonansa, four gruelling, grinding kilometres up a steep hill, off the main road. Bonansa is a lovely little village (take special note of the word 'little') and is well worth a stop for a night or two if you have a good book. The woman who owned the *casa rural,* Doña Pilar, seemed a little suspicious of foreigners (and that meant anyone who lived more than twenty kilometres away) and was particularly put out when I produced a lock for my bike.

'Nobody will steal that here,' she said somewhat testily. 'It's the only bike in the village.' Our conversation did not improve. She was a striding, squinting character, who had clearly knitted her dark-brown sweater by hand. But Doña

Pilar was not a woman given solely to domestic pursuits; Bonansa is a small place and this, no doubt, encourages multi-tasking among its inhabitants. Later in the evening I saw her marching with great fortitude, a hefty sack of logs slung over her shoulder. I had the strong impression she had chopped them herself, quite possibly with a mighty slice of her hard, bare hand.

'Oooaarreeeiahrrroooiiierrrr?' asked Doña Pilar.

I apologized for my poor Spanish and asked her to repeat herself.

'Aaarrrrrooorrrraaaaiiiheerrr?' she implored, rather more loudly than the first time, her eyes narrowing into an ever more mistrustful squint. This, after all, was a woman who, I later discovered when I'd rummaged around in the depths of my panniers and found a Babel fish to stick in my ear, had never been to Sort, a comparatively large town just seventy-five kilometres away. Imagine her suspicion of a person who came from a whole different *country*.

She was asking, it turned out, where I was planning to eat dinner, but her accent was so strong that her words were to me little more than an unintelligible jumble of vowel sounds with a few mouthfuls of tongue-defying rolled 'r's thrown in. I strained hard to understand as, with many repetitions hurled at me at ever-increasing volume, she told me that Bonansa did have a bar and restaurant, but it was closed at present for renovations. I shouldn't imagine the trifling detail of not actually being open was making a great deal of difference to the establishment's profits.

'Oh. I see,' I said.

There was a discouraging silence.

'Right,' I said and paused meaningfully.

A longer silence. Doña Pilar narrowed her eyes and studied me. Oh, to hell with it. I certainly wasn't climbing back on that bike and hacking back up that stupid hill again today. If she wasn't going to offer, I'd just have to ask.

'So, would you be able to give me something simple for supper?'

'Ooooiiiaarrrrrrrhhhaaaeeeeoooouuuiiiieeeerrr?'

'Well, perhaps just a sandwich?'

'Iaaarrrriiiuuuurrr?'

'Well, anything you've got. Do you have any cheese? Or a slice of ham?'

'Oooiiirrraaaaahhhhiirrr.'

And so it was that I ended up with the largest sandwich I have ever seen for my supper. In the end, the poor woman gave up trying to communicate with me and just filled the sandwich with anything she could find in the fridge: cheese, ham, tomatoes and the remains of yesterday's lunch. It was a sandwich of such monstrous proportions that it defeated me entirely, and I had to hide half of it in a piece of tin foil and bury it secretly in the bathroom bin.

The top floor of Doña Pilar's *casa rural* consisted of several en suite double bedrooms, all of which opened onto a sitting room with a sofa and armchairs and a TV. Happily for me, I was the only guest – I don't suppose Bonansa has a booming tourist trade – so I had the sitting room to myself. The French windows opened out onto mountains and fields, and a veritable cacophony of animal noises: the cows and sheep were the lead vocalists with their strident moos and baaas (their articulation, I couldn't help but notice, was very similar to Doña Pilar's); backing vocals came in the form of harmonic cooing from the wood pigeons. On the instrumental front, we had the mellow jingle-jangle of cow bells, while a lively percussion line was played by the woodpeckers.

And so I sat happily in my private sitting room with Bonansa's Animal Symphony Orchestra playing its distinctive version of background music, chomping bravely on my gargantuan sandwich and indulging in a little inspirational reading: Lance Armstrong's autobiography, *It's Not About the Bike*. Lance, for those who don't spend the month of July each year fixated by such things, has won the Tour de France for several years running. This is particularly sensational given that just a few years before his first Tour victory he was diagnosed with testicular cancer that, by the time it was discovered, had already spread to his lungs and brain. The combination of chemotherapy and brain surgery that followed should have destroyed his athletic career (and quite likely finished him off altogether) – but it didn't. He made his remarkable comeback just at the time when the world of cycling really needed a blue-eyed boy: Lance's first Tour win was in 1999, the year following the scandalous drugs bust-up that saw a number of cyclists, managers and *soigneurs* in police cells.

Reading Lance's testosterone-charged life story (a child-hood spent playing catch with flaming, petrol-soaked tennis balls; teenage years hurtling on his bicycle across red-lighted intersections in downtown Dallas; adulthood tearing down mountain switchbacks at breakneck speed, quite literally on one unfortunate occasion), I was much comforted to learn that his bottom too hurts like hell when he's in the saddle for hour after hour, day after day. It just goes to prove that even the hardest of arses gets sore. I was also soothed to read that Lance finds climbing hills slow and painful, just like me, though to be fair Lance's climbing probably features less of the slow and more of the painful than mine does. And I don't think Lance gets to sit down and eat a celebratory banana at the top.

Still, while I wasn't about to win the Tour de France, I was at least beginning to look more like a cyclist. This is not necessarily a good thing; cyclists are the ones, after all, whose appearance has been likened most memorably to that of toasted whippets – something to do with being both grue-somely gaunt and burnt to a crisp. Despite my rigorous application of factor thirty sun cream, I too had acquired extraordinary stripes across my thighs and arms. The latter were brown, my hands milky white, except for a rather strange circle where the hole in the glove comes. As for my face, I was developing what can only be described as a cyclist's nose. And despite the efforts of Doña Pilar's sandwich, I was by the day becoming skinnier and skinnier.

9

Who Let the Dogs Out?

When Louis XIV of France said 'There are no more Pyrenees', he was clearly misinformed. He had blatantly not bundled his freshly powdered wig under a cycling helmet, stuffed his spare velvet knickerbockers into a very tiny pannier and tried cycling from Versailles down to Spain.

On the other hand, perhaps he was dabbling in metaphor. For the date was 1700 – the year the French Bourbon dynasty took over the throne of Spain. Carlos II had died. Carlos had been the pitiful result of generations of in-breeding: a king so weak that he had to be presented at court held up by strings that his nurse worked like a puppet. His jaw stuck out so far that he couldn't chew his food properly, adding indigestion to his seemingly endless catalogue of medical complaints. But the big issue was that Carlos and his wife produced no children as, the history books tell us, neither of them had the remotest idea how to go about it. (Clearly nobody at court thought it wise to inform them.) Carlos appointed the French Bourbon duke Philippe d'Anjou as his heir; when he died, the Spanish branch of the Habsburg house died with him and the Bourbons moved in. Three hundred years later, the House of Bourbon still wears the crown in Spain.

Philippe, who from this point forward was known as Felipe V of Spain, was not amused at becoming king. Spain, he thought, was a nasty, smelly, backward dustbowl and he preferred the elegant surroundings of Versailles. His opinion didn't count for much. At the tender age of sixteen, he was forced to leave Louis's magnificent court and travel on horseback down to Madrid. When he arrived, he found to his horror that his worst fears about the Spanish sense of fashion were confirmed: the nobles actually *wore their own hair*. His humour was doubtless not improved by hiking up and down all those Pyrenean passes on the way.

To this day, I can tell you, there *are* Pyrenees. (Both Lance Armstrong and Miguel Induráin will back me up on this, I'm sure.) I can also tell you that they are big and steep and they make your legs hurt when you pedal up them carrying six weeks' luggage. From the very few lines of notes that I wrote for Friday 5 October, it seems that I cursed my luggage a lot, as swearing about my panniers takes up most of them. I can tell you that I cycled seventy kilometres, burned 1,134 calories if the heart rate monitor is to be trusted, and that it took me around five hours. I can tell you that I ate some toast and jam for breakfast, then a cheese and tomato sandwich, four bananas, some cookies, a plate of pistachio nuts, a plate of prawns and a pizza with cheese, bacon and olives, and drank one beer and one glass of wine. I climbed two mountain passes, but only one of them was marked on the map (had Louis XIV's assertions been influencing the mapmakers, I wondered), an oversight which I felt rather bitter about at the time if the curses in my notebook (another two lines) are anything to go by. Clearly Friday 5 October was not a very articulate day.

As well as being a big day for swearing, Friday 5 October was a big day for frightening encounters with very large dogs. The first one prowled at the end of a remarkably strong-looking iron chain outside the bar I stopped at for my mid-morning sandwich. (How ferocious must this beast be if it needs a chain that thick, I wondered.) I parked my bike up against a railing; the dog stalked over, a moody expression on his face, and started to sniff the wheels in a territorial manner. It took every ounce of courage to steel myself, to stare the beast in the eye and to growl at him menacingly in words he would understand.

'Grrrrrrrr.'

Then I hissed at him threateningly, just to make absolutely sure there could be no mistake, 'Listen here, doggy. If you piss on my nice, new, green bike, I'll bash you over the head with my super-strength Kryptonite bike lock.'

And then I snarled fearsomely for good measure. The enormous dog blinked, then widened his eyes in a doleful expression, let out a pitiful little whimper and scampered away as fast as his great, furry paws could carry him.

I didn't win the second stand-off so easily. I arrived wheezing at the top of the second pass of the day (this was the one they hadn't marked on the map, bastards) in desperate need of a banana stop. I found a suitably positioned panoramic picnic table, tumbled weakly from my bike, and was just opening the bag to fish out a slightly squishy banana when an almighty barking broke out. Split seconds later, from behind the white house on the very summit of the hill rushed three astonishingly large white shaggy dogs. These weren't normal dogs, they were monsters. They were the size of small ponies but with bigger, sharper teeth. I knew about their teeth because they were curling their lips and baring their fangs in a manner that suggested my super-strength Kryptonite bike lock might not be enough to save me. Instantly forgetting my banana, I had just enough time, as the white beasts bore down on me, to yell bravely in the general direction of the white house a line I'd been longing to use all week: 'WHO LET THE DOGS OUT?'

'Woof, woof-woof, woof—'

'*Waaaaahhh!*' I shrieked as I leapt on the bike. This was not a healing primal scream; this was the petrified-to-the-toes-of-my-clippy-clop-bike-shoes variety. I pedalled like crazy and hurtled in abject terror down the other side of the mountain as fast as my wheels would turn.

An hour or two before this, very shortly after cycling out of Doña Pilar's lair fortified by strong hot coffee and toast that she had served to me entirely wordlessly (she was learning), I had crossed the border from Aragón into Catalonia. In bygone times, these two regions were allies and unaffiliated to the rest of Spain. In the twelfth century, a tactically arranged marriage joined the two to create the kingdom of Aragón and Catalonia. With their combined military force, they were able to send the beturbaned Arabs packing and get to work on forging an empire while the rest of the peninsula was still tied up with fighting the Moors.

The first major expedition of this new, imperial force set sail in 1229 with Jaume I, Count of Barcelona and King of Aragón, at the helm. Jaume was thirty-one years old and made a rousing hero if his underlings' accounts are anything to go by.

'This king, Jaume of Aragón, was the handsomest man in the world,' wrote the chronicler Bernat Desclot. 'For he was four inches taller than any other man, very well shaped and endowed in all his members.' Desclot does not divulge how he became privy to such details; perhaps breeches were worn tight in those days.

Mighty members or otherwise, Jaume and his descendants succeeded in conquering the Balearic Islands, Naples, Sardinia and Sicily. Trade flourished and a class of nouveaux riches merchants rose through the ranks. So gauche were these parvenus that one Francesc de Eiximinis found it necessary to explain to them how to behave at table. They should not, he told them, do anything that 'might provoke or move another person to horror or vomit. Nor, for the same reason, should you talk about disgusting things, like shit or enemas or laxatives or repulsive diseases, or about hangings or judicial sentences, or anything else that might cause nausea or vomiting.'

But all good things come to an end. In 1479 Fernando II inherited the throne of Aragón and Catalonia. This was the same Fernando who was married to Isabel, Queen of Castile, and became one half of the despotic 'Catholic Monarchs' duo that finally overthrew the Moors, instigated the Inquisition and gave Columbus his sailing orders. Isabel's family had been firmly opposed to the match; they wanted her to marry Alfonso V of Portugal instead. If that had happened, the whole political shape of the Iberian peninsula would have been changed. Isabel, however, was having nothing of family interference. Fernando was young, smart, charming and handsome; Alfonso was old and ugly. Isabel and Fernando married, still teenagers, in a castle in Segovia. She wore white brocade and ermine; he wore a sable-lined golden robe. The newlyweds, incidentally, were first cousins. This meant that a papal dispensation was needed for the marriage to go ahead. Rather than muck about with the real thing, Fernando forged the paperwork with the help of his father and the archbishop of Toledo. When the Pope discovered their deviousness, he was so put out that he excommunicated the pair of them, a bad start for the couple who would eventually whitewash the whole of Spain with their own unforgiving brand of Catholic purity.

Papal piques aside, the marriage of Fernando and Isabel brought Catalonia once and for all under the Castilian yoke it had fought so hard to escape. One of Fernando's first acts was to set up the Inquisition in Barcelona. The Jewish merchant class, which provided the backbone of the city's financial business, packed its yarmulkes and fled over the mountains to France.

What Fernando didn't banish was the Catalan language – not that he would have been likely to succeed, judging by subsequent attempts. The Catalans take the matter of their language very seriously; it is an outward indication of their autonomy, of their distinction from the rest of Spain. Franco tried to stop them speaking it – in non-Castilian regions his government even posted stickers in public telephone booths instructing users to 'speak Christian', as the regime referred to the Castilian tongue. They went so far as to call Catalan a dialect of Castilian Spanish, a mistake visitors to the region would be well advised not to repeat for fear of violent reprisals.

Catalan is not a dialect, nor is it a mixture of Spanish and French; the Catalan language evolved independently of either. It all comes down to the patterns of Roman occupation. The high-class Romans didn't stop in Catalonia; they preferred the trading and sun-tanning opportunities of the south. In these areas – now Seville, Cádiz, and so on – the upper classes spoke formal, traditional Latin, and this mutated, over the years, into Castilian Spanish. Catalonia for the highfalutin Romans was little more than a gateway to the south. It was therefore inhabited only by lowly legionaries, whose job was to keep the gate securely open. These soldiers and their descendants spoke a more slangy, contemporary form of Latin, which eventually became Catalan. For example, the old Latin word for 'to eat' is *comedere,* which became *comer* in Castilian. The 'modern' Latin word was *manducare,* which turned into the Catalan *menjar* (and, incidentally, the French *manger,* though the French, who are even more maniacal about their language than the Catalans, would probably get terribly uppity if you referred to their tongue's origins as humble foot soldiers' slang). Nowadays, about seven million people speak Catalan and, in 1998, Catalonia passed a law which attempts to ensure that Catalan is the lingua franca of all official activities, and to encourage people to speak it in everyday life. So now it's the Castilian speakers who are miffed and fearful of being sidelined.

But it's not just their language that separates Catalonia from the rest of Spain. The spirit of the people is different too. In Catalonia, there's no *mañana*; everything is done right now. The Catalans don't linger over their lunch when there are deals to be done and money to be made. This attitude, combined with Catalonia's location on the Mediterranean coast, has meant that industry has flourished here and the area has usually been prosperous.

The Catalans put all this down to the characteristic they consider to be their greatest virtue: *seny*. *Seny* doesn't translate exactly but it's a bit like common sense or natural wisdom. Robert Hughes, the art critic and author of *Barcelona*, explains *seny* with the story of a Catalan friend of his who went home for Christmas to his native village and attended midnight mass with his relatives. The church was packed. When the priest brought out a wooden Infant Jesus, the line of people wishing to kiss its feet was so long that the priest realized he was going to be late for his dinner. He whispered to the deacon who slipped into the sacristy and came out with a second Jesus. The kissing was finished in half the time. 'Perhaps only in Catalunya, the first industrial region of Spain, could time-and-motion study be so quickly and instinctively applied to piety,' writes Hughes.

The opposite of *seny* is *rauxa* – going crazy, letting your hair down – and the two can't be separated. A good Catalan will be sensible most of the time, and then release the tension with a *rauxa* attack – getting drunk, spraying graffiti, whatever you can think of to upset the establishment. Of course some people are topsy-turvy and have rather more *rauxa* than *seny*, and that's how Catalonia ends up producing artists like Salvador Dalí, who was as mad as a hatter and demonstrated no *seny* at all. But we'll get to him, his astonishing moustache and his febrile, black eyes shortly.

Back during the Civil War, the Catalan anarchists used to indulge their *rauxa* by burning churches (Orwell notes that during all his time fighting in the area he only saw two or three churches that hadn't been burnt and gutted). Nowadays, however, demolishing churches is unfashionable so the Catalans need another way to let their hair down – and Sort, my destination for the day, is just the place.

Sort is the spot for adventure sports. Everywhere you look there are inflatable rafts or kayaks strapped to roof racks and trailers, and promotional posters for mountaineering, canyoning, abseiling, horse-trekking, mountain biking and every other sort of outdoor adventure. Strangely, there seems to be no mention of the excitement to be had running away from the mountains' four-legged inhabitants, which was by far the most frequent, adrenalin-rich experience I'd had round here, but perhaps I just invite wildlife-related incidents.

I found a hotel, checked in, showered and stretched, and wandered down to the street. Happily installed on a pavement terrace, I sat back and watched the athletic hiking, biking types stroll around and do their thing, drank a couple of beers, and ate a large pile of sticky, garlicky prawns and a plate of the ultimate Catalan snack, *pa amb tomaquet* – bread rubbed with tomato. The Catalans love this stuff. In particularly courageous shows of patriotism, they even eat it for breakfast.

Do not for a moment imagine, though, that *pa amb tomaquet* is anything like bruschetta. For the sake of your own self-preservation, neither should you dare to suggest that Catalan food is a regional variation on Spanish cuisine, or to assume that they might have pinched some ideas from those gastronomes over the hills. Repeat after me: Catalan food is different. And if you think the Catalan *bacalao* seems rather similar to the stuff from Bilbao, or the *arròs negre* looks, well, kind of like the squid-ink rice dishes they serve further south, and the *crema catalana* tastes remarkably like the *flan* they serve with every *menú del día* across the land, you'd be well advised to keep your nasty, centralist thoughts to yourself.

10

Where There Is Hair, There Is Happiness

A mountain pass is an unusual place to take a driving lesson. On the other hand, if you're a mountain person, maybe you need to practise on mountain roads. Still, I was surprised when I stopped at the top of the Coll del Cantó, 1,725 metres above sea level, to be passed by a driving school car complete with a student. It was a precarious spot, what with the sheer cliff hanging down off every switchback, and both the girl at the wheel and the instructor alike seemed to be having a thrilling lesson. Both were ashen-faced; the student was hunched up tight over the steering wheel, clutching it white-knuckled as if her life depended on it – which, I suppose, it did. She veered violently across the road when she saw me. The instructor's eyes widened and his mouth opened and closed very quickly, as if he had just let out an uncontrollable little yelp of terror. I gave the learner a wide berth.

At least the girl didn't bleep me as she drove by – that would have involved releasing her strangling grip on the steering wheel – which made a nice change. I never did work out why so many drivers felt the need to sound their horn as they passed me. I wasn't usually in their way. Were they merely saying hello? Or are Pyrenean drivers angry people with insufficient outlets for their irritation? Or was it merely a hot-blooded Latin male's comment on the desperate pumping of my puny, toasted-whippet legs?

Whatever it was that had them on their horns, it wouldn't be for much longer. Today was my last day in the mountains. Tomorrow I'd be far away from the flat caps and the cow bells, and be strolling instead with the beautiful people down the elegant boulevards of Barcelona. There the drivers would also bleep their horns, but it would be with a big-city, get-out-of-my-way-because-time-is-money tone. Having been a city dweller for many years, that is a bleeping that I'm more familiar with.

There was no fear of a farewell bonk as I was carbo-loaded to the hilt. I ate so much at the hotel's breakfast buffet – bacon and eggs, two slices of apple tart, two magdalena cakes, a few bits of toast and jam, fruit, coffee and juice – that I had to lie down for an hour afterwards. As if that wasn't enough, there were so many panoramic picnic spots along the way that I actually ran out of bananas. Muscles packed full of glycogen, the one climb of the day up to Coll del Cantó seemed a mere trifle. Or perhaps, at last, I was getting fitter. I was beginning to quite like the mountains. There's an easy and predictable rhythm to them: you climb and climb and climb and climb and then you reach the top. Then you eat your banana and take a photo for proof. (When you get home, of course, you find you have rather more panoramic mountain scenes than you can respectably inflict even on your family. The photo viewing session goes something like this: 'Ah yes, that's the view from the top of a mountain . . . Oh, and that's another one . . . This one's a picture I took at the top of a mountain too, but it was a different mountain, though now it does look rather similar to the last one . . . And that's the view off the same mountain, but looking in the other direction . . .' And so on.) Then comes the rather-too-exciting descent, a perpetual battle between the sheer terror of taking a tumble at too many miles an hour and the discomfort of cramping hands from squeezing the brakes for too long. With all that to keep you occupied, the hours simply fly by. And so it was that, in what seemed like a flash but was actually four hours, I landed up in la Seu d'Urgell, Spain's gateway to Andorra.

My first encounter was with an objectionable-smelling man. He was probably in his early thirties though it was hard to tell. People who smell like a windowless room the morning after an all-night party have a habit of ageing badly. He could, by this reasoning, have been about seventeen.

'Excuse me, excuse me,' he accosted me, in English, as I waited at a set of traffic lights on the outskirts of town. I would have cycled off – I don't make a habit of lingering in the presence of strange men who stink – but the fact that he addressed me in English startled me. How on earth did he know? I was so heavily disguised in helmet and cycling glasses that you could scarcely tell that I belonged to the human race, let alone to the British sub-division.

'Plees, I look at your map?'

Goodness, he really did stink. No respectable person ever smelt that bad. He was probably an axe-murderer. Better get out now while I was still in one piece. I started to pedal.

'Wait, wait, you do 'ave a map.' He ran to catch up with me. ''Ere!' And he pointed to my map which, rather too obviously, was displayed for all the world to see in the plastic pouch on my bar bag.

'What the hell are you doing here?' he enquired as he tried to figure out the whereabouts of Lérida.

'Oh, just visiting. Goodness, is that the time? Must be off . . .'

I wrestled my map from his hands and fled.

'Bah! *Me cago en la hostia!*' I shit on the communion wafer! he bellowed after me as I pedalled hotfoot down the street.

That didn't sound like a very nice thing to do. I pedalled a little faster.

My guidebook had led me to believe that la Seu d'Urgell is a lively valley town. Or perhaps I should say misled. While it's not quite the armpit of the earth (I should imagine there are a couple of dustbowls in Mongolia that are worse), la Seu d'Urgell is certainly up there well above the elbow.

Still, the Catalans have a lot to thank the region of Urgell for, for this is the homeland of one Wilfred the Hairy, the man credited with the creation of Catalonia. Between 870 and 878, Wilfred and his brother (I don't know if the brother was also hairy) manfully donned their chain mail and proceeded to stab and axe their way through most of Old Catalonia – ninth-century warfare was nothing if not bloody – bringing the formerly separate counties under a single command.

Wilfred is also credited with the design of the Catalan flag, which features four red stripes against a gold background. The story goes like this: one day, Wilfred was wounded in battle; he had been fighting for the king of the Franks, Louis the Pious. As Wilfred lay in his tent, bleeding stoically through his matted carpet of body hair, King Louis came to visit. By Wilfred's side lay his shield, which was decorated with gold leaf but had no coat of arms. King Louis dipped his fingers in Wilfred's blood and drew them across the surface of the shield: four red stripes against a gold background. And so Catalonia had its flag. Nit-picking historians are quick to point out that this gallant tale can't possibly be true as Louis had died before Wilfred was born, but the story's a good one and the Catalans, not people to

112

be distracted by trifling factual details where patriotism is concerned, are sticking with it.

The big question surrounding Wilfred, of course, is the matter of his hairiness. Popular legend has it that he was separated from his mother at an early age, having been kidnapped by the perfidious French knights who murdered his father. Rather than send him back to his mother, the French took little Wilfred north with them and put him under the protection of the Count of Flanders (with whose daughter he was later to fall passionately in love). So it was that Wilfred didn't see his mother for sixteen years. When they did meet again, she was able to identify her son as he had hair 'on a part of the body where it should not have been'. Quite where that was, nobody seems sure, but popular myth has it that Wilfred was hairy on the soles of his feet. Wherever, the Catalan association with hairiness and manliness has survived across the years. 'Where there is hair, there is happiness,' says the Catalan proverb.

I saw no particularly hairy men in la Seu d'Urgell. Maybe, with the migrations of time, they've all taken up residence in the mountains. In fact, I saw nothing there at all that was worthy of a great deal of comment. La Seu d'Urgell struck me as one of those towns that, the moment you arrive, inspires nothing so strongly as the desire to leave again by the first available form of transport. I'd been planning to poke around the town the next morning and leave by the afternoon bus – the morning one left at dawn. As soon as I arrived I realized that my plan was horribly flawed. It was the weekend. Everything was closed. Tomorrow morning, there wouldn't even be a Spanish-style B&Q or a Homebase to browse around, for the Spanish give such unglamorous pursuits as DIY a very wide berth. How would I rather spend the morning: walking round a shuttered-up hell hole conducting a survey of hairy-chinned men, or strolling down the elegant avenues of Barcelona? I settled my hotel bill, set my alarm clock for five-thirty a.m. and headed out to find some food.

My opinion of la Seu d'Urgell was not improved by the fact that every bar and restaurant was showing football, for the much-worshipped blue and maroon jerseys of FC Barcelona were battling it out against Deportivo La Coruña from Galicia. (Barcelona were subsequently to lose.) But perhaps I should have shown an interest. Football, after all, is an obsession in Spain; it's considerably more popular than bullfighting and held in marginally higher esteem even than cycling. For many fans, football is much more than a sport. Across the hundred or so years that the game has been played in Spain, football has been used to express fervent regionalism, has symbolized the fight against the repression of the provinces, and has been infiltrated by politics of every persuasion.

FC Barcelona, or Barça as the club is commonly known, was set up in 1899, the year after the Spanish lost the last of their South American colonies. Spain was traumatized by the demise of her once-proud empire and the Catalans were eager to distance themselves once more from Madrid, its failures and its shame.

Worse was to come. The football club enjoyed three and a half decades of growth and success; then it, with the rest of Spain, found itself embroiled in bitter, bloody civil war. Barça had always been involved in politics; its management supported Catalan autonomy. When Franco came to power, Barça was investigated by the security police and found to be a dangerous political tool, a hotbed of Catalan separatism.

Franco loved football and used it as a means to unify Spain, to bring the regions together. But he didn't like Barça. The Franco regime's preferred team was Real Madrid. Stories abound of biased referees, unwarranted penalties, and threats from match officials to ensure that Real Madrid and the Spanish national team won. When the European Nations Cup was hosted in Spain in 1964, one senior official even suggested doping the Soviet team, which was to play Spain in the final, just to make sure that Franco didn't have to present the winners' trophy to the communist enemy. (The official was overruled and Spain won anyway.) Whenever Barça met Real Madrid during the Franco years, they came up against similar opposition from the highest officials down. The Catalans, denied even the right to speak their own language in public, vented their rage, their hatred of Franco, on the terraces.

Franco died in 1975 and Spain has been a democracy for nearly three decades, but the intense rivalry and emotion still holds true, and is still expressed on the football pitch. While on an overt political level Spaniards of all persuasions may now collude in the *pacto del olvido*, the pact of forgetfulness (Franco, who's he?), in an attempt to bury the horrors of the Civil War and dictatorship, when Barcelona plays Real Madrid fans of the away team need police escorts. Insults, rocks and bottles are hurled at their buses by the home crowd, and this in a country that scarcely suffers from the drunkenness and hooliganism seen elsewhere in Europe. To many people, it is much more than a game of football.

11

Upwardly Mobile

The journey from la Seu d'Urgell to Barcelona was so easy
that I became suspicious. Had I left my wallet in the hotel?
Carelessly stuck my passport down the side of the bus seat?
Climbed on one going to the opposite end of the earth never
to be seen again?

To start with, there was a perfectly charming young man
at the bus stop, waiting for the same crack-of-dawn transport as I was, who insisted on helping me dismantle my bike,
despite the fact that it made his hands oily. Could *he* be Mr
Right, I wondered as we battled to extract the rear wheel
from the chain and derailleur. He didn't exactly have a bullfighter's bottom, but it doesn't do to be too fussy at this stage
in the game. But the journey was short, there was no time for
informal flirtation and it seemed anti-social to cut straight
to the chase, so I left the nice man in peace.

There weren't many passengers – my desperation to leave
la Seu d'Urgell seemed to be a personal matter – and the bus
driver treated us with a level of attentiveness you would
usually expect from an expensive tour guide. The Spanish
being civilized about their food, we stopped after an hour or
so for coffee and a bun and, when it was time to leave, the

driver rounded us all up and made sure nobody was left behind. My fellow passengers were equally mindful.

'Where's that girl?' barked one rather cerebrally challenged old man, who had earlier been unable to comprehend the complexities of buying his ticket and was now having trouble grasping that I was sitting in exactly the same seat as I had been before. But it gave me a warm glow inside to know that someone was watching out for me, even if that someone was a little bit dim. In Barcelona, two helpful bus drivers directed the re-assembly of my bike from a safe, clean distance.

'You like to cycle?' one of them called over.

Yes, yes, most of the time, when my bottom's not hurting too much.

'That's the back wheel. You need to slot it in . . . put the chain round the little round things . . . yes that's right,' shouted the second.

Thank you, *señor*.

I waved goodbye to the charming man (never to be seen again) and pedalled the short distance to my hotel along a thoughtfully positioned bike track on the pedestrianized avenue in the centre of the Gran Via.

The Gran Via, where the hotel was situated, is one of the main arteries of Barcelona's L'Eixample, or Enlargement. Medieval Barcelona, the so-called Barri Gòtic, was originally a walled city. By the nineteenth century, however, its bricks were bursting. The wall came down and a new city beyond its limits was commissioned: L'Eixample. The contract for the city's design was given to one Ildefons Cerdà, a Utopian socialist. Cerdà's vision was to overthrow class hierarchies, to create through his city planning a society in which no person looked down on another, where there was no wrong end of town. The bourgeois would rub shoulders with the bakers; the butchers and the bankers would live side by side.

'We lead a new life, functioning in a new way. Old cities are no more than an obstacle,' pronounced Cerdà with some zeal in 1860.

His vision was a symmetrical grid with wide streets, gardens and plenty of space. Not everyone approved. Architect Josep Puig i Cadafalch called L'Eixample 'one of the biggest horrors of the world; certainly nothing equals it,' he went on, 'except in the most vulgar cities in South America.' Subsequent architects soon disregarded Cerdà's requirement for low-rise buildings and gardens and cashed in by building on the space. Still, the chamfered corners are still there, allowing a little more sunlight into 'modern' Barcelona – not to mention good spots to park the car.

The job of naming the new streets was given to the poet Victor Balaguer. He took to the task with the fervour of true Catalan patriotism. Not a single Castilian person or non-Catalan event was featured. Instead, the street names of L'Eixample became a resonant celebration of the might of Catalonia past and present: conquerors of yore, such as Roger de Llúria and Bernat do Rooafort, countries of the lost empire, such as Corsega and Sardenya; the sites of Catalan resistance to Napoleon: Bruc, Girona, Bailen. Then there are the poets, the writers, the figureheads, and the political heroes. (Needless to say, the streets were all renamed after Franco's boys came to town.)

Booking the hotel had been no easy matter. The problem is that once you start to introduce other people into your adventures – and more specifically members of your immediate family – you can't just ring the first number in the book and hope they've cleaned the bathroom within the last week. If the mattress is lumpy, or the doorman is grumpy, or the chambermaid frumpy, it won't do at all. Booking a hotel in a city you scarcely know is a risky business. We had ended up in the Hotel Gran Via largely because everywhere else was full, so it was with some nervousness that I arrived on the doorstep, anxious to see if it was up to scratch for the repose of ageing and particular parents.

It turned out to be a charming hotel. Once, in days long gone by, it would have been fashionable, a predicament my parents could relate to and therefore found attractive. Back at the turn of the century, this hotel would have been an elegant watering hole for Catalonia's upper middle classes, whose waistlines and wallets had been fattened by Barcelona's flourishing textile factories and the fume-poisoned proletariat that worked in them. The hotel's glory was faded but nothing much, it seemed, had been changed since the glamorous set of bygone years used to stay here. The towering wooden door was six inches thick, the stair-case presided over by a magnificent balustrade. The salon was filled with period furniture that looked gloriously deca-dent if a little down at heel and uncomfortable to actually sit on. On these ornate chaises longues, beneath this wonder-fully ostentatious chandelier, would once have waited well-to-do factory owners' wives in bow-bedecked hats and narrow 'morning glory' skirts that displayed their impec-cably corseted figures. Towards the close of the nineteenth century, corset makers had developed new, more flexible materials which meant that not just the torso but the hips and bottom could now be squeezed in and shown off to their full effect. As the corsets became longer, the skirts became tighter.

'This very close skirt is not intended for the promenade; it shows to best advantage in a standing posture, and the woman with an eye to grace sits side-wise on her chair in order to prevent it drawing up,' wrote *McCall's Magazine* in May 1908 of the 'Princess gown', the latest in European fashions. Perhaps the uncomfortably upholstered chairs weren't an issue then, if all one could do was perch on them sideways.

Carefully arranged here on these very chairs, the ladies

would greet their gentlemen before an evening at the highly fashionable Liceu opera house on the Ramblas. They would listen to Wagner, whose works were all the rage in Barcelona at the time. The gentlemen wore tails (*never* the American-style tuxedo outside the privacy of one's own home), fiercely starched white shirts and top hats. Wealthy gentlemen were also given to wearing a considerable quantity of hair at this time. Harking back, perhaps, to the legendary prowess of Catalonia's founder, Wilfred the Hairy, bountiful heads of hair were seen to signify strength, virility and prolific energies. Facial hair was particularly *de moda* and was worn in all manner of shapes and sizes – moustaches in elongated puffs, hanging down on each side of the mouth like symmetrical squirrels' tails, or waxed to fine lines of perfection. One of Wellington's infantry soldiers, Private Wheeler, wrote a series of letters about the army's Spanish escapades; he had his own observations to make about the Spanish fondness for facial hair. The occasion he refers to was the arrival of Wellington's troops in Madrid in August 1812:

'As we approached the city the crowd increased, the people were mad with joy. They called us "their deliverours, their Saviours" . . . But amidst all this pleasure and happiness we were obliged to submit to a custome so unenglish that I cannot but feel disgust now I am writing. It was to be kissed by the men. What made it still worse, their breath was so highly seasoned with garlick, then their huge mustaches well stiffened with sweat, dust and snuff, it was like having a hair broom pushed into ones face that had been daubed in a dirty gutter.'

Barcelona's lower classes were put out by their bosses' florid displays of wealth. Workers had a living space of about ninety square feet per person. Poor nutrition and sanitation resulted in epidemics of cholera, typhoid and dysentery; long hours in the factories led to poisoning from toxic dyes and fumes. By the turn of the century, dissent was rife and violent protest brewing. The opera, that favourite hang-out of the bold and the beautiful, was the target: it was, after all, the only place in the city where you could launch a grenade and have no fear of hitting a working man. In 1893, the anarchists bombed the Liceu choosing, symbolically, the opera *William Tell* – the story of patriotic Swiss resistance to a despised Austrian tyrant. The perpetrator was duly sentenced to death, though the executioner was badly out of practice since only one other person had been garrotted in Barcelona in the last thirty years.

I dumped my panniers in my erstwhile fashionable room and left my bike all alone in the small, dark left-luggage area. It would stay here, forsaken, for many days. I had a few hours to spare before going to the airport so I changed out of my oily bike clothes and into my grubby grey cargo pants, which didn't look stylish whether I perched sideways in them or not, and went out to see what the city had to offer.

It was Sunday afternoon and central Barcelona resembled a good-natured street show. I came out of the hotel and headed down Cerdà's wide, generous avenues, towards the Plaça de Catalunya. Outside the Corte Inglés department store, a part of the street had been cordoned off to make room for a rollerblading competition. (Admittedly, Cerdà probably didn't have rollerblading in mind when he designed his ample streets, but the space works well for such activities none the less.) At the top end, women and men in matching outfits tore round the track, synchronized and manically smiling; in another area kids competed in obstacle courses on blades. The first challenge was to skate up a ramp and land on a big foam mattress. Half of them couldn't even get to the top of the ramp, but nobody cared or became overwhelmed by self-consciousness. The big-biceped attendant just hoicked up the weaker ones and the show went on. They all seemed to be having a fine old time.

At the bottom of the Plaça de Catalunya, L'Eixample ends and the Ramblas begin. *Rambla* is the Arabic word for 'riverbed', and that's just what Barcelona's most famous street once was. The old stream ran along the outside of the medieval city walls; it served both as a moat and as a sewer. By the end of the eighteenth century the river was so filled with rubbish and ordure that it no longer flowed so, bit by bit, it was filled in and the waterway driven underground. Still today, if it rains really hard, water from the old stream will glug up into the street through the drainage system. (One of Franco's early press officers, incidentally, blamed the demise of the cities' makeshift sewers for the Civil War. 'Prior to [modern drainage], the riff-raff had been killed by various useful diseases; now they survived and, of course, were above themselves,' proclaimed Captain Aguilera, not a man known for his diplomatic turn of phrase. 'Had we no sewers in Madrid, Barcelona, and Bilbao, all these Red leaders would have died in their infancy instead of exciting the rabble and causing good Spanish blood to flow. When the war is over, we should destroy the sewers. The perfect birth control for Spain is the birth control God intended us to have. Sewers are a luxury to be reserved for those who deserve them, the leaders of Spain, not the slave stock.')

That Sunday afternoon, though, the Ramblas showed no sign of their sloppy beginnings. They were packed with flower-vendors, bird-sellers, street artists and buskers, many of whom were excruciatingly lacking in talent and playing such traditional Spanish classics as Sinatra's 'My Way' and the theme tune from *The Piano*. As I sat and surveyed the scene with a little refreshment in an overpriced and substandard restaurant, a singer serenaded me in a voice so tuneless that I paid him to go away. There were mime artists, kids trying unsuccessfully to breakdance, and Louis Armstrong puppets 'singing' with the help of a synthesizer.

123

There were boot blacks with their polishing kits. (Why do they never offer to polish *my* shoes? Do I look that far past hope?) As for those who were insufficiently talented even to work a synthesizer yet still wanted to earn a few Sunday-afternoon cents, they just painted themselves blue and stood absolutely still, watching while people dropped coins in the hat to reward them, perhaps, for at least having the decency to keep quiet about their shortcomings. Really, Barcelona is a very entrepreneurial place.

This was a far cry from the scene that greeted George Orwell when he arrived in the city in December 1936, at the beginning of the Civil War, when people wore blue in the form not of body paint but of workers' overalls, and political chants rang out in the place of synthesized jazz. 'Down the Ramblas, the wide central artery of the town where crowds of people streamed constantly to and fro, the loud-speakers were bellowing revolutionary songs all day and far into the night,' Orwell wrote in *Homage to Catalonia.* 'Except for a small number of women and foreigners, there were no "well-dressed" people at all. Practically everyone wore rough working-class clothes, or blue overalls or some variant of the militia uniform.'

Orwell returned from the front on leave in April 1937. It wasn't a good time for a holiday. At the beginning of May, street fighting broke out between two Republican factions, the anarchists and the communists. The buzzing streets that I strolled through now were deserted. Trams stood abandoned along the Ramblas where the drivers had jumped out and fled when the shooting began. The only sign of life was the incessant rattle and crack of gunfire.

Off the Ramblas and into the Barri Gòtic, the present-day noise emissions improved substantially. Round by the cathedral a tenor sang quite an impressive rendition of 'Granada'; in the square, a couple danced a red-hot tango. I

124

wandered round the maze of tangled streets, stumbling upon tiny squares I hadn't known existed. There I found, sitting on stone steps or at best a wooden chair, a lone cellist or perhaps a man playing a guitar. There were few passers-by in these more remote spots, and these musicians almost seemed to be playing – far better than most – for their own pleasure.

My parents arrived. I was, of course, delighted to see them, to have someone to talk to other than myself or, at a stretch, a vile-smelling map-reader, but better still, I was pleased to see that my mother had brought with her a spare suitcase containing several changes of clothes – of *my* clothes, at that. For five whole days, I was going to be able to wear something different. I was going to be able to debate the benefits of the blue cotton trousers over the tiny pink shorts, or the white linen shirt over the tight black T-shirt. Oh, great, great, pleasure – for five whole days I would be able to indulge in wardrobe crises.

The arrival of the wonderful clean clothes did not come as a total surprise. I had never for a moment imagined that my mother would be seen dead with me in public in the baggy grey cargo pants (after all, you never know whom you might meet, even in Barcelona), which is funny, really, when you consider that she frequently agrees to be seen in public in the company of my father in his baggy, rust-coloured cords. We'd been having sartorial conversations for days.

'Blippety-blippety bleep bleep.' The phone would vibrate to life.

'Hello, I'm on a mountain,' I would answer.

I think my mother secretly felt quite empowered. The clothes selection was limited, admittedly, but up to a point she was able to ensure that, for five whole days, I wore only the clothes that *she* liked. She hadn't held such an influential role on my wardrobe since I was fourteen years old and insisted on my own allowance with which to buy unsuitably minimalist tops from Dorothy Perkins.

We did the sights. We were told off perpetually. One by-product of the Catalans' much-flaunted *seny* is that if you fail to display the necessary dose of common sense yourself, you will be severely chastised. The Catalans don't smile upon transgression.

'You can't sit there. You'll have to move,' a stroppy woman told my father when he sat down on the wrong chairs in the Park Güell. This made him terribly cross because he doesn't like to be told what to do, especially when his patience is already being amply tested because he's waiting for the female members of his family to work their way to the front of the queue for the loo.

'The reason you can't open the door is because you didn't ask permission,' barked a fierce female attendant when I tried to visit the loo in one of the many bars we patronized. 'If you had asked permission, I would have opened it for you.' And with that, she pressed a little button and, much chastened, I scurried in for my humble ablution.

Down by the marina, we tried to get in the wrong taxi and were shouted at, bustled from the back seat and herded into another car down the street. We bungled the metro so badly we burst into affectionate, familial endearments: 'You great lumbering idiot!' 'You bumbling fool!' and in the end a passing student had to come and help us, and shepherd us patiently through the bemusing turnstile system (you had to insert the ticket into the slot and push the metal bar, it transpired).

In more successful moments, we strolled the streets, laughed at the buskers and, on occasion, even managed to stop humming 'My Way'. We lay on the beach and ate sardines in the sun. My mother and I joined the rest of the female population of the city shopping in Zara, and emerged

126

with satisfyingly bulging paper carrier bags. We ate seafood in the oh-so-chic Port Olimpic; my mother spent the night that followed and much of the next day confined to the bathroom. ('Didn't I see you yesterday?' asked the taxi driver we'd flagged down outside our hotel to take us to the Miró museum. 'Yes! It was you! I picked you up right here in the same place and took you to the Port Olimpic!' It turned out that, out of ten thousand taxi drivers in the city of Barcelona, we'd managed to hail the same one two days running.)

We did the tourist thing and dined in Els Quatre Gats, the beer hall set up in 1897 by the *modernistas*. (It's now an upscale restaurant.) The building has since acquired a nostalgic reputation as one of the great intellectual cafés of the period; between these walls the artists and intellectuals of *fin de siècle* Barcelona (including a very young Picasso) would stage exhibitions, recitals and lectures, and drink and talk and drink and drink. The modernists despised realism; they loved Ibsen and Wagner. The challenge of the modernist, wrote the critic Ramón Casellas in 1893, was 'to pluck from human life . . . gleaming, wild, paroxysmic, hallucinatory visions; to translate eternal verities into deranged paradox; to live by the abnormal and the unheard; to tally the horrors of reason, leaning on the very edge of the abyss . . . Such is the formula of this nebulous and shining art, chaotic and radiant, prosaic and sublime, sensuous and mystical, refined and barbaric, modern and medieval . . .' The *modernistas* were also very fond of adjectives, it seems.

We got lost in Gaudí's Park Güell, whose brightly coloured ceramic benches, extraordinary-shaped houses and ornamental geckos were once intended as a housing estate for well-heeled urbanites. From looking at Gaudí's audacious buildings with their outrageous shapes and flamboyant colours, you'd imagine he was non-conformist, verging on mad. This assumption would be reinforced by the story of his later years and his death. He became so obsessed by his final project, the Sagrada Familia, that he ended up living as a recluse, selling his possessions to raise money for the construction costs. He scarcely ate. He was frequently seen walking, stooped, through the city's streets, dressed in his trademark baggy dark suit and slippers, nibbling on nothing more than a crust of bread. When, on 7 June 1926, he was run down by a tram on the Gran Via, he looked so ragged and destitute that at first nobody recognized him. He was taken to the hospital and put in an iron cot on the public ward among the poor.

But Gaudí was not entirely unconventional. While the surrealists loved him – Dalí positively raved about him – Gaudí would have been horrified by their own anti-religious, anti-establishment leanings. His work had nothing to do with dreams but was based on structural laws, the rules of his craft, and his experience of nature and religion. Gaudí was ardently religious. He had no interest in women (nor indeed, on a sexual level, men); historians believe it quite possible that he died a virgin. By the age of fifty, he was showing signs of severe penitential impulses, living as an ascetic and scarcely eating.

Gaudí's religious sentiment was matched only by his Catalan patriotism, symbols of which abounded in his work. His fervour for Catalan autonomy was such that when he was presented to King Alfonso XIII he refused to speak Castilian and addressed the monarch in Catalan instead. 'Our qualities are not those of the people of the centre – and neither are our faults. We can never unite with them,' Gaudí once said.

Gaudí is the king of Catalan modernism. His work is one of the more spectacular features of Barcelona; unlike paintings, which have to be visited in a gallery or museum, Gaudí's art is right there on the street, for all passers-by to gawp at. In the middle of L'Eixample, on the Passeig de Gracia, sits the house known as La Pedrera with its remarkable wavy façade and elaborate wrought-iron balconies, 'a sea cliff with caves in it for people,' says Robert Hughes. The architect originally wanted to incorporate a ramp into this building so that the residents could drive their cars right to their apartments' front doors, but had to abandon the idea as he couldn't make the ramp shallow enough to be safe. (Gaudí spent some time studying the ramps of other buildings, such as the Giralda in Seville, and concluded, 'Ramps ought to be double, one to go up, the other to go down.' Perhaps he had had the misfortune to visit the Giralda on a day when it was packed full of fat, shuffling tourists, as I was shortly to do.) Instead of the ramp, he built in La Pedrera the first underground car park in Barcelona, though he had to move one column from its original position to allow a resident the space to swing his Rolls-Royce into his spot.

Gaudí's most famous landmark is the Sagrada Familia, a construction that has always created bitter contention in Barcelona. Nobody ever liked it much until it started bringing in the tourist pesetas. Most of the Catalan intelligentsia loathed it from the outset; during the Spanish Civil War, the anarchists hated the building and the values it represented so much that they burned every model, plan and drawing they could find at the site. Gaudí had died ten years earlier, leaving the church unfinished. Now that the plans had been burned, nobody knew how he had intended to continue – not that his calculations would necessarily have helped, as Gaudí was notorious for figuring things out as he went along. His buildings rarely conformed to the limitations of two-dimensional plans, and these were the days before computer-generated models. (When designing the crypt for the church at his patron Eusebi Güell's textile factory, he had to devise a complicated system of string cats' cradles weighted with tiny cotton bags of birdshot to mimic load and thrust.) And so work on the Sagrada Familia still goes on, under different architects, sucking vast sums of money into a project few are convinced by. The mood is perhaps best summed up by Evelyn Waugh, who visited the site in 1930. 'It would be a pity to allow this astonishing curiosity to decay,' he wrote. 'I feel it would be a graceful action on the part of someone who was a little wrong in the head to pay for its completion.'

12

The Town Formerly
Known as Funky

'Use the toilet properly!' instructed a sign on the wall.

'Throw your towel in the bin!' ordered a notice on the mirror.

It was too much to bear. After three days of the Barcelona treatment we felt our deviating characters had been beaten sufficiently into shape. We were chastened, bowed, stooped and sorry. Also, our feet were sore from walking too much. So we bade goodbye to Barcelona, hired a car and drove to Cadaqués, a sleepy little whitewashed town a couple of hours' drive up the coast. How we flew in our little Fiat Punto! Anyone who finds car journeys dull should try taking one after a few weeks of travelling by bicycle. What a delight to zoom along with cushioned seats, temperature control and power at the merest nudge of the foot!

Cadaqués used to be funky. It was Salvador Dalí who started it all. Dalí's grandparents came from Cadaqués and his family kept a house there. As a child, Dalí spent his summers in the house by the sea. 'I spent a delicious summer, as always, in the ideal and dreamy village of Cadaqués,' wrote the fifteen-year-old to his uncle in 1919. 'There, beside the Latin sea, I gorged myself on light and colour. I spent the fiery days of summer painting frenetically and trying to capture the incomparable beauty of the sea and of the sun-drenched beach.'

Ten years later, having been banished from the family and the Cadaqués house by his father (who was nothing short of apoplectic when Dalí inscribed the words 'I have spat on my mother' on a painting), Dalí bought his own place just a kilometre down the coast at Portlligat: a one-storey, 21-square-metre fisherman's shack. As the years progressed, Dalí added floors and extensions and transformed the house into a veritable labyrinth.

Dalí's visitors included the surrealist painter René Magritte, the photographer Man Ray, and André Breton, the founder of the surrealist movement (he thought the place decrepit and was irritated by the flies). Walt Disney and the Duke of Windsor came here in the fifties (though not together, I think), followed by Mick Jagger and Gabriel García Márquez a couple of decades later. Spain's most prestigious poet and playwright of the twentieth century, Federico García Lorca, came to Cadaqués several times; Dalí and Lorca had an intimate friendship as young men though Dalí, whose sexuality was always ambiguous, was terrified of succumbing to the homosexual impulses that Lorca stirred in him. In later years, the painter was visited at home by Catalan Prime Minister Jordi Pujol, and even King Juan Carlos and Queen Sofía.

But despite its position as a playground for luminaries, Cadaqués never lost its fishing-village feel. Its fishermen may have whiled away afternoons with Dalí's wife, the insatiable Gala, at her personal residence (for Gala was a racy character and Dalí couldn't take the pace); the old folk from the village may have appeared in one of the most talked-about intellectual films of the time, Buñuel's *L'Age d'Or*, parts of which were filmed here, but still Cadaqués didn't cash in on its celebrity status. Even today there are no glitzy hotels, no million-dollar yachts, no casinos. The restaurants are all still small, family-run affairs offering simply grilled fresh seafood served with a bottle of local Penedès. Painted, wooden fishing boats are still hauled up on the beach. As for nightlife, forget it. When we asked the hotel receptionist if the seafront rooms were noisy from revelry down below he looked quite astonished.

'Not in Cadaqués,' he said.

We'd booked into the Hotel Laguna, in the rear part of the town. The guidebook reckoned it had good rooms; we believed it – until we arrived. Now I have to say that Hotel Laguna might be utterly enchanting. For all I know, its beds could be made up with crisp, Egyptian-cotton sheets; there may be complimentary cashmere dressing gowns for the guests to wear while they pad around on the deep-pile carpets sampling the free Clarins cosmetics in the bathroom. But I don't know, because we didn't go past the door.

We found the place with little enough trouble tucked away up a tiny back street. We unloaded our remarkable number of bags from the car and staggered towards the entrance. Then we faltered and then we stopped. We peered into the spartan hallway and wrinkled our noses at the musty smell emanating from within, which spoke of damp patches and peeling wallpaper.

'It only has one star!' shuddered my mother, blinking at the sign on the wall.

'Has anyone seen us?' I asked. A quick glance around proved that the reception was deserted.

'Quick! Run!' instructed my father.

We tottered back to the car rather faster than we had left it, leapt in and lurched guiltily away. We spent the next two nights instead in the delightful beachfront Hotel Playa Sol. Our balconies looked onto the bobbing boats in the bay; we fell asleep at night to the sound of lapping waves. We ate vast breakfasts, swam – very briefly – in the icy cold swimming pool and then sat on sun loungers in our sweaters. I called the Hotel Laguna and explained that, due to an unfortunate incident involving a close encounter with a thundering mountain pig, we would no longer be able to make it to Cadaqués. And, honour restored, we settled down for a gin and tonic on the balcony and admired the sun setting over the bay.

We passed over the bottle of red wine at the breakfast buffet the first morning – a tremendous feat of abstinence – and opted instead for orange juice and invigorating cups of coffee. (Tea should be avoided at all costs in Spain. Queen Victoria visited the country in the 1890s and commented that she found the tea undrinkable. Nothing has changed.) We drove up a tiny, steep, winding road to the monastery of Sant Pere de Rodes, which is now deserted, though monks may still have been living there in Dalí's day if his friend Amanda Lear can be believed.

Lear was a Franco-Oriental transsexual and drag cabaret performer with whom Dalí was very taken. According to her book on Dalí, *Le Dali d'Amanda,* he asked her to be united with him by the church in 'spiritual marriage'. To this end, they rode a donkey up a mountain to consult a hermit in a remote hillside sanctuary. The hermit, apparently, was in favour of the union but told them to seek the blessing of a monk at the monastery of Sant Pere de Rodes. We know no more of the incident and, as Dalí's biographer Ian Gibson points out, the whole story could well be as tall as the mountain they climbed, for Lear was no more reliable a diarist than Dalí himself.

We drove over to Cap de Creus, the rugged, rocky headland that Dalí called a 'grandiose geological delirium'. The landscape here is dark and foreboding with little in the way of vegetation. The low, dry-stone walls from the old vine terraces still stand, casting black shadows on the dark soil under the midday sun, but the vines are long gone, victim to the phylloxera vastatrix that plagued these hills in the 1880s.

The aphid had already reared its ugly antennae in France in the 1860s, wiping out most of the French vineyards. (After this, many French winemakers moved south to Spain to continue their trade, principally in the Rioja region. It's unwise to enter into this line of argument if a Spaniard is in earshot – you might have the misfortune to find a bottle or two hurled forcefully in your direction – but outside Spain it's generally agreed that the quality of wine production in the region improved dramatically after the French came to stay.) The French disaster created euphoria among Catalan winemakers as the realities of supply and demand inflated their prices. When the resented Madrid government ordered them to clear a fifteen-mile vine-free zone at the foot of the Pyrenees to stop the critter creepy-crawling its way into Spain the winemakers ignored the rule – to their own downfall. In 1879 the louse made its first appearance in northern Catalonia and in a little over ten years wiped out nearly a million acres of vineyards. Vast tracts of land – like these around Cap de Creus – were never replanted.

It was this weird and wonderful scenery that provided Dalí with inspiration for many of his paintings. And it was the rocks around the Cap de Creus headland that inspired Dalí to paint the first of his soft watches.

On the way back to Barcelona, we stopped at the Dalí museum in Figueres, the town where the painter grew up. Dalí created the museum himself, down to the hanging of the last wooden chair and the final model loaf of bread, so it's a truly kooky place. Dalí, after all, has always been associated with the bizarre, if not the downright crazy.

'These pictures from the subconscious reveal so skilled a craftsman that the artist's return to full consciousness

135

may be awaited with interest,' jibed the *Daily Telegraph* in response to Dalí's contribution to the International Surrealist Exhibition, held in London in 1936.

'That boy looks like a fanatic. Small wonder that they have a civil war in Spain if they look like that,' Sigmund Freud is said to have whispered when he met Dalí in London in 1938.

Catalan art critic Sebastià Gasch wrote of his first meeting with Dalí in 1926: 'In that waxen child's face, hard, inexpressive and stiff, there shone, with extraordinary intensity, two minuscule, febrile, terrible, menacing eyes. Terrifying eyes, the eyes of a madman.'

As for Dalí, who was never one to deprive the world of his opinion, he said, 'The only difference between me and a madman is that I am not mad.' And he didn't just say it once. He first uttered that sentence in 1934 – and he was so pleased with it that he repeated it again, and again, and again . . . for the rest of his life.

We left Dalí, his stark staring sculptures and his peculiar paintings to fly away with the fairies, content in the knowledge that, even in our most deranged moments, we would never sculpt loaves of bread onto the heads of classical statues. Oh no, *we* weren't *that* mad. I waved goodbye to my parents at the airport and ventured into the hotel's luggage room to look out my sadly neglected bike. Tomorrow I would fly down to Granada and continue my cycling journey across the south of Spain.

13

'Grana-a-a-a-da'

The check-in girl gave a harrumph of a sigh; her pancake mix of foundation and face powder juddered so that it almost, but not quite, betrayed a facial expression. She shrugged her tailored shoulders vigorously and threw her heavily made-up eyes to the heavens.

'The flight to Granada is a hundred and fifty-three places overbooked. You're on the waiting list.'

She glared at me accusingly, as if the fault were all mine, as if only a simple-witted buffoon would expect a seat on a flight for which they had paid for a ticket. I'd arrived at the airport at eight in the morning, two full hours before my flight was due to leave, to be told that the computers were down while they 'adjusted' the ticket allocation. When the computer came back to life, I had been bumped off.

'With a bit of luck,' Little Miss Pancake Mix scowled as if hexing me against all hope, 'you might get on the after-noon flight. It leaves at half past four.'

Half past four? I'm sorry, *señorita,* but you don't seem to understand. By half past four, I'm meant to be well into my fourth or fifth beer on a sunny Granada terrace, gazing contentedly at the dusky-red walls of the Alhambra palace.

'If you've got a problem,' she sniffed, 'you can go over to counter one and talk to the man from PR.'

Problem? You bet I've got a problem. What you don't realize, Pancake Mix, is that my calm, reasonable exterior is only a shallow façade. Underneath it all, I'm very highly strung indeed. It doesn't take much to send me plummeting over the edge. *Talk* to the man from PR? Huh! I'm ready to bash him on the nose.

I stomped over to counter one, where I joined the back of a very long queue of, oh, say about 152 very irate people. Their eyes were bulging with anger, their white-knuckled fists clenching ready to fight.

'Es indignante.' It's disgusting, muttered the hordes of Bloody Annoyed from Barcelona.

Wow, I thought, that PR man must have the worst job in the world. Previously, I had thought that the worst job in the world was held by Paul from Wandsworth Borough Council who is obliged, every now and then, to attend meetings to explain the council's shortcomings in maintaining the local-authority-run building I used to live in. Other than Paul, and on the odd very entertaining occasion in the past myself, the majority of meeting-goers are Old Women With Attitude, ex-council tenants who have bought their flats under the Right to Buy scheme. Handbag-bashing council employees is their number one favourite pastime.

Poor old Paul sits there and smiles weakly, doing his best to say nothing incriminating (this restricts him to saying nothing much at all) while thinking instead about the steaming plate of pie and peas his wife is right now preparing for his tea. And really, Paul is lucky, because he only has to sit and be screamed at by the battleaxe brigade for half an hour once every few months; after that, he can return to his nice, safe office at the council and continue to do very little. The PR man from Iberia Airlines, on the other hand, has to

138

sit at Barcelona airport's counter all day long, day in, day out.

Finally, I arrived at the front of the queue. I rather crossly explained my predicament, my annoyance that I could be bumped off the flight when my ticket was reconfirmed and I had arrived at the airport a full two hours before take-off. The PR man pursed his lips and tapped his computer keyboard.

'No,' he pronounced. 'You did not arrive two hours before take-off. According to the computer records, you attempted to check in at eight-fifty. That is one hour and ten minutes before take-off.'

The blood started to tear round my body, turning my face pink. My heart began to beat in that scarily fast way that indicates moments of extreme stress, such as when you're being chased by a tiger or when a greasy scumbag who ought to be on his knees with contrition wrongfully accuses you of lying instead. My sympathy was evaporating fast.

'But that's because your computers were down for nearly an hour,' I spluttered. 'I arrived at eight o'clock. I was told to wait.'

'No,' he said tersely. 'No you did not. You arrived at eight-fifty.' And then, the final insult. 'You will take the ten-fifteen flight to Málaga and continue to Granada by bus.'

I had missed Málaga from my itinerary on purpose. I don't like the place. The airport – the only tiny spot of the city I was to see on this particular visit – has especially little to say for itself. Its bars provide sustenance to British and German holiday makers, either translucent-pale or lobster-red depending on the stage of their journey, as they travel to and from the vast numbers of other bars propping up the economy of the Costa del Sol. But the airport's architects at least thought to draw the travellers' attention to the one good thing the city produced. They built the Pablo Picasso Terminal.

Picasso was born in Málaga in October 1881. He was still-born. (Interestingly, so was Frank Sinatra until his grandmother chucked cold water over him. Can we detect a pattern here? Do all recovered stillborns turn into hell-raisers?) The midwife gave up on the dead baby and turned her attentions to the mother; it was Picasso's Uncle Salvador, a doctor, who brought him to life. Leaning over the unbreathing, blue baby, Uncle Salvador puffed cigarette smoke into his nostrils. Pablo Ruiz Picasso screamed and turned pink. And he kept on screaming, wailing, ranting and raving for the next ninety-one years.

Picasso was not an easy man. On meeting his first bride to be, Olga Chochlova, Picasso's mother told her, 'You poor girl, you don't know what you're letting yourself in for. If I were a friend I would tell you not to do it under any con-ditions. I don't believe any woman could be happy with my son. He's available for himself but for no-one else.'

For the first ten years of the painter's life, the Picasso family lived in Málaga; after that they moved north to Galicia and then to Barcelona, following Picasso's father's jobs as a drawing teacher. But although he only spent his very early years here, the sharp Mediterranean light of the city, at that time a racy and cultured place without the merest twinkle of a package tourist, influenced Picasso for the rest of his life. He was a gifted painter from the start. 'I never drew like a child,' he once said. 'When I was twelve, I drew like Raphael.' Certainly, he was precocious. His first word, his family says, was 'piz', his childish articulation of *lápiz* (pencil). He was terrified of the classroom and a dreadful student – the young Picasso couldn't understand the concept of arithmetic, and saw numbers only as shapes; for example, a seven was for Pablito an upside-down nose – so his father enrolled him in a private school where the

140

headmaster allowed him to spend all day drawing in the kitchen with his wife.

By the end of the century, Picasso was uncomfortable with the kind of bourgeois values Málaga's middle classes had come to represent. He felt more at ease with the intellectual circles of Barcelona and Paris. His last visit to the city was in 1900 when he was just nineteen. Four years later, he settled in Paris for good; when Franco came to power in Spain in 1936, the artist swore never to return to his homeland while the dictator ruled. (In the end, Franco outlived Picasso by two years.) I took the maestro's lead and, following a harassed, uniformed woman, headed straight for the chartered bus that was to ferry me to Granada.

When I eventually arrived in Granada some hours later, I was still feeling grumpy. The flight had been freezing and had boasted a higher-than-respectable quota of purple-faced, wailing children. It took all my powers of grown-up self-restraint not to join in the chorus. The bus trip had been sweltering, and presided over by a bossy, uniformed woman who competed only with the odious PR man (may he sit on that hard plastic seat and be bawled at for eternity) for the title of World's Most Deserving Official Of A Handbag-Bashing.

I climbed on my bike and cycled to my *pensión,* on the second floor of a rickety old building. The lift was tiny. I heaved open the ten-tonne metal door, piled in my bike and my panniers. And then I realized – there was no space left for me. What was I to do? Surely not carry all that lot up two floors? I mean, I was getting fitter, but I had my limits and I'd been through a lot that morning.

Oh hell, I was going to have to race the lift. Hadn't I had enough exercise for one month? I leaned in, pushed the second-floor button, leapt out and slammed shut the heavy metal door, then started up the slick, marble stairs at a sprint. Sliding on every step in my slippy, clippy bike shoes, I skidded round each corner, clinging to the banister for dear life, praying desperately I'd get there in time, before someone else summoned the lift and threw my precious bike out or, worse yet, acquired it for themselves. It was a precarious ascent. As I skated round the first turn in the stairs, I nearly collided with a very elegant Spanish couple wearing well-tailored leather coats and smoking matching cigarettes.

'*Dios mío*,' muttered the man as he put a protective hand in front of his girlfriend. They stopped, stared and flattened themselves against the wall.

'Ah, so sorry,' I puffed as I slithered, red-faced, past them, spraying their stylish ensembles with flecks of sweat. They looked on, horrified.

I arrived on the second floor somewhat worse for wear, and successfully retrieved my belongings from the lift which ding-donged to a stop just as I arrived. Sadly, the *pensión* turned out not to be worth the effort I'd put in. My room was brown. The first time I used the lavatory, the chain came off in my hand. It had one of those old-fashioned wall-mounted cisterns and after the demise of the chain I had to flush the loo by standing on my tiptoes and pulling the cistern lever. It was that kind of establishment.

On the door of the first-floor apartment below was taped a sheet of A4 paper.

'We have moved Felipe González,' it announced.

Moved him? Where on earth to? How many people did it take to carry him? Did he put up a struggle? Whatever the case, it didn't seem a very respectful way to deal with the country's ex-prime minister. And then I figured it out. There was an address underneath. The apartment's former inhabitants had missed out a vital colon. The rooms within used to house some kind of business enterprise called Felipe González. The notice should have read, 'We have moved: Felipe González, 1 Anystreet, Anyplace, etc.' But this was

142

Spain where little heed is paid to precision, where four o'clock means half-past six, and what are a couple of tiny dots between friends? *Hombre!* Stop fussing and have another *cerveza.*

What with the flight, the bus, the hotel and the sad collapse of the bathroom facilities, cheering myself up was a challenging business. Fortunately, yet another atrociously talentless busker came to the rescue. The hapless character who entertained me in the bright sunshine of the Plaza Nueva, where I drank my consolatory beer and ate an edifying plate of grilled *calamares,* juggled with fire. His eyes bulged with terror. His palms perspired; his fingers fumbled. Again and again, he failed to catch the flaming batons and had to hop ashen-faced out of the way as they fell around his feet. My sense of humour was slowly restored.

At a judicious distance from the bungling juggler, buskers bashed through poorly crooned Sinatra imitations and vendors sat at their stalls or, where they had no stall, displayed their wares on mats on the floor. They sold the ubiquitous jewellery, Alhambra-esque knick-knacks, and pseudo-Moorish boxes and pots dated circa 2001. For now I was in Andalusia, the gateway to Africa, the part of Spain on which the Moors left their most indelible stamp.

Here the Muslims reigned for nearly eight hundred years, long after they'd been hacked and harried from the rest of the peninsula. Here they had their capitals: the earliest caliphate reigned in Córdoba; later dynasties set up throne in Seville and lastly, when everywhere else was lost to the Christians, the Nasrid empire ruled from the most bewitching palace of them all, Granada's Alhambra. Here in Andalusia, the Muslims built their magical palaces, replete with blossoming gardens, trees and bushes moulded into archways and labyrinths, and flowing fountains that provided a haven of cool against the blistering sun. Around these gardens the Moorish enchantresses shimmied in seductive silks and mysterious veils, refreshing themselves, perhaps, with a fig, a handful of almonds, a goblet of wine. In the background, musicians strummed on pear-shaped lutes which they plucked with a trimmed eagle's feather while others played zithers and reed pipes, or beat out a hypnotic rhythm on tablah drums.

Al-Andalus, as the Muslims called their kingdom in Spain, is recalled by novelists and their florid pens as a fragrant, mystical, sensuous kingdom. The Arabs encouraged religious tolerance, learning and beauty. Córdoba, which reigned briefly as a superpower in the tenth century, 'has no equal in the Maghrib, and hardly in Egypt, Syria or Mesopotamia, for the size of its population, its extent, the space occupied by its markets, the cleanliness of its streets, the architecture of its mosques, the number of its baths and caravanserais [inns],' wrote the tenth-century geographer Ibn Hawkal. Córdoba's caliph, or leader, 'Abd al-Rahman III (who was in fact only a quarter Arab and had to dye his red hair black to bolster his image), built a glorious palace in the city. The main hall's roof and walls were built from tinted marble so fine they appeared translucent; in the centre of the room stood a bowl of mercury that, when rocked, reflected sunbeams that darted around the room like lightning. The palace's fish ponds were said to be so extensive that the fish alone ate twelve thousand loaves of bread a day. Later the Nasrids, the last of the Muslim dynasties to rule in Spain, built the Alhambra in Granada. In the early nineteenth century American novelist Washington Irving lived for a period in the Alhambra's Royal Palace. 'Such is the Alhambra – a Moslem pile in the midst of a Christian land, an Oriental palace amidst the Gothic edifices of the West, an elegant memento of a brave, intelligent, and graceful people who conquered, ruled and passed away,' he wrote.

But the Moorish occupation of Spain was not all beauty

144

and books. The Muslims fought not only the Christians but also each other. Over the eight hundred years of occupation, several different Arab dynasties came and went. According to Muslim legend, when Allah created Earth, he granted each place five wishes. Al-Andalus asked for a clear sky, a beautiful sea full of fish, ripe fruit, fair women and good government. Allah granted all but the last, because, he said, to allow a country this would be to create heaven on earth.

Although religious tolerance was the norm within Moorish cities – intercommunal relations were apparently so cordial that some of the more wealthy Muslims used Christian monasteries as wine bars, for there they could drink the elixir forbidden by their own laws these were turbulent times; religious wars were rife and the battles were bloody. After one particularly gruesome slaughter of Christians near Pamplona in 920, the Muslims found they had chopped off so many Christian heads that they couldn't make room for them all on the mule-train that was to transport them back to Córdoba so they could be displayed on stakes around the city walls. Muslim wealth came from plunder and kidnapping eminent Christians. It worked the other way round, too. Catalan troops were so enthusiastic in their looting following a battle with the Muslim Berbers near Ronda in 1010 that, when they tried to swim across the river Guadiaro, many of them drowned because they were so weighted down with gold and silver.

After the Christian Reconquest religious tolerance hit an all-time low, even before Fernando and Isabel came to power, for the northern half of Spain was back in Christian hands by the middle of the twelfth century and even the southern cities of Seville, Córdoba and Jaén were embracing the cross by 1250. Laws were passed to make sure the Mudéjars – Muslims living under Christian rule – didn't mix with the Catholics. They could only use the bath-house on their religion's allotted day; Muslim men caught having sexual relations with Christian women were stoned to death.

I spent the afternoon tramping around the sights. It was a Saturday afternoon; Friday had been a public holiday to celebrate El Día de la Hispanidad, the day Columbus landed on the island of San Salvador and 'discovered America'. Half of Spain seemed to have taken advantage of the long weekend to visit Granada. I braved the crush to climb the tiny, rickety streets of the Albaicín, the old Islamic quarter, with its breathtaking views of the golden-red walls of the Alhambra. I battled around the narrow, cobbled streets of the town centre, which opened out unexpectedly onto pretty shaded squares peppered with flower stalls, newspaper and bread kiosks and cafés. I joined the queue to look at the tombs of the Catholic Monarchs.

These two, Fernando of Aragón and Isabel of Castile, are credited with the union of modern-day Spain. Their marriage, as we saw when we were up in Catalonia, joined their two kingdoms much to the displeasure of Isabel's family, the wrinkled Alfonso of Portugal (whom Isabel's family preferred to the racy Fernando) and even the Pope. Having combined their forces, Fernando and Isabel finally threw the Moors out of Spain after eight hundred years of occupation. Granada was the last, stubborn stronghold; the Catholic Monarchs were determined to take it. In a moment of misguided resolution, Queen Isabel vowed not to change her blouse until Granada was conquered. (Her husband wisely dissuaded her.)

Eventually, in the closing months of 1491, Isabel and Fernando – with a little help from their armies – negotiated the city's surrender. In January 1492, they triumphantly entered the city and sent the last emir, Boabdil, packing with thirty thousand gold coins to cover his immediate expenses. (His mum went with him; she was not amused at the prospect

146

of ending her days in dusty Africa: 'You do well to weep like a woman for that which you failed to defend like a man,' she chastised her son when he turned round and shed tears at the sight of the glorious city he had left.)

The same year, Columbus sailed the ocean blue, and Fernando and Isabel expelled the Jews from Spain (despite the fact that it was those same Jews who had financed the *Reconquista*'s final push). Ten years later, they got rid of the Muslims too, ordering that they convert or face banishment. Given that emigration was only an option for those who paid a considerable sum into the Catholic Monarchs' coffers, and agreed to abide by a number of other rules – such as leaving all their children behind in Spain – nearly all the Muslims chose the former. In one year alone, an estimated three hundred thousand Muslims converted to Christianity, and became known as Moriscos. But the story doesn't end happily there. Islam continued to smoulder behind closed doors (Moriscos would have their children baptised, but wash off the holy water the moment they arrived home, for example) while in the street outside, the Inquisition blazed. This was another of the Catholic Monarchs' legacies – in their eagerness to cleanse their newly unified country of so-called heretics they introduced the Inquisition to Spain in 1478, a time when it had largely burned itself out in the rest of Europe. The Spanish Inquisition was to last three hundred years, killing twelve thousand people. Suffice to say, the Catholic Monarchs weren't exactly pussycats. Strong leaders, maybe. A couple you'd want to invite over to help stoke the flames on Bonfire Night, perhaps not.

To judge by the queue outside the Capilla Real, where they – or what little is left of them – lie in lead coffins, modern-day Spain is pretty interested in its infamous monarchs. On the ground floor of the chapel lie the ornate marble tombs, not only of Isabel and Fernando but of their

147

daughter Juana la Loca (Joan the Mad) and her husband Felipe el Hermoso (Philip the Beautiful). Poor old Juana, incidentally, had a bit of a rough ride. Her older brother died, literally going out with a bang, or so the story goes: the doctors blamed his death on too much sex with his wife, the insatiable Margaret of Burgundy. As these two left no heir despite all those hours in the sack, Juana became queen of Castile when Isabel passed away – but not for long. She was passionately in love with her womanizing husband Felipe (who happened to be Margaret of Burgundy's brother – a liking for sex clearly ran in the family), but she couldn't hold his attention for long. Unrequited lust addled her mind. Poor old Juana went mad and was declared unfit to rule.

When Felipe died suddenly a couple of months later, Juana lost her sanity altogether. Still fiercely possessive of her husband, she refused to allow him to be buried and, following the advice of a deluded monk who claimed her husband would come back to life, Juana embarked on a tour of Spain with Felipe's fast-rotting corpse. The cortège featured eight black horses to draw the hearse and a parade of torchbearers. Every so often, Juana insisted on opening the coffin to gaze at her husband's maggoty body.

In the end, they managed to wrestle the mouldy Felipe from her in Tordesillas, northwest of Madrid, where Juana lived for the next forty-six years under house arrest. Felipe's body was eventually moved to Granada, and here they all lie in the Capilla Real, one happy royal family in death if not in life. Their actual coffins lie not with the tombs on the ground floor, though, but in a basement crypt.

There was a long, long queue to file down there – Spaniards, I assumed, eager to pay respect to the couple that created modern-day Spain. Finally, my turn came to descend down into the dark depths, where the great king and queen lay. I craned my head to see through the metal grate

148

and into the dim, cavernous crypt beyond. There, in a tiny, unadorned room, lay the family's plain, austere lead coffins. Holiday-making Spain, used to the glitter and gold of the Catholicism that Fernando and Isabel so single-mindedly espoused, was unimpressed.

'Bah, it's nothing,' the woman in front of me spat in disappointment. We filed up the stairs on the other side, and that was the end of that.

Next door at the cathedral, I found myself queuing behind yet another group of pensioners. One old woman, I noticed, had broken with convention in a very daring moment and had a *purple* rinse. They were, as usual, geriatric and garrulous, too involved in exchanging tortilla recipes and relating the terrible scandal of María who lives at number sixty-two to realize that anyone might be trying to edge past their bulky forms. Shepherding them was a booming tour guide, waving her brightly coloured umbrella and bellowing heartily. She made no difference.

The cathedral was worth the rabble, though. Construction started just thirty years after the Christians reconquered the city, and they were determined to outdo the Moors in architectural ostentation. Given that the Alhambra was just up the road, this took some doing. The result is quite staggering – and shockingly opulent. The building is vast. In dramatic contrast to other Spanish cathedrals, which are often rather dark because of the screened choir in the middle that blocks the light, the one in Granada is flooded with light; it's almost luminous, with white walls and gleaming marble surrounding remarkable stained-glass windows and priceless paintings.

I only managed to hold out till eight-thirty before I had no choice but to eat dinner. Because of the unfashionably early hour, my fellow diners consisted entirely of middle-aged fellow tourists. The temperature dropped dramatically once the sun went down – it *was* late October – and we sat wrapped in anoraks and shawls, insistent on eating outdoors. This was Spain, after all.

'What do you think *cava* means, dear?' the man on the next table asked his wife, as he peered at the menu over his bifocals.

'I don't know, dear,' she replied, drawing her sensible woollen shawl more tightly around her. 'Let me look it up in the phrase book.' She rummaged around in the bottom of her large, practical bag for several moments, unearthing such travel necessities as the digital camera neither she nor her husband seemed to have the first idea how to use, and a half-eaten packet of McVitie's digestive biscuits. Finally she emerged from the depths with a tiny, dog-eared book printed, probably, in the 1960s when she and her husband first went to the Costa del Sol. (In those days, it was considered off-beat and gloriously hip.) She rustled the pages for a good while.

'Well, I don't know, dear,' she eventually admitted. 'It doesn't seem to be in here. I think perhaps it's a kind of fish.'

Cava is not a kind of fish; it's a kind of bubbly wine. *Cava* first popped its cork in Spain – in Catalonia, where 99 per cent of the stuff is still bottled – towards the end of the nineteenth century. The vineyards of the Penedès area had been ravaged by the phylloxera aphids. When they were replanted, white grapes replaced many of the traditional red-grape vines.

Over the other side of the Pyrenees, the French were all in a lather about their champagne, which they had discovered rather by accident two hundred years previously. (The Pyrenees are very tall, as we have already seen, and news takes time to travel.) A few barrels of still wine from the Champagne region had been shipped before fermentation was complete, the theory goes. It was wintertime, so the yeast would have been dormant. But when the barrels

150

arrived at their destination in the spring, the warmer weather breathed life back into the yeast. These lucky barrels, then, went through two fermentations instead of the usual one – and when they were cracked open, the wine was found to sparkle.

'*Mon Dieu!*' proclaimed the French nobles with a great Gallic flourish and a wobble of their wigs. 'Zees wine ees feezy.'

And, because the French can't bear to do anything that is not the very height of cool, they instantly pronounced it fashionable.

Fast forward two hundred years and, in the tiny Catalan town of Sant Sadurni d'Anoia, a group of winemakers known as the Seven Creek Sages sat swirling and sniffing and swirling and sniffing some more. They were trying to figure out what to do with their new white grapes. It might be rather nice, they thought, to make some of their new wine bubble, just like that funny fizzy stuff over the hills in France. But how could they make a sparkling wine in Spain of a quality that would rival French champagne? After much thought, and no few litres of lubrication, they hit on a master plan.

'I know,' cried one, with the excitement of a man who has hit on a very big idea indeed. 'Let's do it exactly the same way the French do it.'

And so they did.

After the first pressing, they fermented the grape juice in barrels in cool, temperature-controlled cellars (in order to achieve this in steamy Spain, unfortunately, they had to dig a very deep hole in the ground, during which they must have worked up quite a thirst). After blending, in December and January, they bottled the wine, adding yeast and sugar, which produced a second fermentation. It's this second fermentation that creates the fizz, as the French discovered all those years ago. Once the wine has matured (this takes at

151

least nine months) the bottles are laid neck downwards so that the sediment collects. The bottle necks are then frozen, opened and . . . POP! The carbon dioxide bursts the frozen sediment out of the bottle. Then the bottle is corked again and left to age.

After that, there was only one thing left for the Seven Sages to decide. What on earth were they going to call their new, frothy wine? They each poured themselves a glass and settled down for a good, long think. Inspiration did not strike. They cracked open another bottle with a lovely, resounding, celebratory pop and then, as it sounded so nice, they drained another. Their addled brains whirred and clicked. And then one particularly creative sage leapt to his feet.

'I've got it!' he exclaimed. 'We'll call it *cava*,' which, in English, means 'cellar'.

And so they did.

I wandered home to catch the weather report: tomorrow I was back on the bike. I was becoming pretty good at the weather, understanding those funny wavy lines, the bands of high pressure and low. I was even starting to figure out the weather girls' rota.

In my brown hotel room, an exceedingly fat cockroach had taken up residence. I'm an experienced cockroach-basher (my Hong Kong flat was full of them – I even found one inside the washing machine once) so I entered gamely into the sport, chasing it round the room and brandishing a shoe in a ready-to-wallop position for a good fifteen minutes. For while these insects can apparently withstand a nuclear holocaust, few of them have ever withstood a mighty smack of my shoe. Round the chairs, through the bed legs and into the bathroom we went, the cockroach scuttling nimbly as I crashed my way bruisingly between the furniture muttering threats that were supposed to inspire surrender.

'I'm going to get you, you little sod . . . Won't be moving so fast with your innards sprayed over the carpet, will you?'

The cockroach tried a tactical diversion under the bed where it could see I wouldn't fit; undefeated, I hurled myself flat across the mattress, head and walloping arm hanging off the end, ready to strike the second it emerged. In the end, though, the brute got away. For sure, this was one athletic cockroach.

At two a.m., I woke to find that not only was my bathroom falling apart, and my hotel room brown and inhabited by a fat but fast cockroach, but it also overlooked a very noisy bar. The noise from the revellers below was deafening. These were people who had drunk a whisky and Fanta orange or two more than was good for them.

I was up early anyway. My destination for the day was the Alpujarras, the jumble of valleys south of the Sierra Nevada that have had more than fifteen minutes of fame over the centuries. It was here that Boabdil, the last Nasrid ruler of Granada, was exiled when Fernando and Isabel conquered the city. (He lasted only a year in the hills before heading back to Africa.) The writer Gerald Brenan lived here for a number of years in the 1920s and '30s. His house guests included Virginia and Leonard Woolf, the painter Carrington and her friends Ralph Partridge and Lytton Strachey. Strachey was apparently unimpressed. 'When . . . Leonard and Virginia Woolf were preparing to come out and stay with me, he advised them strongly against it, declaring in his high-pitched voice that it was "death",' Brenan wrote in *South from Granada*.

If I thought I'd met some unsophisticated people on my trip, Brenan's tales go to show that Spain's rural folk have come a long way in eighty years. In his day, the villagers' lives were governed by witchcraft and omens. When Brenan confessed to the priest that he was a Protestant, the priest 'brushed this aside as a matter of small importance and, patting me on the back, said, "Never mind that, man. You come to mass and you'll find it will do you no harm. But a word in your ear. Don't tell people that you are a Protestant. The country people are very ignorant and won't understand." ' On enquiring, he was told that some of the villagers thought that Protestants were people with tails.

The locals' grasp of world events was such that, in the early 1920s, many of them had no idea that the First World War had taken place and assumed that the war in which Brenan had taken part was against the Moors.

More recently the Alpujarras have provided the backdrop for Chris Stewart's *Driving Over Lemons.* Things had come along a bit in sixty or seventy years – but not much. When Stewart bought the heap of bricks he called a house in the 1990s, there was still no road, no running water and no electricity, and there were plenty of peasants still suspicious about modern ways.

It seemed to be the general consensus, among everyone except the person who drew my map, that the only way to Pampaneira, the Alpujarran village I was heading for, was by the *autovía.* The problem was that I didn't want to take the *autovía.* I wanted to take that nice little wiggly white road on the map, the one with the green line down its side which, according to Messrs Michelin, designated a scenic route.

The man at the hotel reception, at least, was honest with his directions. He'd only ever been to the Alpujarras on the *autovía,* he said. He didn't know any other way. I hit the road, hoping to find somebody to give directions *en route.*

The suited lady in the street, who walked with brisk, efficient strides as her vertically challenged poodle skipped alongside, had no idea what I was talking about so she in turn collared a young white-coated male nurse standing on a nearby doorstep, who was waiting to attend to a sick nun in an apartment within.

'Oh yes, there did use to be another road,' he said. 'I think you want to go down there' – a vague flourish – 'over the roundabout, and just kind of keep going.' But then the buzzer to the sick nun's apartment buzzed, the lock on the door was clicked open, and he disappeared before he could offer any more explicit instructions.

The sexagenarian cyclist I asked at the next red traffic light simply thought I was mad and therefore refrained from offering me any directions at all.

'*Hostia*,' he exclaimed. (*Hostia* is a Spanish swear word meaning 'host' – as in body of Christ, not poor soul besieged by guests. Admittedly, it loses something in translation.) 'Pampaneira must be at least eighty kilometres away!' At that moment the light turned green and he wobbled off in his circa-1960 sunglasses, his great, billowing gut hanging out over his tight Lycra shorts.

I have no idea whether the two cardigan-clad old men sitting on the park bench, debating their bowls tactics perhaps, knew where the road was or not because I couldn't understand a word they said. They bellowed toothlessly, enthusiastically waving their walking sticks in the general direction of the mountains. I followed the sticks and, after a couple of misjudged meanderings, happened upon the road and the Sunday-morning bicycle brigade in force and full regalia. The rest was perfect cycling – long, flat, well-surfaced roads and not a car in sight. They, of course, were all on the *autovía*. I pedalled through stone-terraced olive groves, the trees heavy with the black and green fruit, through pomegranate orchards and tiny whitewashed villages set against the backdrop of the snowcapped Sierra Nevada.

It was not until I'd covered about fifty kilometres that I committed my most terrible social *faux-pas* yet: I overtook another cyclist. This man had much better kit than I had (bright green Lycra shorts and a matching green-and-white 'Caja Rural' cycling jersey) so to go past him really wouldn't

155

do. What's more he was male. I had entirely forgotten the Spanish rules *of machismo*.

'*Hola*,' I called out as I passed him labouring up a hill. I might as well have insulted his mother's home-cured ham. Señor Cyclist called up the resources of every tortilla-loaded muscle to hammer down on the pedals and draw back even with me.

'Where are you off to in such a hurry?' he demanded, vainly trying to control his heaving breath. What could I say? The truth was, I wasn't in a hurry at all and, while I had until this moment been fully convinced that I was the least competent cyclist on earth, it now became blindingly apparent that during those weeks in the Pyrenees my quadriceps must have grown. There was now at least one person on the face of the planet who cycled more slowly than I did. Belatedly mindful of the unwisdom of entering into a contest with *machismo,* I slowed down, tucked in behind him, and told him I was going to Pampaneira.

'Pampaneira,' he choked. '*Hostia!* It's twenty kilometres straight up a hill like this.'

He held his hand almost vertical. But I had learnt by now that the Spanish are prone to exaggeration. I smiled as sweetly as I could manage and thought quietly to myself, Tough talk, mountain man. This is the girl who conquered Cotefablo, who nailed Navarre, who pounded the Pyrenees. And, if my legs were quivering like a custard *flan* when I got to the top, well, he need never know. He wasn't going that far.

The first ten of those twenty kilometres turned out to be glorious freewheeling through rugged mountain valleys, over yellow, crumbling stone bridges and spectacular, rocky gorges. The hill – a mere eight kilometres – was a little on the steep side. I didn't bonk, I didn't even have the pleasure of foreplay, but by the time I arrived at the top I was having something equivalent, perhaps, to a peck on the cheek. I

156

refuelled my sugar and fat reserves with Coke and crisps in a flower-bedecked restaurant, and dwelt on the fact that there was not another cyclist in sight. Clearly, I thought smugly, they're all kit and no quads in this part of the world.

Pampaneira's whitewashed houses cling for dear life to the side of the mountain, their window boxes of begonias and geraniums dangling vertiginously over the void. When I arrived, the village was seething with people and stalls selling every kind of handmade ware you could possibly imagine, and some that you shouldn't even try to: shaggy carpets that resembled unkempt sheep, shoes that have never been fashionable, poorly executed paintings of the local villages, cheeses pungent enough to evict the neighbours, vegetables and fruits, bread, jams, and, of course, the ubiquitous ceramics. Today, it turned out, was Pampaneira's annual arts-and-crafts fair and everyone within a hundred kilo-metres had come for their piece of the action. There were hippies and hitchhikers by the score, local groups with overexcited children on a rare outing beyond the boundaries of their five-family village, and quite probably hundreds of tourists from farther afield who, like me, had come to see what the likes of Gerald Brenan and Chris Stewart were harping on about.

It didn't seem a very safe environment in which to abandon a lone, lithe, pale-green road bike. I battled through the crowds to find a table for lunch, somewhere I could lock up my bike and still keep an eye on it. A terrace table came up for grabs; I bustled in and snatched it. Those Hong Kong elbowing lessons weren't for nothing, then. These super-relaxed Spaniards didn't stand a chance against *me*. I propped my bicycle up against a wall about fifty metres away. I was feeling fiercely protective, ferociously pro-prietorial. I was neurotic about my bike.

No sooner had I sat down than two small boys sidled up to the machine. I directed at them my most terrifying stare.

They poked its gleaming green frame with their curious little fingers. I narrowed my eyes and scowled. They prodded the bike computer clipped to the handlebars. I gave dagger looks. They gave a bit of a shove – and the little computer fell off. Their parents at the next table did nothing at all. I had to take matters into my own hands.

'Get your filthy little hands off my nice clean bike,' I hissed at them, sprinting over to save it. 'It's *mine*.'

'We didn't touch it,' squealed little boy number one. 'It broke by itself.'

'Well it's *mine*. You can't play with it. So there.'

'We were just looking,' squeaked little boy number two. 'We were nowhere near it.'

Their parents were well into their third bottle of house plonk and didn't give a damn. This is Spain, after all, where children of all sizes are given the benefit of free expression. After all that excitement, I only had ten minutes to spare before the bus left for Granada. Given that there were only two buses a day and I didn't really feel like cycling the seventy-odd kilometres back into town, I was eager to catch it.

I managed to procure the front seat on the bus, which made for a rather more thrilling journey than I'd bargained for. The ticket machine was playing up and the driver seemed to think this warranted more attention than the steering wheel as he hurtled hair-raisingly round the hairpin bends.

'C'mon, you stupid machine,' he muttered, one hand on the wheel, the other jabbing at buttons on the keypad. His eyes were not on the road.

His mobile phone rang. '*Diga* . . . Hey! Conchita! Great to hear from you . . . yeah . . . great . . . yeah. I had a good time too . . . hey, Conchita, what you doing tonight?' With one hand holding the phone, and the other still jabbing at the ticket machine, there didn't seem to be many fingers left for steering the bus round mountain switchbacks.

Finally, having arranged to meet the lovely Conchita at a bar called La Alhambra at ten p.m., the driver smiled flirtatiously at the handset, bade it *adiós* and had just returned his mind to the steering wheel when another bus came careering round the bend in the opposite direction. The brakes squealed. We passengers gasped and gripped our seats. The drivers, though, weren't so easily cowed. The other bus's driver roared with laughter; ours grinned wryly and gave the sign of the cross.

'*Que te den por el culo!*' May they give it to you up the arse! he muttered at the ticket machine, still grinning. (He made no such lewd comment to the mobile phone.)

Who are these guys? Retired rally drivers looking for a little spice to keep their engines oiled? Maybe when Lance Armstrong gets too old to make it up those hills with just his legs to power him he could consider the wildly exhilarating life of a mountain bus driver as a second career.

On Monday morning I had an appointment with the Alhambra, the glorious palace of the last Moorish dynasty – but first I had to pay a visit to another bike mechanic. My gears were rasping and the chain was clattering. Perhaps my highly strung thoroughbred of a racing bike didn't think much of being treated like a pack animal and was putting up a fight. Whatever the reason, the gears needed tuning and I'd learnt from bitter experience that I wasn't the woman for the job. And, although I hadn't had a single puncture, the tires could none the less do with a bit more air, and the guys in the shop were so much better at pumping than I was.

I headed off down a maze of back streets trying to find the shop the hostel owner had suggested. I was hoping, it has to be said, to meet another incarnation of Javi, the saint from San Sebastián. I found the shop and pushed open the door.

'What?' a surly character in oily overalls barked at me from the corner of the shop. He didn't smile engagingly as Javi had done.

'Er, I was wondering, could you mend my, um . . .' I realized I didn't know the word for gears and pointed at the lever.

'What?' The oily man glared.

'Um, this thing, er . . .'

The oily man gave that universal, multi-lingual, withering look that says, 'Stupid woman,' and said, 'Leave it there. Come back after four.'

He then glared at me once more for good measure. His assistant stood and gawped. I left the bike as instructed and made good my escape. It looked as if Javi had been a one off. And so I did what stupid women have done for centuries when needing to console themselves after run-ins with nasty men. I went in search of chocolate.

Drinking chocolate in Spain is far, far different from the version in northern Europe. It's usually served for breakfast, is thick as mud and fabulously rich, and comes served with *churros*, strips of hot, light, crispy, deep-fried dough.

Spain was the first country in Europe to relish the joys of chocolate, although even here it took a while to catch on. It first came to Spain with Columbus: he brought cocoa beans back from the New World and showed them to King Fernando, explaining that they were a form of currency. Fernando thought they looked like boring little brown lumps. Gold was so much prettier and glitterier. And so no more was said.

Nearly twenty years after that, Hernán Cortés, the intrepid, gun-toting explorer, landed in Mexico. By an incredible stroke of good luck for Cortés, the Aztecs worshipped a god called Quetzalcoatl who, legend had it, was tall, had white skin and sported a beard. They were ecstatic at the sight of Cortés, who was also tall, white-

160

skinned and bearded, and welcomed him with their most precious commodity – chocolate. Oops.

The Aztecs revered cocoa beans. They used them as a form of currency, as Columbus had seen, but also in religious services. Chocolate was consumed as a drink only by nobles and warriors. The beans were roasted and ground into a paste, then mixed with water and maize, flavoured with chillies and beaten to a froth. The Aztec ruler Montezuma and his court consumed up to fifty pitchers of the 'xocolatl' drink each day (Montezuma particularly liked to drink a cup before entering his harem, as he believed it increased his virility). The elixir was served in goblets of solid gold, which were used just once, and then cast with breathtaking extravagance into a nearby lake.

Because the Aztecs had yet to work out that Cortés was not a god but a nasty, marauding interloper, and that the long, tubular, metal thing he carried was not for communicating with the heavens but a rather vicious, new-fangled instrument called a gun which would soon blow their centuries-old empire to smithereens, they treated him to several cups of their precious drink. And Cortés, once he was done with killing his hosts and nicking their treasure, returned to Spain with galleons loaded with cocoa beans and chocolate-making equipment. Chocolate soon became a fashionable drink in Spain (they left the chillies out and added nuts and honey) and its recipe was kept a closely guarded secret. Even so, people soon became so addicted that it came to be viewed by puritans as an evil poison. Spain's Princess María Theresa was obsessed by the stuff and made chocolate the rage of Europe when she presented cocoa beans as an engagement gift to Louis XIV. Apparently, she herself drank it every day and it was thought to be the reason all her teeth fell out.

I headed to the Plaza Bib-Rambla whose elegant *chocolaterías* provide the first fat and sugar buzz of the day to

Granada's beautiful crowd. Taking a window seat, I surveyed the scene in the tree-lined square outside. Fruit vendors and flower sellers busily set up their stalls on the freshly hosed cobbles around the ornate fountain and lush flowerbeds that dominate the square. In the street beyond, schoolchildren with bulging backpacks were bundled onto school buses, while lethargic-looking students with their folders tucked under their arms shuffled to class, weary after the demands of their social lives the night before.

The waiter appeared, a vat of steaming, chocolatey goo in one hand, a plateful of sizzling, crunchy *churros* in the other. The first few mouthfuls zapped my early-morning taste buds and sugar-thin blood like a drug. After I finished, of course, I felt faintly queasy and had to ask whether toast and orange juice might not have been a more sensible option.

Slightly nauseous, I made my way to the Plaza Nueva and climbed aboard the 'Alhambra bus'. We wended our way up the narrow, cobbled street, through the palace's arched stone gateway and up the magnificent tree-lined drive. This was my first visit to the Alhambra, and I was very excited. I was also a little afraid that it wouldn't live up to its sensational reputation – but I needn't have worried. Just to add to the hyperbole, I'll say that the Alhambra is magical, radiant, dazzling, heavenly and that it blew me away. I'll also say that it's full of very friendly cats, the significance of whom I never worked out. I recommend you drop everything and go there tomorrow.

14

Close Encounters
With the Tarmac

If you've ever had trouble finding your way out of a strange city in a car, you shouldn't try it on a bike. Almost every route is motorway, streaming with drivers on a mission to test the shockproof qualities of a cyclist's helmet. Nobody you ask for directions, of course, has the first idea why you might want to take a bumpy little side road when you could glide along gleaming asphalt instead. They send you straight to the motorway. I even tried pre-selecting candidates for directions by only asking those over seventy years of age. They, at least, I thought, ought to have been around before the motorway was built and remember the old road out of town. And perhaps they did. The problem was, most of them had very few teeth and strong Andalusian accents and I couldn't understand a word they said.

After some hours of touring through suburbs and back streets, following signs to nowhere and doubling dizzyingly back on myself again and again, I found myself, thanks to some small miracle, on the road to Fuente Vaqueros, the birthplace of Federico García Lorca. Lorca is generally acknowledged as Spain's greatest twentieth-century poet and playwright. His plays include *Blood Wedding*; he penned the *Gypsy Ballads* poems. He might have written a good deal more – 'I'm in love with the ones I haven't written yet,' the artist told a journalist who asked him which of his plays he liked the best – had the Nationalists not shot him dead in the opening days of the Spanish Civil War. He was just thirty-eight years old.

Lorca stood for everything Franco's right-wing army was against. He was an intellectual with left-wing inclinations; his name appeared on a 1933 register of the Association of Friends of the Soviet Union. He was homosexual: the firing squad put an extra couple of bullets up his anus to demonstrate their open-mindedness. He spoke out against the conservative values of Granada's bourgeoisie.

'It was a disastrous event, even though they say the opposite in the schools,' Lorca said of the 1492 Reconquest of Granada in an inflammatory interview with *El Sol* newspaper two months before his death. 'An admirable civilization, and a poetry, architecture and delicacy unique in the world – all were lost, to give way to an impoverished, cowardly, narrow-minded town, inhabited at present by the worst bourgeoisie in Spain.'

But Lorca was about as apolitical as it was possible for a writer to be amid the turmoil and uncertainty of 1930s Spain. He repeatedly refused to join the Communist Party; he was concerned with human rights, not political rhetoric. 'As an observer of life, the artist cannot remain insensitive to the social question,' he believed. But when asked about his political beliefs, he told a friend, 'Look, I greet some people like this' – raising his arm in a Nazi salute – 'and others like this' – clenching a communist fist. 'But to my friends, *this*,' he cried, and held out his hand for his friend to shake. Lorca declared himself too frightened to participate in politics. Certainly, he was a fearful – and childlike – character. (One of his favourite tricks was to sit in the corner of a restaurant, pretending to compose spontaneously a poem which he had, in reality, written some time previously.) His greatest fear of all was, ironically, his own death. As a young man living in Madrid's Residencia, a boarding house for budding intellectuals, Lorca would ritually throw himself across the bed feigning rigor mortis and encourage his friends to enact his funeral procession through the streets of Granada. When he visited Cadaqués, he would insist on holding Dalí's and his sister Ana María's hands. Ana María later recalled that he was deeply afraid of dying, and that holding their hands seemed to him to provide a connection with life. At the beach he would only venture into the shallowest water: he was terrified of drowning.

As the Civil War began to brew, Lorca anxiously fled the turbulence of Madrid and took up residence at his family's summer house just outside Granada. They listened incessantly to the radio; from Madrid came the rousing voice of communist leader Dolores Ibarruri, La Pasionaria, calling on women to prepare vats of boiling oil to hurl at the Nationalist troops. 'Better to die on one's feet than to live on one's knees,' she proclaimed along with her most famous rallying call, '*No pasarán!*' They will not pass! (In response, the right spread rumours that she had once cut a priest's throat with her teeth.)

But Granada provided Lorca with no refuge. In days the city fell to the Nationalists. The Republicans dropped bombs in retaliation; Lorca huddled, petrified, with his family, hiding in terror under the grand piano during air raids. The family house was searched several times: Nationalist soldiers accused Lorca of spying for the Russians. Fearing for his safety, he took shelter in the house of right-wing Falangist friends. It was not enough. On 16 August 1936, Lorca was arrested by Nationalist soldiers. 'He's done more damage with a pen than others have with a pistol,' announced the arresting officer, Ruiz Alonso, who had his own arguments with the Falangist leadership and was happy to embarrass them by making an arrest at the house of high-profile members. Lorca trembled and wept as he was bundled into the officer's car; two days later, he was driven six miles to Víznar, in the foothills of the Sierra Nevada, and executed beside a stand of olive trees.

Fuente Vaqueros, where Lorca was born, betrays none of the violence that its most famous inhabitant faced nearby, sixty-odd years ago. It's a charming little village with tree-lined avenues, a large square with plenty of benches well utilized by numerous old men in their ubiquitous flat caps, and a monument to Lorca at one end. Lorca called it a 'quiet, fragrant little village' in his account of his childhood, 'My Village', which he wrote aged nineteen after his family had moved to Granada. He looked back on his rural childhood as a lost paradise, a time of unconditional love and happiness. Years later, when Lorca was famous, a street in the village was renamed after him and he came to speak at the dedication of the local library. He promised his audience that, wherever he went, he would always acknowledge the place of his birth, 'so that whatever glory or fame I might achieve will also belong to this friendly, this modern, this tantalizing liberal village, Fuente Vaqueros.' He subsequently said that he could never have written *Blood Wedding* and his rural tragedies had his childhood memories not been infused with the 'flavour of the earth'.

Lorca came from a well-to-do farming family. The house where he was born has now been turned into a museum. Its curators have tried to keep things just the way they were when the family lived there, from the furniture to the pots and pans. The actual bed upon which Lorca came into this world is still there, too, though thankfully somewhat cleaner than it must have been on that doubtless messy day. Visitors tour the bedroom next door, where the young Federico slept and where, each morning, his mother would stride to the

166

window, throw open the shutters and proclaim, 'May the grace of God enter,' before crossing herself and leading her children in prayer.

Upstairs, they've transformed the granary into a tiny shrine to Lorca with low-key but none the less charming exhibitions of handwritten letters, programmes and newspaper clippings. In another room, above the old stables, the guide shows a 1930s piece of film of a stage performance by La Barraca, the student theatre group that Lorca set up and directed, which embodied all his ideals about the theatre. The group travelled round Spain, from village to village, performing for free.

'We will remove plays from the libraries, take them away from scholars, and restore them to the sunlight and fresh air of the village square,' Lorca declared. The characters of the film flit about in that old-movie, too-fast way against upbeat background music, reflecting the exuberance and optimism of their director.

Back on the bike, I pedalled along tiny back roads through cornfields and poplar orchards. This was the *vega,* the fertile plain of Granada irrigated by the melting snows of the Sierra Nevada whose echoing birdsong and poplar fields Lorca so loved. The terrain was flat. There was no traffic, there were no people. The birdies chirruped, the little goats frolicked in the fields and all was well with the world.

And then I saw it. About four feet long and as thick as my wrist, the snake lay in its tell-tale wavy S-shape across the road.

'Aaaah!' I screeched, flinging the handlebars to the left, throwing myself and the bike into the opposite carriageway. I gripped the brakes and sent the bike into a tyre-burning skid. With a resounding crunch, the bike and I crashed to the ground.

The snake was not moving. It was curious that it should

remain inert in the face of such frenzied activity just a metre or two away. And then I realized why. It was not a snake. It was a piece of old rubber lying in the middle of the road.

Somewhere deep within me, my Asian demons still were lurking – for in Asia, snakes were a regular feature. My conscious mind might be learning to relax, but my unconscious clearly had some way to go. What on earth would the psychoanalysts have had to say about this sudden onset of hysteria combined with snake delusions? The doctors of centuries past reckoned hysteria was created by 'vapours' from the womb travelling to the brain. It was the baleful result of sexual abstinence in women not temperamentally suited to that way of life, they said. The terrible conclusions they might they have drawn about the craziness going on in my subconscious didn't bear thinking about.

The goats in the field looked mildly surprised that I'd thrown myself so excitedly from my bike, but fortunately there was nobody else around to see me so I sheepishly brushed the grit from my legs, concluded my grazes weren't life threatening and climbed back onto the bike. I set off again with a jaunty whistle, supposed to imply to nobody in particular that I was really very relaxed and not remotely concerned about uterine vapours, and soon I was gobbling up the miles at such a rate I was afraid I'd arrive at my stop for the night, Alhama de Granada, ahead of schedule. I didn't want to spend too much time in Alhama de Granada. I didn't have high hopes for the town. The woman in the Granada tourist office had told me it was 'not exactly the nicest town in the area' and its one and only hotel was inexplicably full, so I had had to book into a one-star *pensión* at twelve euros a night. I was prepared for the worst.

I shouldn't have worried about arriving early. I should have known the easy roads wouldn't last long. I'd only covered about ten kilometres when I arrived at Láchar, where I had to cross underneath the motorway. It looked easy enough on the map. My tiny, wiggly road should have slipped simply underneath the six-lane, fume-spewing, tarmac monster and popped out the other side. But it didn't.

I arrived at a roundabout, to find only one signpost – to the motorway. There was just one other road, so battered and beaten it bore no signpost at all. It was a skinny, wizened little thing. Its tarmac was cracked and pitted, neglected, no doubt, in favour of the brash new motorway next door. I set off, over the potholes and pebbles, my confidence diminished. In taking this rickety old highway I was all alone and there was nobody to ask.

After several minutes of self-doubt, I spied a man in the distance. He was as shrivelled and sunken-eyed as the road itself, trying, as he hobbled down the lane, to herd a small flock of scraggy, gaunt goats. He had with him a dog, who was doing his best, but the poor mutt was almost as ancient as its owner. Its coat was mangy and thin, its eyes were red-rimmed and rheumy, its legs were lame.

'Excuse me,' I started when the pair drew close. Neither man nor dog so much as blinked. 'Excuse me' – a little louder this time. The old man looked up, startled. It was then that I noticed that he had just three, very long, extraordinarily brown teeth.

'Is this the way to Peñuelas?' I hollered. He wrinkled his crow-footed eyes in consternation. I drew a deep breath. 'PEÑUELAS,' I bawled. The old man looked taken aback.

'Yes, yes,' he said quietly, and with a wave of his age-spotted hand added, 'It's just down there.'

What he didn't tell me was that a few hundred metres further on, the road ran out and turned into tumbledown track. The old man and his goats, I dare say, could negotiate it, but it was quite impassable for anything with wheels. I got off the bike, picked my way over rocks and boulders, then clambered up a bank pulling machine and luggage behind me. At the top I found myself, despite all my efforts, on the

169

hard shoulder of the motorway. Peñuelas, unfortunately, was on the other side; to get there, I had to hammer frantically up a steeply inclined motorway exit and over a bridge that crossed the road.

The flat roads of the beginning of the day soon came to an end and meandering ups and downs through olive groves took their place. The bent, knarred trees laden with under-ripe fruit sat perfectly spaced for as far as the eye could see, like a gigantic grid of dark green dots against a sandy yellow background. The roads undulated gently at first; then they took on more demanding profiles. From each small summit stretched kilometre after endless kilometre of olive groves, their spotted fabric rising and dipping in waves as the hills rose and fell towards the distant horizon.

The olive trees that made up this interminable, arid grid had probably been here for quite some time, for an olive tree can live for more than a thousand years. Just think, then, of the triumphs and disasters these knobbly branches have seen. Perhaps some of these same trees bore their first fruit when the Arabs ruled; perhaps it was a beturbaned head that tended them, a brown-skinned hand that carried the long pole to shake the fruit from their branches. Perhaps these very trees stood by and watched as the Christian armies swept from the north and, slowly, slowly vanquished the Moors.

Spain's first olive trees arrived on the peninsula well before Moorish times, though. They made their maiden appearance in the wheelbarrows of the Romans; now the country is the world's largest olive oil producer. Spain's dry, dusty hillsides are covered with 292 million olive trees – and most of them are in Andalusia. The Spanish olive industry presses up to a million tonnes of oil in productive years. Some of it gets exported, but much of it stays at home, to be poured liberally down the gullets of the oil-adoring Spanish. The International Olive Oil Council reckons that the average

Spaniard guzzles 13.68 kilograms of olive oil each year. They pour it freely over their salads, with just a nip of vinegar alongside. They fry just about anything they can find in it. They dip bread in it. They make breads and pastries with it. And, of course, with a glass of wine or a cold beer before lunch or after the evening *paseo*, they devour olives whole.

Given the life-enhancing qualities of the green grease, it's a wonder the Spaniards don't live for ever. Olive oil, they say, reduces the amount of cholesterol in the blood and contains anti-oxidants such as vitamins A, D, E and K. It stimulates the absorption of minerals. It helps digestion, disposes of gastric acid and helps in the healing of ulcers. It relieves constipation and is good for the pancreas, liver and gall bladder. It strengthens bones and enhances skin — this stuff is not only good for you, it also makes you beautiful. Sadly, for all its life-enhancing qualities, it contains plenty of calories. Olive oil may make you fit but it will make you fat, too.

If these hills kept up, though, I'd be able to drink olive oil by the bottle and I'd still lose weight. None of them was particularly long, but these slopes were steeper than anything I'd encountered in the Pyrenees. The lactic acid started to pulse through my muscles as I spent more and more time out of the saddle just to get to the top, and the roads were in such dreadful condition that I couldn't take the descents much faster than the climbs. At one point, a slew of gravel across the road threw me from the bike; after that I went even more cautiously. Out here in the middle of nowhere would be no place to buckle a wheel or, indeed, to break a leg.

The landscape became sparse and dry. It was a desolate spot. There were few road signs, and none of those friendly little roadside stumps I'd relied on in the north to reassure me that I was on the right road, that rewardingly knocked off the kilometres one by one. An hour could go by without sight of another person or a car: the only features of this landscape were the dark-leaved, never-ending olive trees. Even the villages were deserted for the most part. The high point of the afternoon was when I passed *three* people tilling a field. They stopped working, stood up and stared.

'Look!' exclaimed a woman brandishing a hoe. 'There's a girl on a bike!' This part of Andalusia was obviously not the most action-packed place on earth.

In the one-mule village of Castillo de Tajarja, I asked an old man with a dark brown, deeply wrinkled face if I was going the right way to La Zahora. He was overcome by the sense of social occasion and delighted in drawing it out for as long as he could.

'Just go straight,' he said. 'There's a turning to the right. Don't take it. After a couple of kilometres, there's a turning to the left. Don't take that either. Then you go over a hill, and down the other side. You'll know you're going the right way when you pass the white house on the hill. Then there's another turning to the left. Don't take it . . .'

He had a heavy accent, but I reckoned I'd understood. 'OK,' I said, just to make sure. 'So I go straight, then I turn right and after a couple of kilometres I go left.'

'No . . .' He looked at me steadily, his eyes narrowing slightly as if he were mildly insulted that I had failed to comprehend such simple directions. 'You just go straight like I said.'

On arrival at the hostel, I had another unexpectedly close encounter with the tarmac. I'm blaming it on surprise. After all that fuss, the *pensión* was clean and bright. I was so astonished as I pulled up outside it that I entirely forgot to unclip my cleats and the bike and I – much to the astonishment of the old man and his equally ancient poodle tottering by – crashed as one to the ground. The startled old man offered no help or sympathy as I lay there in my oily, skin-grazed state; he and his poodle just stopped and stared as if they had seen no stranger event in the whole of their hundred years than a clearly deranged woman throwing herself wilfully from her bicycle. Luckily, there was no harm done apart from a bruised elbow. I brushed the grit from my face and went in. They didn't seem to be expecting me.

'There's a girl here says she booked a room,' the old man at the desk shouted to his wife, tucked away in some sanctuary in the back.

'*Booked a room?*' exclaimed the woman. She waddled out of her refuge, duster and apron flapping, to take a look at the strange creature who had done such a remarkable thing.

'Well, actually, yes,' I confirmed. 'I phoned yesterday.'

'Ah,' she said. 'So you're the one who phoned yesterday.' There was a long, consternated pause during which she regarded me suspiciously. Then she said the five most beautiful words I had heard all week: 'I was expecting a foreigner.'

I won't get carried away on a cloud of self-congratulation. She had only heard me speak a couple of words and she was probably hard of hearing. But this was a new experience for me. Usually, when I open my mouth and try to speak Spanish, not only do people know I'm foreign, they often laugh like drains. I've become used to providing entertainment when I try to negotiate my way through life's mundane little tasks. After six months of living in Spain when I was a student, I found I'd been using the wrong word when buying chicken breasts. '*Hola,*' I had for months cheerfully greeted the girl behind the meat counter. 'Please could you give me two chicken's bosoms?'

'So where are you from?' asked the deaf hostel proprietress.

'I'm English.'

'Oh, really? English from England?'

173

'Well, yes, actually.' I paused a moment – was it just me or was that a strange question? 'Um . . . where else would I be English from?' I asked very politely and Englishly.

'Well!' retorted the woman, rolling her eyes as if to say I might be English but I was also incredibly slow. 'You could be English from Scotland, or English from Ireland, or English from America, or English from Australia . . .'

'Or from Canada, or even New Zealand, though that's a very long way away,' her husband threw in, so as not to be outdone.

Ah.

Still, I felt pretty smug about my linguistic success, even if the woman who'd mistaken me for a Spaniard was not the most geographically informed person in the world, and I was unable to loathe Alhama de Granada quite as much as the woman in the slick city tourist office would have liked. It's not up to Granada's palatial standards, perhaps, but this small town has played its meagre role in history: the defeat of the Moors here in 1482 severed a vital supply link between Granada and Malaga, effectively cutting the Moors off from all links with Africa. Their 780-year-civilization would fall just ten years later. The loss of the town was such a strategic disaster for the Muslims that people started writing poems about it. Even Byron had a go.

I sat on a terrace and munched my way through yet another cheese sandwich from a bar overhung with yet more legs of ham and patronized by the usual glut of old men drinking their afternoon tipple – that's the one that comes between the post-prandial digestif and the early-evening aperitif. These old men, though, weren't your average flat-capped brigade. Some of them wore fedoras and a very few went really overboard with a sturdy number that was nearer to a top hat. Hats are just as important for the Andalusians, it seems, as berets are for the Basques.

I took a walk round the town, which didn't take long.

Alhama de Granada had fallen some way since its heyday in the fifteenth century. It seemed to be playing host to no other visitors – which made me wonder how the main hotel could possibly be full – apart from one very blond, very lost-looking German family whom I found disconsolately wandering the streets. We briefly exchanged notes about getting lost (a mutual experience) and the inaccuracy of the road signs (hard for the Germans to fathom) and our itineraries for the days to come (theirs rather more painstakingly thought out than mine). It was at this point that the blond German *Frau* figured out that I was making this trip all alone.

'*Um Himmels willen!* You cycle all that vay all by yourselff? You haff no husbant?' Her big, blue eyes popped in horror. She looked protectively at little blond Gretchen by her side, clearly hoping that her own little treasure would never do anything so ridiculous – whether that be to cycle round a foreign country alone or to reach the age of thirty-one without a husband, I couldn't quite be sure.

'You haff much courage,' she concluded, still looking appalled to the roots of her blond, blond hair. And with that, she protectively rounded up her family and herded them off, away from my wayward influence.

I continued my wanderings, past a smattering of shops selling clothes so unsightly you'd rather walk round naked, dusty electrical stores that might just have discovered the transistor radio, and others that sold hideous porcelain statues of biblical figures. There was also one very dingy and dilapidated nightclub, whose entertainment my landlady must have had in mind when she asked if I'd need a door key to come in after midnight.

'Midnight? In this town?' I wanted to ask. I assured her I'd be tucked up in bed by ten-thirty. And so I was.

15

A Lost Woman

The moral of the story is never to be fooled by flattery. The morning following my little linguistic triumph, I still felt such glowing goodwill towards the landlady who thought for a fleeting moment I was Spanish that my reason deserted me entirely. Instead of seeing the stark truth – that she was a deaf old fool who couldn't have heard a foghorn if her head was jammed in its bell – I took a liking to her. Worse still, I believed her directions without checking the map.

I packed up my bike after breakfast and the nice *señora* cheerily waved me off.

'Go down there, turn right at the junction, and follow the signs to Loja,' she beamed, benevolence oozing from every pore.

I thanked her warmly and pedalled away in the direction she pointed.

To say things went downhill from then on would not be entirely accurate. Metaphorically, yes, I dived headlong into a ravine. Literally, however, I battled up an interminable, perpendicular hill in a drizzle that soon matured into a wholehearted downpour. Rivulets of water streamed off my helmet and ran down my nose. Every passing car churned filthy spray onto my legs and into my shoes until my feet were each sitting in its own personal, sloshy little pool. After an hour or two, I slithered a long way down a steep, wet slope and arrived at a town called Salar.

Salar? *Salar?* Where on earth was Salar? I had been expecting to arrive at a small village called Ventas de Zafarraya, on the edge of a scenic country park full of frolicking fauna. Salar, on the other hand, seemed to be a large, sprawling, moderately ugly town whose most promising signs of life were two unwashed children sullenly kicking a deflated football. It was now, and only now, that it dawned on me to check where this place Loja – to which I had followed the signs – might be.

I pulled out the map. I looked along my route. I widened the search. I was just about to give up hope altogether and ask an unsuspecting passer-by when I found Loja – and Salar just a stone's throw away. I had gone 180 degrees in the wrong direction. After all my careful planning of a route that took in hills and vales and gambolling goats, I had, at the first word from some deranged stranger who happened to have complimented my Spanish, abandoned my fastidious plotting and pedalled all the way . . . to the motorway.

The nice *señora,* you see, wasn't wrong when she told me to go to Loja. I had told her I was heading for Antequera and *if* one were to travel by car, *if* one weren't on a bicycle, *if* one didn't mind having one's brains dashed out on the motorway tarmac after being squashed flat by a lunatic lorry driver with a schedule to keep, well, that might have been quite a good way to go. But I didn't want to take the motorway, so I unkindly cursed the stupid woman and felt rather pleased when, later that evening, I found that I had inadvertently walked off with her hostel room key.

According to the map, all was not lost and I might avoid the motorway yet. According to real life, all was irretrievably, irredeemably, unsalvageably doomed to damnation and beyond. The road that was meant to neatly bisect the motorway and lead me to an alternative, scenic route soon petered out into a mud track. The pebbles became rocks, then boulders. I had to abandon cycling and, for the second day running, took wearily to pushing the bike through the dirt. Just when I thought the situation couldn't get any worse, a vast German shepherd dog charged at me, barking ferociously, baring his pointy white fangs with murderous menace.

In the nick of time, moments before I made a nervous lunge with my super-strength Kryptonite bike lock and hurled the brute onto the fast lane to doggy heaven, his owner appeared. I asked him the way.

'Ah, you'll need to take the motorway.'

'But what about this nice little white, wiggly road here?'

I pointed to the road on my map. The man squinted, took the map and held it at a full arm's distance, then tilted his head to one side and squinted again.

'Haven't got my glasses,' he said. 'Can't see a thing. But really, *señorita,* I would advise you to take the motorway.'

'On a *bicycle*?'

'Oh yes, you'll have no trouble. Really, the motorway is the best way. Much quicker. Now, let me see . . . take the motorway to here,' he jabbed his finger on the map, at some indiscriminate spot about a hundred kilometres from where we were standing, 'then come off and follow this road,' he prodded the map somewhere on the south coast, 'and that'll take you to Riofrío.' He pointed decisively at a town called Baena in Córdoba province. 'From Riofrío, you can take this road,' he jabbed his finger somewhere near Jaén to the north, 'all the way over here to Puerto de los Alazores.' He took a stab at Pinos Puente, on the outskirts of Granada. 'So you see, you need to take the motorway in the Seville direction. It's the only way.'

At last, the motorway conspiracy had won – but only for one kilometre. I tucked tight into the hard shoulder and concentrated on not being sucked in by the rush and the roar from the lorries thundering by and, thankfully, soon arrived in Riofrío without great incident. Unfortunately, though, the road ended there. I cursed the long-sighted man with his fantastical directions and turned to a man chopping wood.

'Is this the road to Puerto de los Alazores?'

'Oh no,' the man replied, laying down his axe. 'You'll need to take the motorway if you want to go there. Come off at the next exit.'

'In the Seville direction?'

'No, no. You need to go back towards Granada.'

Which, if I wasn't mistaken, would take me to Loja, the very town from which I had just spent an hour trying to escape.

In the end, the axe man came up with an alternative route. I could, he said, just follow the road to the top of the village and then, when the road ran out, follow the little path which would join up with the road to the *puerto*. But, he added, he didn't think the path was very good for cycling.

I should have taken heed. The path ran out and became track; then the track ran out and became open field. I pushed on. And on, and on. And on some more. Still, there was no road in sight. I clambered over chains fencing off a railway line, heaving the bike and my luggage over. I hauled the bike up a ridiculously steep, grassy hill. I had no doubt that I was irretrievably lost in the middle of nowhere, never to be seen again, condemned for the rest of time to eating berries and small fluffy birds killed and plucked with my own butchering hands. I only kept going because I didn't have any better ideas. And then, miraculously, I came to a path, and then a road.

'Excuse me,' I said, approaching a group of field labourers taking a rest under a tree. I was getting good at this by now. 'Is this the road to Puerto de los Alazores?'

'That's right,' one replied, while the rest just sniggered. 'It's up there – twenty kilometres straight uphill.'

Oh yes, and there was a howling headwind. Eventually, after four hours of cycling I arrived at Puerto de los Alazores. I was back on track, thirty-six kilometres from where I'd started.

On the final, murderous hill up into the village of Villanueva de la Concepción, I got off the bike once more and pushed. I was not in a happy mood. As I stumbled, tired and fractious, through the village's deserted outskirts, two teenagers on a moped passed me. They laughed. I snarled. They drove to the end of the street, turned back towards me and then, tucking in close to me and my luggage-laden bike, they passed once more – and the kid on the back reached out and smacked me soundly round the side of the head. The two kids howled with laughter at their daring escapade. I, on the other hand, was apoplectic.

'*You stinking little toads!*' I screamed at them as they swung round for their third drive-by.

I staggered into the middle of the road and with a new burst of energy began to wave my arms about like a madwoman, stabbing my finger at them in what I hoped was a forceful and threatening manner.

'*You obnoxious little toerags!*' I bellowed. 'You come near me one more time and I'll have you and your pathetic, pop-popping moped. Just think about touching me once more and I'll pummel the pair of you into pulp! Think I look too tired to fight back, do you, you vile, greasy-faced scumbags? Well we'll see about that, won't we. We'll just see how much damage I can do to a couple of spotty little teenagers, shall we? You dare lay a puny *finger* on me, and I'll show you just how much energy I've got left, you FUCKING LITTLE DICKHEADS!'

I think there may have been one or two words towards the end of my diatribe that they even understood. Really, though, they should consider themselves lucky. They received a hands-on, real-life lesson in the English vernacular – from a native speaker, what's more, and that usually costs extra. Thinking better of a third ride-by, they laughed some more and sputtered off down a side street.

My self-esteem was shattered, my body destroyed. My mental recuperation had taken a kamikaze nosedive. I limped on up the hill towards El Torcal. El Torcal, I discovered afterwards, is renowned for its astonishing limestone rock formations. The sierra is known as a kind of 'stone museum', where the porous stone has been shaped by millions of years of sun, wind and water into fantastic formations that have been given names such as 'Lizard' or 'She-wolf'. I almost noticed. As I cycled by, I had a brief, flickering shadow of a thought along the lines of 'Funny-looking rock, that.' And then I went back to wondering if I was nearly there yet.

I fell into my hotel in Antequera – literally. My cleated shoes slipped on the marble ramp in the doorway and I landed with a bump in an oily, unsophisticated little heap. To collapse on arrival two days running didn't seem terribly auspicious, but the receptionist was a kindly man who called me *'guapa'* (beautiful) even though I clearly was not. Spaniards are nice like that. Or perhaps they're just lecherous. Or maybe there are lots of them that have very bad eyesight. He told me how much he, too, loved to cycle and, since I didn't have the heart to tell him that I didn't hold it in terribly high regard myself right then, I just nodded weakly, then hobbled off to shower and stretch.

The hot water of the bath felt so good it gave me goose bumps. By the time I'd managed to drag myself from the tub and make myself presentable for a public appearance, it was seven-thirty, so I didn't see a lot of Antequera, and none of it at all in daylight. But from my one-hour evening stroll I can say this: it is a very lovely town. The Moors built an imposing fortress here; subsequently, it was an important base for the *Reconquista* and, as such, enjoyed prosperity between the fifteenth and eighteenth centuries. Many of the town's landmarks date from this period: glorious old churches with delightful belfries, impressive stone houses and public buildings with wrought-iron grilles covering the windows. If you peek discreetly through somebody's open front door, you'll see wonderful marble patios, Moorish-style, bedecked with plants and ornate wrought-iron adornments. The shops were full of things I would have been in severe danger of buying had it not been for the horror of having to carry them: ceramics and clothes, tasteful vases and elegant homeware. The pride of the town, though, is a one-and-a-half-metre bronze Roman statue of a patrician's teenage toy boy. The real thing was dug up near Antequera in the 1950s and resides in the town museum but, if you can make do with a replica of a replica of a toy boy, in Antequera you can find him pretty much any way he pleases you – on the face of a plate, as a painting, or on a T-shirt ready to be plastered across your chest.

16

Lance, Would You Mind
If We Swapped Legs?

As I picked myself up off the tarmac for the fourth time in two days, I was willing to bet the sheep standing by the side of the road laughed at me. It stopped chewing its grass, lifted its dumb, woolly head, kind of raised the corners of its mouth and then bleated something that sounded very like 'Haaa-haaa'. But perhaps I was just being paranoid.

I'd only just started – I was less than a kilometre from the hotel door – and I'd stopped for directions halfway up a steep hill. My jaded, incapacitated legs hadn't worked up enough power to get me going properly again, what with the hill and the cursed luggage. I tried to pedal, and went nowhere. The bike teetered a little, then toppled to the ground taking me with it.

It was no use being tired. I had ninety-five kilometres to cycle today, following on from yesterday's 109. I had to haul myself and my luggage to the top of two mountains. I had firm words with my legs, told them to toughen up, and began again my long day's trudge.

To be fair, the scenery was breathtaking. It even made me forget about my shaky legs for a while. This is the land of turquoise-blue rivers and stomach-lurching limestone gorges. (The wild mountain scenery of this part of Andalusia has often been favoured by film makers of 'paella westerns'.) Following my abject failure at rock-appreciation yesterday, I was keeping my eyes peeled and paying due attention, but even I couldn't have missed the gorge at El Chorro. Just a few metres wide and, in places, a staggering four hundred metres high, it's a popular haunt for rock climbers – who must, quite frankly, be out of their minds to climb up such a high, sheer face. Cycling these roads was quite scary enough for me. The route down into the gorge was a terrifying head-over-handlebars descent, a true brake-pad-burning extravaganza. On either side of the road, the hillsides were peppered with white, bougainvillaea-clad mansions, the holiday retreats of the rich who invite their friends to lounge around the pool and flex their perfectly tanned muscles. Today, though, the villas were all shuttered up, and the tycoons were back in their oak-panelled offices making megabucks to spend on another holiday home they'd never use, an apartment on Palm Beach, perhaps, or an expensively restored farmhouse in Tuscany.

When I stopped for my ritual sandwich in El Chorro village, I was surrounded by vanloads of long-haired Aussie mountain bikers, who'd driven over to the gorge with their bikes in the back of the van. This, it dawned on me, is the right way to cycle. Too late, I realized that it's entirely ridiculous actually to carry your luggage. It's much better to stick a very large suitcase containing several changes of shamefully glamorous clothes – a couple of pairs of kittenish Blahnik mules, perhaps, or some tight little Gucci hipsters at the very least – and all the toiletries of your most fresh-faced dreams in a nice big van, drive to a pretty location, go for a brief but beautiful bike ride, and then motor comfortably back to your luxurious hotel and eat a sinfully large dinner to replace any calories you might have mistakenly burned. I made a mental note to remember this for next time.

Just a couple of kilometres up the road from El Chorro lies the village of Barbastro, once the stronghold of the folk-loric bandit Omar Ibn Hafsun. Ibn Hafsun was Spain's Robin Hood of the Dark Ages. A ninth-century Muslim (his family had converted to Islam from Christianity in the early days of the Moorish occupation), he was a wild and warlike young man. When he killed his neighbour, his father disowned him and he fled to Morocco, then returned to Spain the following year and set up fort in Barbastro. His cunning and courage gained him control of vast tracts of land, stretching from Cartagena to the Straits of Gibraltar – that's most of the south coast of Spain – and inland to Écija, Baena and Jaén. But despite his cut throat ambition, Ibn Hafsun was reputed to be a gentleman. He was said to be so respectful of women that any one of them could travel through the lands he controlled without fear of attack.

Bandits, along with smugglers, hold a special romanticism in Spanish folklore, and they didn't die out with Ibn Hafsun. This remote, mountainous area remained big on heroic rogues right through to the twentieth century: the 'last bandit', nicknamed Pasos Largos or Big Steps, died in 1934 during a gun fight with the Guardia Civil. Yes, they were savage, barbarous, thieving and murderous. They could be bloodthirsty and cruel. They liked robbing people, and punching the living daylights out of a rich man was all in a day's work. But the bandits were virile and valiant. They fought like heroes, struggling against authority to help the poor and the oppressed. This, after all, was a world where men were *real* men, and women merely ran the place. And the Spanish have always been suckers for *machismo*.

Take, for example, Diego Corrientes, known to folklore as 'the Generous Bandit'. Corrientes, the storybooks tell us, never seriously injured his victims, and he never killed a soul. He robbed the rich to feed the poor. The local nobleman,

Don Francisco Bruna, didn't like him much and had the misfortune to ride past him in his carriage one day. Corrientes was on horseback and recognized him.

'What a pleasure to meet you here, Don Francisco,' Corrientes exclaimed, beaming broadly. 'My boot lace has just come undone. It's so convenient of you to appear like this. Now you can tie it for me.' And with that, he stuck his foot up on Don Francisco's carriage window sill, leaving him with no choice but to tie the lace.

Another tale tells of how Corrientes managed to rob even Don Francisco himself. With much audacity, he showed up one day at Don Francisco's home.

'Is it true, sir, that you have promised ten thousand *reals* to the man who hands over the thief Diego Corrientes?'

'That's true, and here's the money to prove it.'

'Then give it to me – because *I* am Diego Corrientes,' declared the fearless bandit, and by the time Don Francisco had recovered from his shock both Corrientes and the money were gone.

Perhaps the most famous of all bandits, however, was José María 'El Tempranillo'. His nickname, which means the young one, was given to him on account of the early age at which he took to the land of the lawless. Soon he became king of the mountains. With his sleek black hair, blue eyes, pearly-white teeth and fair, dainty hands, he would dress in a finely woven shirt, a velvet jacket with silver buttons and leather chaps. He was as handsome and brave as ever a robber could be. When he ambushed a stagecoach, so the stories go, he invariably helped the ladies down and settled them comfortably in the shade before proceeding with his business. He always left his victims with enough money to travel safely to the next village and he never allowed any of his band to steal a jewel that held sentimental value.

Once, high on a mountain pass, El Tempranillo happened upon a poor muleteer on a lame, decrepit horse, transporting a few skins of vinegar to his village. El Tempranillo roared with laughter.

'What are you doing riding on that old donkey, my friend?'

The muleteer was offended. 'You may laugh,' he said, 'but this old horse, though ugly, is the only thing that stands between me and the grave. Without him to help me, I'd die of hunger. He's my only means of working, and I have no money to buy another.'

'Take this bag,' said El Tempranillo, handing him a heavy sack. 'Go to the house of the rich old man Herrera. He's got a horse for sale. Pay him exactly one thousand five hundred *reals* for it. Mind you do as I say, though. If I find you on this old mule tomorrow I'll chuck both you and the donkey into the ravine.'

The muleteer did as he was told, went to old Herrera's house, and paid him exactly one thousand five hundred *reals* for his horse. The next night, two men broke into Herrera's house, punched him and blindfolded him.

'Quickly, hand over your money.'

'Please, let me go, I don't have a cent in the house.'

'You lying fool. We know you sold a horse yesterday for one thousand five hundred *reals*.' And so the money landed back in the hands of José María 'El Tempranillo'.

El Tempranillo eventually met a violent end when he was murdered by a former bandit comrade. He had, ironically enough, taken a job with the Guardia Civil and his nemesis objected to his new allegiance. The Guardia Civil was then a brand-new rural police force, founded precisely to stamp out the bandits and highwaymen that plagued the mountain roads. If the Guardia Civil was created as a force to uphold an oppressive authority, it's not a reputation it shook off easily. For nearly forty years of the twentieth century the Guardia Civil were Franco's henchmen, the men responsible for imposing his draconian laws. They had fortress-like headquarters in every small town from which they patrolled the countryside in pairs. The prime minister responsible for founding the force, Narvaez, was not exactly a pushover either. As he lay on his deathbed, the priest in attendance asked him if he had forgiven his enemies.

'I have no enemies, Father,' Narvaez replied. 'I've had them all shot.'

And so I trudged through this new set of mountains, up and up and up and down and down and down. It was about halfway up the second major hill that the bad thoughts started to set in.

'You could always hitch a lift,' a wicked little voice whispered from deep within my soul.

I pedalled a little further, the head wind powering down on me.

'C'mon,' whimpered the neurons in my legs. 'You could wave down any one of these passing vans.'

'Wave down a van, wave down a van, wave down a van,' the whining little muscle cells Chinese-whispered their way up to my hips, along my spine, through my neck, to my brain.

'Push off,' said my big, strong brain.

'Just think,' my legs whinged and wheedled. 'You could be there in twenty minutes in a van as opposed to two hours on this horrible, hurtful bike. In twenty minutes, you could be in a nice hot bath, nice hot bath, nice hot bath, nice hot bath, nice hot bath . . .'

The real test of mettle, though, was when a taxi with its 'vacant' light on passed.

I made it to Ronda on two wheels, triumphant in spite of the mutiny. I had decided that after my arduous time in the hills I deserved a small reward in the form of a hotel that was guaranteed to be delightful. I had therefore booked in to the Hotel San Gabriel, a gloriously converted old Andalusian mansion. Each room, they say, is different, though I can't vouch for that as I only set foot in my own. But that alone was magnificent. I booked and paid for a single room, but it was palatial, the five-foot double bed almost insignificant among the expanse of tasteful terracotta tiles and furnishings. The shower was large enough to party in. There was even a tiny wrought-iron balcony in the shadow of an orange tree. The reception area was no characterless counter. At this hotel, a tiny plaque in the hallway directed you to a well-appointed room that had all the features of a gentleman's study: a leather-topped desk and walls lined with brimming bookcases. The woman behind the desk smiled and invited me to take a seat on the velvet-upholstered armchair while she completed the check-in procedure. Not for the first time, I felt underdressed in my grimy, oil-besmirched Lycra and wondered if, after I'd sat on it, they would have to burn that elegant, velvet chair.

I didn't throw a party in the shower – for that, I'd have needed friends – but I did crack open a beer from the minibar and drank it all on my own in the long evening shadow of the orange tree. For today I felt I had something to celebrate. I had turned the corner; I had beaten the wicked cycling demons and my own torturous self-doubt too. Today I'd been tired, but I'd battled on. I'd kept my spirits high, right to the end. I'd pushed through the physical boundaries and come out the other side.

Eat your heart out, Xena Warrior Princess! You may battle the spectres of your past in your tight little leathers and remarkable breast armour, you may kick butt with your whips and chains, but you can't raise hell on a bike because in your time they hadn't invented them yet. Wham bam Lara Croft! You can blow to smithereens all the stumbling, stony monsters in Cambodia if you think it will do any good – but I've conquered mountains, overcome my fears, pushed on through *real* pain and come out the other side – without a

191

belt full of guns and the help of a comforting pair of powder-blue silk pyjamas. And get this, Lara: unlike you, I'm for real. When *I* bungee jump among the chandeliers in *my* mansion, *my* breasts *move*.

And so it was that, very pleased with myself and a tiny bit pickled, I put on my trusty grey cargo pants and black vest top and wandered out to see what Ronda had to offer.

Ronda is famous not only for bandits, but also for bull-fighting and for its very deep gorge. Blend all that with its proximity to the tourist havens along the Costa del Sol, and you'll understand why it's jam-packed with tourists every day of the week. The good news is that a lot of them are day trippers who jump on their bus and go back to the rollicks and frolics of the coast the minute the sun dips down behind the pinky glow of the mountain tops.

It's the gorge that started it all. It really is very deep – as you peer over the edge of the Puente Nuevo (which literally translates as 'new bridge' despite the fact that it's really quite old, although not as old as the old bridge), your tummy gives a little lurch. But whereas most modern-day tourists concentrate on what a bad idea it would be to drop one's camera or how it would really spoil their day out if little Carlos fell over the edge, early civilizations saw things in a rather more positive light. They thought the gorge was quite splendid, because nobody could climb up it and attack them. In the days when settlers couldn't conceive of man flying through the air, a town positioned on top of a gorge like this would be virtually impregnable. And so they built one.

There's a sinister side to Ronda's gorge, too. During the first month of the Spanish Civil War, 512 people are said to have died here, cruelly thrown from the high stone bridge to be dashed to death on the rocks below. Ernest Hemingway's famous scene in *For Whom the Bell Tolls* is meant to be based on the savagery that took place in Ronda. The Republicans herded their Nationalist neighbours into the town hall, then arranged the villagers in the square into two rows. The villagers, armed with flails, clubs and pitchforks, beat the right-wing landowners who were forced to walk the gauntlet between them, then hurled them over the cliff edge.

The Republicans weren't the first to throw people to their deaths this way. Back in the eighteenth century, the bull-fighter Pedro Romero chucked his wife into the gorge after he found her in bed with another man – an unjust demise, one has to conclude, when one learns that Pedro himself is said to have ripped off his pink silk tights to sleep with both the Queen of Spain and her arch-rival, the Duchess of Alba.

But perhaps Pedro was forgiven his adultery on account of his status for, while horns are firmly locked between Ronda and Seville about who invented bullfighting, here in Ronda nobody would dare doubt that the modern-day *corrida* began with the Romero family. In the early eighteenth century, Pedro's grandfather, Francisco Romero, came up with the idea of using a hat, and later a cape, to lure the bull away from a matador who'd been toppled from his horse. Francisco's son Juan then introduced the *cuadrilla*, the support crew, and finally Pedro was the first to tackle the bull on just his nimble, slipper-clad feet. He's said to have killed 5,600 bulls without suffering any kind of injury and was still battling the beasts in the arena at the age of eighty.

If you go to the bullring in Seville, on the other hand, they'll point to a seventeenth-century painting on the wall showing soldiers practising their lancing skills against wooden replicas of enemy heads. The guide tells you that this (which looks nothing whatsoever like bullfighting and doesn't even feature a bull) led to the advent of bullfighting as a sport when they introduced the animal to make the jousting more difficult. It's a tenuous story – after all, bull-baiting on horseback was popular even in ancient Rome – and is believed only by the inhabitants of Seville.

17

The Mountain Rescue

I awoke in my gloriously large bed in my magnificently large room to an ominous patter on the window. It was raining. I had indulgent plans for the morning – to drink coffee and read the paper on a sunny terrace overlooking the gorge, and then to visit the famous old bullring and the bullfighting museum next door. It wasn't to be.

I scuttled through the rain to a café and ate an overpriced breakfast while gloomily watching the downpour. I drew out the breakfast experience as long as I could, but the café wasn't a place for lingering. Both the bullring and the museum were closed for half an hour yet. My enthusiasm took a dive. All the signs were that it was going to be a godawful day and I thought I'd better get on with it.

The delightful receptionist at the hotel, whose name, I think, was José, asked me where I was heading. I explained my route: over the hills to Grazalema and El Bosque, both of which are reputed to be exceedingly pretty. Then I would continue on to Arcos de la Frontera, my stop for the night. José poked his head out of the doorway, into the wet, wet world outside.

'Ah, Grazalema. Did you know, the village of Grazalema has the highest rainfall in the whole of Spain?' he asked with an unnecessarily broad smile. 'In Grazalema, they have two thousand litres of rainfall a year, compared to Ronda's six hundred.' He grinned cheerfully. It was pouring with rain in Ronda. Things did not look good.

And so I started to ride. It wasn't too bad to begin with. There was a steady drizzle, but nothing ferocious, a bit like your regular day out in the Lake District or the emerald-green bogs of Ireland. Having cancelled my morning's activities, I had more time than I'd bargained for, so I thought I'd use it up with regular stops for warming cups of tea. My first tea stop was in the infamous Grazalema. It was raining, predictably enough, though I could see that if you managed to pick a sunny day it would be a lovely little place, with its whitewashed houses and cobbled streets.

'Not a great day for cycling,' said an elderly man in a flat cap as I emerged from the café in which damp, disheartened hikers were seeking refuge alongside the regulars. Very observant, *señor*.

'Oh well,' he said in a rare outbreak of optimism for a Spanish bystander. 'It's not far up to the *puerto* from here. After that it's all downhill.'

Maybe if you live in a rainy place you have to look on the bright side.

I climbed up. The rain came down. I went higher. The rain pounded harder. As I neared the top of the mountain, the grizzly little drizzle had developed into a raging tempest. The rain was whipping down, the trees overhead were bowing abasedly to the fearsome wind and, with one gust, I was swept across the road and into the ditch.

The storm was lashing and crashing and thrashing. I couldn't see a metre in front of me. Forget cycling; it was a challenge even to *walk*, the winds were so strong. I battled along the side of the road on foot, my feet sloshing around in shoes full of water. And then I realized – something unfamiliar was going on. I was alone on top of a mountain.

Litres of water were bucketing horizontally across the road, vicious winds were felling trees all about me, branches were being hurled through the air and crashing around my feet. I was surrounded by pandemonium, on the brink of decapitation by a flying log – and I was utterly calm. What had happened to my usual, panic-first-think-later approach to life? How on earth could I, in the middle of this frenzied hullabaloo, be so utterly *in control*? A little sunshine, plenty of exercise, a couple of beers in the evening, and I was a new person, reinvigorated, rejuvenated, regenerated.

A car ground to a sploshy stop beside me. A window wound down.

'Er, um, hold on a minute, nearly got it, um . . .' muttered the voice from within. I peered through the rain to make out a head buried in what looked remarkably like the Lonely Planet *Spanish Phrasebook*.

'Um, um, oh dear, um . . . *Hablaah inglays?*' Do you speak English? said the voice, and then the head lifted, a face emerged complete with the beaming smile of success, of a few words spoken in a foreign language. The head was wearing a baseball cap with 'Canada' embossed large on the front.

'Yes, yes, yes, *yes*, YES!' I bellowed elatedly through the storm, losing hold of my self-control for just a moment, and before Canada and her companion had a chance to take back their offer of a ride in their warm, dry car, I had leapt nimbly into the back.

Shannon and Chris, for these turned out to be their names, even had a bike rack fixed on their roof. And while I sat and made a puddle in their car, Chris, who turned out to come from Tamworth, just thirty kilometres from the Derbyshire village where I grew up, very kindly drenched himself to the skin attaching my bicycle to the rack. And then, because they were nice like that, they drove me all the way to my hotel.

What was it they said about Franco? That he had two trays on his desk, one labelled 'Problems that time will solve' and the other 'Problems that time has solved'. He took great pleasure, apparently, in moving papers from the first tray to the second. And I had to concede that he might have had a point. Don't panic. Plod on. Go with the flow, even if it is flowing rather faster than you'd like. And then, eventually, you'll be rewarded. Chris, Shannon and the Canada cap will appear.

The Hotel Los Olivos in Arcos was a pretty little place. The French windows from my room opened onto a central court-yard with trees, flowers, tables and chairs. It wasn't the hotel's fault that it was raining. Maybe it was the rain's fault, though, that the staff were so grumpy. What is it with Spaniards and bad weather? A couple of drops of rain, and the whole country falls to bits. Everyone hunkers at home and argues with their in-laws. Nobody goes shopping, nobody, God forbid, goes out to the bars. A few days of rain in Spain and the economy is in a state of near-collapse.

The girl on the front desk of Hotel Los Olivos was clearly a victim of RAGE (Rain Affective Glares and Explosions). As I limped damply through the door, she hurled a wrathful glower in my direction, and puffed out a mighty, indignant sigh. I meekly joined the little line at the desk, behind the terribly polite middle-aged British couple who were apolo-gizing profusely in loud, clear English for the fact that all the lights in their room had suddenly gone out with a fizzle and a poof. The Rabid Receptionist flung her best scowl at them and snapped that she'd look into it. The Terribly Polite Couple gathered their umbrellas, map books, and reading glasses and pottered cheerfully into the rain. They looked like the type who cut out *Daily Telegraph* coupons and invest them in short breaks in Scotland, and so are unfussed by such trifling inconveniences as having to wade down the street waist-high in water. As they left the building to brave the deluge outside, the Rabid Receptionist swept up the telephone receiver.

'Those mad old bats in room 132,' she barked at whichever poor soul was on the other end, 'have got it into their heads that the lights in their room aren't working. Go and check it, will you. I'm sure there's nothing the matter. Fat old trouts look about a hundred and six years old and have the brains of a week-old potato tortilla. Why can't they just go back to their own—'

And then she remembered that I was standing there. What really irked me, though, was not her behind-the-back bitching about my fellow countrymen, but the fact that she charged me an extra two euros for an overnight 'parking space' for my bike.

The receptionist's temper apart, I believe that Arcos de la Frontera is a pleasant place. It stands, apparently, on a narrow wedge of rock, and towers impressively above the plain as you approach. It's a tangle of tiny streets and historic buildings – or so they say. I tried my best to go out to verify all of this. I valiantly picked out of my drenched luggage the clothes that were merely damp as opposed to downright soggy and took to the streets. The deluge persisted. I took refuge in an internet café, drank yet another cup of tea and checked my e-mail, thinking the squall might ease. The rain poured, pounded and pelted. Bits of tree crashed disconcertingly to the ground. I ducked out to buy a newspaper and sprinted to another bar – deserted, of course, because the regular bar-dwellers wouldn't venture out in *this* – where I downed a beer. The rain became still stronger and steadier. Now my damp clothes were wet, and I was beginning to shiver. CRACK! Another branch hurled itself past the bar window and onto the tarmac outside. This place was becoming a little more exciting than I'd anticipated. I gave up on Arcos and made a run for my hotel. Once in my room, I took off all my clothes, and sat huddled in the armchair wearing nothing but the blanket from my bed. For the first time all day, I was warm and dry. I thanked God I wasn't camping.

On the television they were scheduled to show bullfighting. This week was the annual *feria* in Jaén; as at all major festivals, the bullring had been opened to some of the best matadors in Spain and the TV cameras were rolling.

So far today, however, there had been no bullfighting in Jaén because it had been raining there too. Where there should have lain an arena of perfectly raked dry sand were muddy puddles of brownish slop. As I tuned in, though, the rain had just stopped and the arena's attendants had driven a vast truck full of sand into the ring and dumped it in the middle; men with rakes were desperately trying to soak up the slosh with the fresh, dry load. Anybody, surely, could see that it was a hopeless task from the beginning. The cameras kept returning to pan the slate-coloured skies. The commentator stated the obvious over and again: the rain wasn't going to hold off for long.

The new sand made little difference but the toreros came out to inspect the ring anyway and, incredibly, pronounced it fit for the fight. The commentator muttered unhappily; even I, perhaps the most inexpert viewer in the whole of Spain, could see it wasn't the best decision ever taken.

The first bull came raging out of its door. Almost immediately a light drizzle set in, progressing to a steady stream of rain. The *banderilleros* skipped in and placed their darts; the picadors took their turn to gouge and weaken the bull. By now, the bull, bloodied and drenched, was slipping in the squelching mud. The bull is bred to be brave, dominant and ferocious. This poor animal fell again and again, his glistening black hide coated with slop.

The first matador came in for kill. He had to remove his

shoes: slick, flimsy little slippers totally unsuited to wet conditions. He hopped about in his pink silk stockings, the sodden sand caked on his feet and spattered up his calves. The glorious *traje de luces*, the incredibly tight and glamorous bullfighter's costume, didn't glitter. It was a crude and clumsy spectacle. The matador gave a few turns of the cape. The bull's horns kept snagging the fabric so the cape slipped from the matador's hands – and then the inevitable happened. Maybe the wet slowed the matador's movements, maybe he lost his footing, it happened too fast to see. In an instant, though, he was no longer performing his damp little dance on the sand. He flew instead high into the air, his inner thigh hooked on the bull's horn. As the bull tossed him his limbs flapped like a rag doll's, while his own blood spurted from his leg with such force that his face was sprayed crimson. The *cuadrilla*, the matador's support crew, rushed in with their capes and distracted the bull; in moments five or six of them had lifted the matador and set off at a sprint towards the bullring's infirmary, a thick trail of blood flowing behind them.

It now fell to the second matador to kill the bull. It was a slow and grisly affair. The matador attempted to insert the sword into the *rubios*, that point between the bull's shoulder blades where the sword should enter to sever the pulmonary blood vessel. He missed. The ugly business went on for some minutes, the animal wandering dazed in the pouring rain, darts and swords flapping from his punctured body. It took a few more attempts before the 'brave bull' lay limp, wet and muddy in a puddle of sand. 'Play' was suspended.

Later we learnt that the bull's horn had severed the first matador's femoral artery; he spent one and a half hours in the bullring's own operating theatre before he could be transferred to the general hospital for further surgery. The prognosis, according to the next day's *El País*, was grave.

Done badly, bullfighting can be a shambolic butchery.

201

The worst are often *novillero*, or apprentice, fights in which younger, less threatening bulls are used. Even the top matadors frequently fail to kill the bull with the first sword; apprentices are notoriously less skilled. Small bullocks, mere babies, lie weakly in the sand letting out increasingly pitiful, plaintive moos with each clumsy stab.

If you see a good bullfight, though, when the bull is *bravo* and the matador courageous and skilled, the excitement is palpable. An elderly armchair aficionado in Madrid once derided to me the modern enthusiasm for football. Bullfighting, he believed, was a truer sport.

'When a footballer makes a mistake,' he said, 'he loses a goal. When a bullfighter makes a mistake, he loses his life.'

But if the matador can play the bull right, if he struts boldly across the ring in his tiny, tight trousers and drops to his knees with his back to the raging beast, the bull's horns nudging his shoulder blades, and then rises gracefully to play the bull closely and skilfully with his *capote*, it's hard not to be carried away on the wave of the crowd's emotion. The band strikes up a *paso doble*, the spectators wave their handkerchiefs in wild approval and take a swig of wine from a *bota* in between roaring, heartfelt *olés*.

Go to a *corrida* in which the fearless nineteen-year-old heart-throb El Juli is taking part, and the crowd is guaranteed to go crazy. With his floppy black hair, boyish good looks, pert physique and youthful vigour, his breathtaking daring, stylish exploits, and unbeatable skill in the ring, El Juli leaves the girls drooling and the boys dreaming. Which left me wondering . . . perhaps it was El Juli that Sheena back in Hong Kong had her prophetic dream about. You know, the dream in which I had a steamy fling with a bullfighter. I must drop her an e-mail, I thought, and ask her what the bullfighter in the dream looked like. A fling with El Juli, now that was worth thinking about. Admittedly, he's a bit young

– he's not even twenty yet – but naivety has its charms. Of course, *he* might take one look at *me*, the dark circles and crow's feet just beginning around my eyes, and run screaming from the room like a man being chased, well, by an angry bull. Still, there could be no harm trying.

The butchery on screen had, unfortunately, failed to kill my appetite (to be truthful, it had been quite exciting, even more exciting than *Lois y Clark: Las Nuevas Aventuras de Superman*), which meant that I had to abandon my warm dry blanket, put on wet clothes and venture to a restaurant in the street outside. My choice of establishment was not a gastronomic decision. I went to the nearest place. There were only two other tables taken, with a couple on each. It wasn't a big night for eating out in Arcos. It was a night for huddling round the *brasero*, the fire under the family's round table which is covered by a long thick circular blanket that you can draw up onto your knees to warm your bones.

The couple at the nearest table, middle-aged Americans, spoke in hushed tones and snuck sidelong peeks at me. I seemed to provide them with some kind of delicious but disapproving fascination such as one might normally reserve for other people's extramarital affairs. What on earth could a young woman (and a wet young woman at that) be doing eating alone and, worse still, *drinking* alone? Clearly I was fast on my way to the gutter. But I didn't care. It had been a demanding day and I had calmly overcome the obstacles. I felt I deserved a glass of wine, or two or three, to celebrate my survival. I asked the waiter if they served half bottles.

'No,' he said, 'but I'll give you a whole bottle and you can just drink half of it.'

It was a light, crisp local wine, a blend of Palomino and Riesling grapes grown and bottled right there in Arcos. It tasted too good and the half bottle turned to three-quarters. But the Spanish aren't ones to trouble themselves with accuracy where clocks or wine are concerned. The waiter charged me for half the bottle – a mere four euros – and I tottered back to my hotel to dry out in more ways than one.

18

Meeting Michael

The rain was still pounding the next morning. I was bound for Jerez, the land of sherry, and had intended to travel by bike, but I was loath to invite a repeat of yesterday's escapades. For although yesterday I had managed to avoid brain damage inflicted by a flying lump of tree, it wouldn't do to test my luck too hard. And anyway, my bottom hurt. I bottled out and took the bus.

The bus timetable seemed to be open to interpretation. The woman on reception assured me that buses left for Jerez at ten-fifteen and ten-forty-five. After something of a circuitous route, I arrived at the bus station at ten-sixteen. The ten-fifteen had left on time.

'The ten-fifteen? 'Fraid you've missed it.' A skinny old man in a shabby raincoat rubbed his hands with apparent relish. He was one of those pensioners who hang out in busy places populated by the bored and the desperate because it's the only way they can find people who will talk to them. These guys don't even get invited to the group sit-and-stare sessions. Could have something to do with the raincoats.

'The next bus isn't till eleven-twenty-five. You'll have to sit here and wait with me,' he grinned. He seemed rather pleased with himself for having collared a companion, and one in a shamelessly tight Lycra outfit at that.

The timetable on the wall didn't agree. It reckoned the next bus to Jerez would come at eleven-fifteen, while another, rival old man swore blind there was one at eleven o'clock. Of the ten-forty-five, there was not a whisper. I settled down with my newspaper – and I would have read it, had not old man number three felt ripe for a chat.

'So, you like to cycle . . .' he started out, with a nod to my heavily laden machine. 'I used to like to cycle myself, you know . . .'

And he told me all about his old mountain bike, which he used to ride each Saturday morning high into the hills, a breath of fresh air, a taste of freedom after a long, dirty week in the bottling factory.

'Ah, how I loved that bike. I cared for it better than I ever cared for any woman,' he sighed, a faraway gaze of nostalgia in his eye. 'But then, the doctors told me I had a problem with my heart, and I had to give up such strenuous pastimes.'

The old man managed to spin out his tales of past loves and escapades for half an hour or so. We moved on to world politics.

'The Middle East?' said the man. 'Bah, what a mess. And look at Afghanistan. That's a mess too. And that terrible business with ETA. *Dios mío*, a *terrible* mess.'

Eventually, at eleven-fifty, a bus arrived. It finally left for Jerez at twelve.

Jerez de la Frontera is a wealthy, elegant old town, full of history. First and foremost, it's the home of sherry, but it's known also for its nimble-hoofed dressage horses and as a hotbed of flamenco. General Miguel Primo de Rivera – leader of the bloodless coup of 1923 and head of the six-year dictatorship that followed – was a Jerez man. He was an archetypal old-school Andalusian aristocrat – he chased women, loved horses, swilled liquor, and bellowed a hearty *olé* at the bulls. He was the prototype of macho: his new government, he declared, was 'a man's movement. Anyone who feels his masculinity is not yet fully defined should wait patiently for the good days we are preparing for the Fatherland. Spaniards! Long live Spain and long live the king!'

Despite his less than modern approach to gender politics, Primo de Rivera was a considerably softer touch than his fellow dictators who followed, and he instigated some good things – the network of state-run *parador* hotels among them. But he wasn't strong enough.

'Spain needed an iron surgeon and got a quack dentist instead,' philosopher Miguel de Unamuno said.

In 1929 Wall Street crashed; the temporary prosperity that Spain had enjoyed in the 1920s took a tumble too. King Alfonso XIII, with whom Primo de Rivera had always been in cahoots, dismissed the dictator, who went into exile in France. Dividing his time between the church and the brothel, Primo de Rivera was dead within months. Jerez still remembers him, though. In the middle of the main square, the Plaza del Arenal, stands a grand statue of the old dictator on his high stone horse. From his still, sculpted head pours the white stain of pigeon excrement, like a bucket of paint in a cheap slapstick comedy.

I checked into my hotel, then ate an excellent lunch. A dish of seafood salad was served on the house. Then came a *plato ibérico* – ham, cheese, chorizo, salami and bread, and this was followed by dogfish in brandy sauce with chips and then a *flan*, or caramel custard. It was a bit of a struggle to finish it all, but I made a heroic effort and, after I'd washed everything down with the requisite glass of *fino*, I was ready for a short siesta.

But all this constant travelling, this cycling tourist's habit of spending each night in a different bed, was beginning to addle my mind. I stood at the hotel reception. The receptionist raised his eyebrows, waiting for me to speak.

'Oh, *buenas tardes*, please could I have the key for room . . . er . . . um . . .' Was is 110? No, no, that was last night. 326? No, that was the dingy brown room in Granada. Try 102 . . .

Will I one day guess wrong? Would the receptionist correct me – is this business of having to declare your room number really a test that you can pass or fail? – or would he have no idea, and blithely allow me to stroll away with somebody else's key, to walk in on some husband having it away with the chambermaid while his wife's out shopping?

I once knew a man called David who travelled a lot on business, who spent night after night in a different hotel, a different room number, a different bed. David wasn't an easy man – he was the type who creates very loud scenes in restaurants when he doesn't get the window table – and on this particular day he was feeling even grumpier than usual. He stomped into his hotel, stamped up the stairs, and tried to insert the key card into the slot. Nothing. He tried it upside down. Still nothing. Fuming, David strode back down to reception.

'This key doesn't work!' he yelled at the girl on the desk. 'Get me the manager.'

'But sir—'

'Don't "but sir" me! I'm not taking any excuses! I'm fed up with your poor service! Get me the manager!'

'But sir—'

'I SAID GET ME THE MANAGER!'

Finally the manager appeared. 'But sir,' he said. 'This isn't a key from our hotel. Your key comes from the hotel next door.'

What David needed was a little cycling therapy.

*　　　*　　　*

By the time I'd woken up from my siesta (in the right bed, thank goodness), spent half an hour cleaning my bike and then double that time cleaning the oily grime off the hotel room floor, it was six o'clock, the sky had cleared and it was time for an evening *paseo*.

It was Saturday evening and the people of Jerez were getting married. A ribbon-bedecked bridal car glided to a halt alongside a church in the old quarter; from the doors of the cathedral boomed the celebratory chords of the 'Wedding March.' Sartorially impeccable latecomers scurried from hastily parked cars; the well-heeled ladies tottered on the cobbles in their shoes not made for walking as they gripped the arms of their more sensibly shod partners for support.

I wandered through the tiny, narrow streets of the old quarter and into squares overshadowed by grandiose old buildings with ornate stonework surrounding their iron-studded wooden portals. On the terraces, those Jerezanos who hadn't been invited to weddings sat under orange trees heavy with still-green fruit and chatted over a beer, a coffee or an ice-cream. For it was the weekend and, at weekends, Spaniards relax. (I have absolutely no idea when they wash their cars or put up useful shelves.)

Saturday evening was a busy time, too, for Jerez's internet café, which was packed with teenage boys noisily playing computer games and groups of girls giggling over online chat rooms. The Spanish government was in the middle of a campaign to encourage people to become computer- and internet-literate. According to the papers, it wasn't working. People still didn't have computers in their homes and weren't going online. Maybe the government pollsters should have tried putting their heads round the door of any of the small-town internet cafés I visited on my trip, because one thing I can vouch for: the teenagers of Spain know how to use an internet chat room – for hours and hours and

209

hours. Groups of fourteen-year-old girls sit huddled around the same screen giggling, gasping and checking their hair. I suppose it's the perfect teenage chat-up tool. The person on the other end can't see your spots.

I took in a movie at the out-of-town multiplex which, with its McDonald's, its Mexican theme bar, its hypermarket and its mall-based cafés, could have come straight out of middle America, and afterwards headed back to the town centre for dinner. At last, I seemed to be working on a Spanish timetable. Everywhere I had been today, Jerez had been there with me. I'd had to wait for a seat at lunch and took the last table for dinner. It was ten p.m. and, for once, I ate my *raciones* of garlic prawns and salad on a terrace in the town's old quarter surrounded by Spaniards rather than tourists – or, in areas with no tourists, quite alone. Groups of friends lined their stomachs before a long night out; couples nibbled on shared plates of food as their nocturnal children toddled between the tables tripping up the waiters. A group of freshly groomed guys in their early twenties sauntered past, dribbling and passing a windfall green orange on their way to a long Saturday night of drinking and dancing.

On Sunday morning Jerez was closed. And so, newly attuned to the Spanish way of doing things, I did what other people do in Spain on a Sunday. I went on a bike ride.

My idea was to cycle round the three towns that make up Spain's 'sherry triangle' – Sanlúcar de Barrameda, El Puerto de Santa María, and Jerez de la Frontera, and to drink a glass of the local sherry in each of them. I wasn't quite sure what effect three glasses of sherry were going to have on my cycling technique, but any slight wobbles, I thought, should be compensated for by the fact that – great joy – I wouldn't be carrying my luggage. In any case, I was only following in the tracks of the best. In the early days of the

Tour de France, riders used to stop regularly for a slurp of pain-relieving wine. As recently as the 1980s, French rider Bernard Hinault was said to fill his last water bottle of each day of the race with champagne. Back in the sixties, Briton Tom Simpson was found to have high levels of alcohol in his blood – though, on the downside, this was only discovered during his post mortem.

Still, I wouldn't be drinking ordinary old wine or common champagne; I would be drinking sherry, which comes exclusively from this part of the world – apparently the chalky soil that soaks up the water suits the Palomino grape. The drink is named after the town: the word 'sherry' is the British attempt to pronounce the word 'Jerez', and it was the British appetite for the drink which led them to pour their money into Jerez's bodegas. They were already drinking sherry in Shakespeare's time ('A good sherris-sack . . . ascends me into the brain; dries me there all the foolish and dull and crudy vapours which environ it,' declares Sir John Falstaff in *Henry IV Part Two*), but it wasn't until the early nineteenth century that British wine merchants formed partnerships with the Spanish, married their daughters into wine-growing families, and helped the sherry bodegas to blossom into flourishing empires. If you think only an octogenarian would be seen dead with a glass of sherry in his hand, try taking a bar crawl round Jerez – or any other town in southern Spain. Here, sherry is enjoyed by everyone from retired field hands taking their morning tipple to the best-dressed ladies sipping an aperitif in a cosmopolitan bar. Served chilled – and most important, freshly opened – with a hunk of chorizo and a bowl full of olives, it's a different drink altogether from that warm bottle of Harvey's Bristol Cream you've had festering at the back of the cupboard since the last time your grandmother came for lunch.

It's only twenty-two kilometres from Jerez to Sanlúcar, and the road is straight and flat. Where there weren't potholes – and there were many – the cycling was tremendous. Without the luggage weighing me down I zipped along fast and light. Maybe my panniers had provided good strength training after all.

The countryside was flat and whitish in colour, the fields in between jobs – a situation with which I could empathize – lying fallow between the autumn harvest and the replanting in January. Every now and then, the scenery was punctuated by grand, wrought-iron gates with curved brick surrounds, which gave onto long, straight driveways through the vineyards leading to imposing limestone *cortijos,* the country residences of the vine-owning families who, I would think, must enjoy eating their breakfast while looking out on their fortunes literally growing as far as the eye can see.

At Sanlúcar, I headed straight for the beach. More river mouth than sea front, this is the point where the sea meets the Guadalquivir river, the grand waterway that carves across southern Spain and upon whose banks the great southern cities of Córdoba and Seville are built. The Sanlúcar bank of the estuary used to be the town's fishing quarter; now its long stretches of deep yellow sand are flanked with upscale restaurants whose white linen tablecloths flutter in the sea breeze. It's a wonderful spot overlooking the water, the colourful fishing boats and, on the far bank, the Parque Nacional de Doñana, one of Europe's most important wetlands. The park's most celebrated inhabitants are the pardel lynx and the Spanish imperial eagle, but species of more lowly plume come for a paddle here too. They reckon that 80 per cent of Europe's wild ducks take their winter break among the park's marshes and drifting sand dunes. There must be almost as many wild ducks here as there are old ducks wintering a little further down the coast in the gin-swamps and sand bunkers of the Costa del Sol.

I rolled up in time to watch Sanlúcar taking its pre-lunch

stroll along the palm-flanked waterfront promenade. It was midday, which seemed to me an entirely respectable hour for my first *copa*. The restaurant I chose to patronize clearly thought otherwise. I selected my spot, parked my bike up against the nearby wall, and waited. Admittedly, I was the only person to take a seat along the entire strip and I was rather dirtier and more casually dressed than most of the elegant Sunday-morning strollers.

The waiting staff observed me from a distance, exchanged glances with each other and giggled uncomfortably. I smiled at them with what I hoped was an engaging expression. They looked at their feet and shuffled off inside, where it was cool and safe and there were no oil-smeared weirdoes in unsightly tight clothes. It was some time before, finally, the oldest man among them worked up the courage to approach me.

'Ah, *buenos días*.' I greeted him with my best smile. 'Could you give me a glass of manzanilla and, perhaps, a tapa?'

'*No hay tapas*,' said the man. 'It's too early. The kitchen's not open yet.'

'A bag of crisps?'

'No. Like I said, the kitchen's not open yet. I'll bring you the manzanilla.'

Some minutes later, he reappeared with a glass and a bottle of manzanilla, the delicate, straw-coloured sherry specific to this town. Some people say that its flavour – slightly different from the finos of Jerez – is due to the sea breeze. I'm no expert on sherry, though I found this more mellow on the palate than the straightforward finos. One thing I can say with some authority, though. The sherry in Jerez tastes very like the stuff from Sainsbury's.

Did the painter Francisco de Goya and his high-class mistress, the Duchess of Alba, slurp aphrodisiac oysters with their sherry on this very waterfront as a prelude to their celebrated entanglements, I wondered. We met Goya when we

213

were up in his native Aragón; the Duchess of Alba, who had an estate here in Sanlúcar, was for a time his lover.

The duchess was one of the most glamorous and alluring women in all Spain. 'The Duchess of Alba possesses not a single hair that does not awaken desire,' wrote Fleuriot de Langle, a Frenchman who visited Spain in the early 1780s. 'Nothing in the world is as beautiful as she . . . When she walks by, all the world stands at the window – even children, who stop playing to gaze at her.'

Goya, on the other hand, was a ruddy-faced, provincial hick whose combination of remarkable painting skills and cloying brown-nosing abilities had earned him the position of court painter. This, then, was the ultimate uptown girl, downtown boy liaison.

It wasn't out of the ordinary for high-class ladies to take consorts and even lovers in the late eighteenth century, for marriages were tactical arrangements, the alliances of clans; once the deal was done and a woman was safely spoken for she was free to be seen in public with other men. What was unusual in this case was that in 1796, when the steamy seduction took place, the duchess's husband (a man to whom she had been married off at the tender age of fourteen and with whom she was entirely incompatible) was scarcely cold in his grave. Additionally, of course, there's the fact that Goya could scarcely be considered a good match, even if he was a dab hand at dipping his brush.

Nineteenth-century grapevine gossip had it that the affair first sparked in the winter 1792–3; Goya accompanied the duchess to Sanlúcar, the chatterers said, after she had had a row with the queen. (The queen and the duchess were sworn rivals, especially with regard to the affections of bullfighter Pedro Romero, whose lithe, silk-clad body both women are said to have coveted. Romero, you might remember from Ronda, was the first bullfighter to step into the ring on foot, threw his philandering wife over the precipice, and was said to have killed 5,600 bulls without suffering so much as a scratch.) During the journey, so the story goes, an axle broke on the duchess's carriage. Goya helped to mend it but he caught a fever in the rain, which resulted in his serious illness that winter and subsequent deafness. More recent historians, however, refute this as both the Sanlúcar estate and the duchess's summer house outside Seville were occupied by other people at the time and the duchess, we have to surmise, wouldn't have been one for rumpy-pumpy among the Palomino vines. What is certain, though, is that Goya spent some time with the duchess at Sanlúcar in 1796, for he produced a series of drawings, known as the Sanlúcar Album, and you don't have to study them deeply to work out that Goya didn't limit his activities to the drawing room. There is a naked woman bathing at a fountain, two naked women sitting back to back on a bed – all rousing stuff, no doubt, for a simple gilder's son.

'His knees shook. Every hair, every pore of her skin, the thick arched eyebrows, the breasts half-exposed under the black lace, aroused in him unbounded desire,' writes Lion Feuchtwanger in his fictional account of the affair, *This Is The Hour: A Novel about Goya* (Viking, New York). Whether their philanderings were quite this inflamed, we'll have to leave to the imagination. After all, Feuchtwanger, a twentieth-century writer, wasn't there either. But Goya's portraits of the socialite duchess give the game away. His 'Portrait of the Duchess of Alba in Black', which was painted the year following his dalliance in Sanlúcar, depicts a big black beauty mark by the duchess's right eye: this, we are told, denotes passion in the person wearing it. The duchess is wearing two rings on her right hand; one carries the name of her recently deceased husband (the duchess was clearly not one for hanging around and letting the bed go cold); the second ring on her index finger bears the name 'Goya'. And, in the sand by her feet, are engraved the words 'Solo Goya' – Only Goya. After Goya completed the portrait, someone painted over the word 'Solo' pretty swiftly, so that just the artist's signature remained. The incriminating word was only uncovered when the painting was restored in the 1950s. It was also found that the paint used to cover over the word dated back to the time of the portrait's execution – in other words, it was either Goya himself or a close contemporary who covered up the indiscretion.

Had Goya's ardour cooled? Was such a public display of affection considered inappropriate? Or had, as seems more likely, the glorious dowager duchess merely become tired of him? After all, she was thirty-six years old and the most desired woman in Spain; he was fifty-two and deaf. Perhaps the real clue comes from Goya's etching 'Tantalus', dated 1797–8, in which an old man is tormented by the unrequited love of a younger woman – in this case because she is dead. 'If he were a better lover and less boring, she would revive again,' declares the Prado museum's commentary. The wording is assumed to be Goya's own.

The Duchess of Alba herself, by the way, didn't exactly rest in peace. She died in suspicious circumstances after weeks of agony, delirium and tremors just a few years later. The common people believed she had been poisoned by the nobles; at court, they blamed the servants.

The rumours weren't finally silenced until 1945, when the then Duke of Alba ordered that his ancestor's remains be exhumed and tests carried out to find out how she died. The tests concluded that there was no poison: the duchess had died of encephalitis. But they also found something else when they dug up the body: both her feet had been sawn off – and the left one was missing. It turned out that forty years after the duchess's death, the church where she was buried was in need of renovation and, in order to carry out the work, her body was disinterred and moved to another cemetery. Once there, the movers found that they'd ordered her new coffin nine centimetres too short. None of the family was present and so, the theory goes, rather than bother with a replacement coffin they just chopped her off at the ankles. But what of the missing foot? Did they carelessly forget to put it in the coffin, or is it still to this day hidden away somewhere in a jar, satisfying that most peculiar of Spanish tendencies, the fondness for collecting severed body parts? Whatever the reason, it was an ironic end for those most sought-after and pampered of feet.

It might have been nice, I thought, to forget about the rest of the trip and settle down in one of those Sanlúcar restaurants to a few plates of freshly caught seafood. But duty called. I was a little woozy when I got back on my bike, what with just having knocked back a glass of 17.5 per cent alcohol on an empty stomach while my blood was tearing energetically round my body thanks to the cycling. Maybe that was why I managed to get so lost finding my way out of Sanlúcar, which had seemed a smallish town on my way in. Or maybe it was just because, yet again, I made the mistake of asking the way.

This time, I managed to attract a whole crowd of locals, all eager to add their two cents' worth to my map-reading attempts. It turned into a veritable streetside conference featuring a couple of housewives, two power-walking twenty-something women out for their morning stride, and a lone van driver.

'*Leave town?*' exclaimed Housewife Number One as if it were a most unusual thing to wish to do. 'Well, let me think. What do you reckon, Inmaculada? If she took the road past Paco's place, then went left at the greengrocer's—'

'Oh no, that way's too complicated, Concepción. She'll never find it. How about sticking to the main road as far as—'

'But the main road's miles out of the way. Far better to take the short cut over the park, past Eduardo's bar,' chipped in one of the power-walkers.

Given my navigational advisers' inability to agree on the way out of town – and they *lived* here, for heaven's sake – it's a miracle that I ever ended up on any road at all, but finally the van driver won by virtue of having a louder and deeper voice. The posse of women agreed that he might have a point, after all, in saying that I could just go up the road and turn left, and off I went.

I took the scenic route to El Puerto de Santa María. On the main road it's only twenty-three kilometres but I cycled almost double that. I wended through green pastures and crop-planted fields, took an unintended detour round a small beach town, and eventually ended up in a seafood restaurant at the port in El Puerto in time for lunch. To accompany my glass of fino from Pavón (which, I can tell you with some authority, was a pale straw colour and tasted very like a glass of sherry) I asked the waiter to recommend a fish for grilling.

'Oh, they're all good,' he replied eagerly. 'It depends which one you want.'

I took a wild guess from the long list of words I couldn't understand – any old grilled fish will do, I thought – and ordered a *choco* which, to my great surprise some minutes later, turned out to be a vast, betentacled and besuckered whole squid. It was fresh and tender, if not quite the soft, flaky creature I'd been hoping for. Twelve kilometres later I was back in Jerez, where I allowed myself a shower and a stretch before the third glass of the day, the perennial favourite Tio Pepe, which I drank in a cobbled square as dusk fell to the music of hundreds of tiny bats clamouring among the trees.

Tio Pepe, I found out the next day as I sat aboard a cheery red tourist train which trundled its way around the González

218

Byass bodega, was a real person. He was the uncle of Manuel María González, the man who founded the company (*tío* means uncle in Spanish). Uncle Pepe was good enough to invest some money in his nephew's fledgling bodega. In return, he's become the most famous uncle in the sherry world. It was a curiously entertaining little tour. Not only did we chuff around on the little red train, we also got high on the sherry fumes in the cellars where the oak barrels are stacked three high.

Jerez, no doubt, is full of people who know their *jerez* but up there with the best of them must be the smallest residents of the González Byass bodega. Twice a day, the staff leave out a fresh glass of sherry on the floor of the cellar, and balance a tiny ladder from the ground to the lip of the glass. This is the tipple for the mice who live among the barrels; they've acquired quite a taste for it over the years, they say. There are even photographs of the mice dropping by for a drink. And, this being Spain, the staff leave them a little tapa – in this case a bowl of nuts – to go with it. Apparently during the early morning tours, the guides manage to coax the mice out of their lair to perform tricks for the crowds. By the later tours – one of which I was on – the poor mice are a little worse for wear and are snoring off the rigours of the morning behind a barrel.

It was on the little red train that I met Michael. Michael was an American writer from Texas who was spending four weeks in Andalusia in search of a flamenco guitar. In order to find it, he had to hang out with lots of flamenco types, drink vats of whisky, smoke Cuban cigars and anaesthetize his brain cells – all four of them – with dope until dawn each day.

Michael invited me to go with him that evening to a flamenco bar where, I imagined, grizzled old guitarists with long, greasy hair and calloused fingers would tell their exuberant tales in the deep, rasping voices of men who had spent a few years too many in bars thick with smoke. Some time after midnight, the party in full swing, they would grab their guitars and strike a passionate chord . . . A young Latin sex god with the muscular midriff and moody expression of Joaquín Cortés (I saw him dance at the Royal Albert Hall once and he has been on my Suitable Sex God shortlist ever since) would emerge from their midst with a twirl and a stamp and a flick of his gleaming, jet-black hair . . . 'You cannot dants *ze paso doble?*' he would murmur softly in my ear, rather like the old guy in *Strictly Ballroom*, but younger, better-looking and without a wife or kids. And then he would whisk me away in his arms across the worn wooden floor. I, of course, would master the *paso doble* immediately and would not once tread on the sex god's perfectly formed toes. I accepted Michael's invitation straight away.

The one thing that is certain about flamenco is that it arouses the passions. Everything else seems a little hazy. The gypsies are fervently of the opinion that they started it all, that flamenco is theirs. The deep emotion that the music releases is a result of the ongoing suffering of the gypsy population almost from the moment they set foot in Spain in the fifteenth century, they say: the Catholic Monarchs imprisoned them; later Carlos I passed a decree condemning to the galleys any gypsy man between the ages of twenty and fifty who had no profession or employer. The gypsies didn't fare well in enclosed spaces, let alone prison and galley ships, and, being musical types, they learned to wail in tune.

A number of flamenco enthusiasts from the *payo* or non-gypsy side ardently disagree: gypsies, they say, settled in many European countries, not just Spain, and no music similar to flamenco has grown up among the gypsy groups in, say, England or France. No, proclaim the *payos*, flamenco has its roots in the harsh, hot soil of Andalusia and its melting pot of cultures: Byzantines, Romans, Arabs, Jews and, lastly and in very small letters indeed, gypsies.

Blas Infante, the Andalusian Nationalist lawyer, had an

interesting theory: Andalusia, he pointed out, has a much stronger Arabic heritage than the rest of Spain – the Moors ruled here for several centuries after they'd been driven from the northern cities and their musical traditions left their mark. In 1609, the poor old Moriscos were finally expelled from the country (the Moriscos, if you remember, were the ex-Muslims forced by Isabel and Fernando to convert to Christianity in 1502. They carried on celebrating Islam behind closed doors until, in 1609, Felipe III forced them to leave Spain altogether). They had nowhere to go – many of those who ended up back in Africa were murdered or sold as slaves – and so a number of them fled to the hills of Andalusia where they lived in hiding. Here they were protected by the gypsies, themselves nomads and outcasts, and the gypsies assimilated the rhythms of the Morisco music: the word flamenco, it has been suggested, comes from the Arabic *felah-mengu*, which means 'fleeing field workers'. Unfortunately for Blas Infante, his ideas about Andalusian roots didn't go down well with Franco's soldiers; they executed him in 1936, so he was unable to say any more.

However it started, the first written record of flamenco music can be traced back only to the eighteenth century. In the years that followed, the first flamenco schools were established in Jerez, Cádiz and the Triana area of Seville. (These three cities, needless to say, disagree wholeheartedly about which one of them started singing and stamping first.) As time went on, it developed into its present form, consisting of three parts: song, dance and guitar. Now you can go to flamenco shows and workshops all over the world, ranging from the festive, danceable *sevillanas* to the agonizingly sorrowful *cante jondo,* or deep song (which, to those with untrained ears, can sound something like the wailings of a lustful-but-rejected tomcat). But, say the aficionados, you can't experience real flamenco by going to a performance. *Real* flamenco, they rasp, can only take place some time after midnight, when a group of friends in a dark, dingy, basement bar bursts, with the help of a skinful of local liquor, into a frenzy of simultaneous flamenco expression, stamping and singing and working out their pains and passions.

I harbour severe doubts about the direction in which Michael was intending to angle his own passions that night. We started the evening off with dinner, which took some time. Michael laughed at all my jokes, which I took to be a bad sign, but I held out, eager for the flamenco bar. When I enquired after it, Michael stalled.

'Well,' he said, 'I'll have to phone Boris, this guy I met last night. I think he might know where it is.'

Boris? That didn't sound like a very good name for a sultry, swarthy flamenco sex god. A second-hand Volkswagen dealer, maybe. A sauerkraut salesman, perhaps. A hot-blooded, sexy *guitarrista* with large quantities of dark, virile chest hair bursting forth from his alluringly unbuttoned, ruffled shirt? I don't think so.

'Hey Boris,' said Michael to the mobile phone. 'Yeah, hi, it's me, Michael, remember? From last night? . . . Yeah, wow, was that good ganja, man . . . Yeah, well, I was just wondering what you're up to tonight? . . . Just staying in? . . . Yeah, I've got this girl . . . Yeah, we'd love to come round . . . Be there in an hour . . . Great . . . Yeah . . . Bye now.'

We? An hour? Got this girl? Go round to Boris's place? Call me mistrustful, but could Michael and Boris be a partnership of perverts who delight in luring young girls (oh, all right, not-so-young women) into their dungeon, drugging them and tying them up in chains for weeks on end while they torture them with tunes from their flamenco guitars? Or could this whole flamenco thing be a sick ruse in itself? Perhaps there was no flamenco. Perhaps there would just be another synthesized rendition of 'My Way' with a Scotch and Fanta orange chaser. Was I being excessively cynical –

or was Michael just trying to get into my pants? The decision wasn't hard: 'My Way' . . . or the highway?

'I'm terribly sorry, Michael,' I said, digging deep for self-control. 'It's a long time since I've had sex, but I'm not so desperate that I'm going to go off with a man who has friends called Boris. Try me again when you've got the phone number of a bullfighter called El Juli.'

And with those proud words, I held my head high and turned my back on Michael, on Boris and his dope, and strutted back to my solitary, single bed, the TV remote control and the late-night weatherman.

19

On the Banks of
the Guadalquivir

My arrival in Seville was a little more exciting than I'd bargained for. My map showed my insignificant little B-road turning into an inconsequential little dual carriageway.

'No, no dear, not an *autovía*,' the Michelin men mollified me with their soothing, yellow road-colouring pencils. 'It's a trifling two-lane affair leading straight to the heart of the city.'

The Michelin men were deceptive, fickle and cruel.

A few kilometres outside Seville, the traffic started to reproduce. What had once been a paltry little B-road became choked with lumbering lorries and pert little Puntos, all of which surely should have been sputtering their fumes on the perfectly good motorway which my map said ran parallel. The lanes split; the traffic divided, gestated, procreated. I tucked nervously into the hard shoulder. And then the hard shoulder dislocated. It veered right and slipped away towards Granada, taking the two right-hand lanes of traffic with it.

Now, you will remember that I had already been to Granada. I liked it very much but I hadn't been planning

225

to go back there so soon. I especially wasn't planning to go back there today on my bicycle via the bold, blue-signposted motorway. I had somehow to bolt across the two errant, right-hand lanes of hurtling Seats and Opels to join the left-hand lanes and their incumbents bound for Seville city centre. I stopped, studied the scene, and swore. And then I threw myself and my bike into the fray, sprinting across the motorway as fast as my slippy, clippy-clop bike shoes would allow.

A trauma of that level deserves a treat, so I decided I'd better find myself a decent hotel. Admittedly, my treats were getting somewhat out of hand and were becoming alarmingly close to being the norm, but the bank manager was a very long way away and credit cards are lovely things. Anyway, I didn't want to risk ruining my Seville experience with yet another damp and dingy, brown hostel room, so I checked in to Las Casas de la Judería.

As its name suggests (if you're Spanish, that is) the hotel comprises a huddle of renovated old houses in the Barrio de Santa Cruz, Seville's former Jewish quarter. Going from one house to another – or indeed to the world outside – is a business fraught with navigational challenges as you have to wend your way round tiny back streets, through imposing wooden gates, across cobbled patios, and through another tangle of narrow lanes until you are well and truly disoriented. Because of this, the hotel has to employ a whole team of staff who seem to be dedicated solely to leading guests from one part of the hotel to another and answering their questions: 'Excuse me, but how do I get *out*?' 'Where *has* the reception gone to?' 'Where on earth have I left my brain?'

The rooms look out onto elegant courtyards, some with fountains, all with delightful trees and plants. In the patio outside my room lay a vast copper basin brimming with fresh oranges. I couldn't quite figure out if they were meant to be ornamental or if one was allowed to eat them, so I snuck a few into my room and ate them anyway. They were warm and sweet and quite delicious.

My room was dominated by a glorious four-poster bed with a pile of puffy white pillows. The bathroom featured a colossal shower with a head a foot in diameter and an enormous bath with shapely golden taps. Oh God, life was hard! What on earth was I meant to do? Rip off my clothes and leap into the great big shower? Roll like a contented cat all over the bed; lose myself in the vast, soft pillows? Recline sedately on the pillow mountain and channel-surf cable TV? Tear energetically into the streets and check out everything Seville had to offer?

In the end, though, the bathtub won because it had one of those Jacuzzi functions. I poured in a couple of bottles of complimentary bath foam and leapt eagerly into the tub. The white, sculpted peaks rose high above my head, the steam billowed around me. Entirely delighted with myself and my ridiculously ambitious credit card limit, I gave the Jacuzzi button an enthusiastic push – and all hell broke loose. And then it dawned on me: it might be better to have the jet-blowing holes *under* the water, rather than just skimming the top. With a whoosh and a blast, water and foam sprayed all over the room, coating even the opposite wall with damp little white globs and adorning the floor with a series of warm puddles. My magnificent bathroom was suddenly rather a mess.

It took most of the generous supply of fluffy white towels to clean up the bathroom (I was ashamed to let the hotel staff know that I had both stolen the oranges *and* destroyed the bathroom within the same hour) but I was finally fit to go out for dinner on a terrace just outside one of the hotel's many doors, in the Barrio de Santa Cruz.

The old Jewish quarter where the Barrio de Santa Cruz

now lies hasn't, in fact, been home to many Jews for some five hundred years. Their demise started well before that, though, on a steamy summer's afternoon in 1391: the Christian population of Seville was incensed by a tax increase and the tax collectors were Jews. The Christians stormed the *barrio*, killed almost four thousand Jews and destroyed the synagogues. During the course of the summer, the Jewish quarters of Córdoba, Valencia and other cities were also attacked.

The Jews took fright and, to save their skins, began to convert to Christianity. But many of them converted in name only. The *conversos* continued to observe the Jewish Sabbath and to circumcise their children rather than baptize them. Worse still, according to the Christians, their lip service to Christianity meant that they could now hold high positions at court, forbidden to *bona fide* Jews. (By this time, Seville was ruled by Christians; the *Reconquista* took the city from the Moors in 1248.) The Christian population seethed with resentment towards the Jews' wealth and prosperity and accused them of using the church as a ladder for social climbing.

Discontent brewed and hatred simmered until, towards the end of the fifteenth century, a Dominican friar persuaded the Catholic Monarchs to instigate in Spain an Inquisition modelled on the system that had so successfully massacred swaths of French 'heretics' since the beginning of the thirteenth century; the Pope backed the proposal and the infamous Spanish Inquisition stoked its fires.

The first office of the Inquisition was set up in Seville in October 1480. Four months later, six people were burned at the stake in the first *auto da fe,* or act of faith, as the Inquisitors perversely called the ceremonial burning of heretics. Over the next seven years, seven hundred executions and five thousand 'lighter' punishments were carried out in Seville alone. In Castile as a whole (the kingdom that stretched from the Bay of Biscay in the north to the Sierra Morena in the south) two thousand executions and fifteen thousand other punishments had been meted out by 1490. The Inquisition had no powers over followers of non-Christian faiths, but now that so many Jews (and, after 1502, Muslims) had converted, it could hunt them down and punish them for supposed non-Christian practices – which could be as minor as reading the wrong books, or even fabricated altogether, as the Inquisition refused to reveal its evidence and sources. Almost all the victims were converts.

The Inquisition was devilishly corrupt and greedy. Jews were wealthy; by denouncing them, the Inquisitors and the Crown could get their mitts on their money as mere suspicion of heresy was enough to guarantee the confiscation of all one's assets. For this reason, the officials tried to round up as many 'heretics' as they possibly could. The idea was not just to catch one person and get him to admit his guilt, but to force him to implicate others in his crime as well. The Inquisition, though forbidden from spilling blood, worked out a whole series of imaginative, non bloody torture devices to make sure an interviewee gave plenty of names.

The way it worked was this: the Inquisitorial authorities would descend on towns and villages every few months or so and hold a compulsory mass in which members of the congregation were invited to come forward and admit their 'infection'. If they did so within the so-called period of grace – about a month – they got off with a mere penance on the condition that they denounced others. In the end, of course, the Inquisition became an outlet for petty rivalries and revenge. Sometimes whole sections of the community would confess themselves guilty *en masse* to prevent somebody else from denouncing them first.

If you did admit your 'infection', though, even the lighter penalties were so grim that being roasted alive on a bonfire might have seemed preferable. From the early days of the

French Inquisition, the most popular punishments were lengthy pilgrimages and vigorous whippings. Each Sunday the penitent would arrive at mass carrying a rod, with which the priest would enthusiastically whip him before the entire congregation, with further public whippings scheduled for the first Sunday of every month and all feast days. What's more, these punishments didn't have any set time frame. As Michael Baigent and Richard Leigh explain in their book *The Inquisition,* these ordeals would be suffered by the penitent for the rest of his life unless the Inquisitor happened to come back into town, remember him, and release him from his sentence.

If suspects didn't confess, of course, they weren't rewarded with such gentle treatment. They were burned on the stake or, if they confessed at the very last minute, the Inquisition generously granted them the favour of being strangled before their bodies were thrown on the flames. The Inquisition was not formally abolished until 1834, although the last victim to be burned at the stake met her demise some years before that, in 1780 and again in Seville. She was an old woman accused of 'having carnal converse with the Devil and laying eggs that had prophecies written on them'.

Fortunately, I managed to forget all about the unappetizing subjects of flagellation and incineration as I ate my dinner even though it, too, had been a little too enthusiastically fried. Sometimes, when eating abroad, it's a pleasure to be presented with little gastronomic surprises, to find that the succulent medallions of pork you thought you'd ordered have turned out to be fricassee of pig's tail (which, I can assure you, looks nothing like as pretty when it's cooked as it does in its natural curly, gravity-defying state stuck on a piglet's behind). Sometimes you're in the mood for a little experimentation – and sometimes you're not. Sometimes, especially when you're about five weeks into a trip full of surprises, you find yourself starting to behave in gastro-nomically self-destructive ways. One minute you're debating how many days old the breadcrumbs in a *gazpacho* should be, the next you find yourself ordering a filled-crust pizza with extra cheese in Pizza Hut.

This meal then, though in a pleasant and historic location, fell into the latter category of unwanted surprises. The white wine turned out red; the waiter asked if I'd like it room-temperature or chilled and I mistakenly opted for the latter. The 'San Jacobo', which had been advertised to me as chicken with ham in a cheese sauce, came as crispy bread-crumb batter with oil sauce, and something tough and indistinguishable on the inside. The *gazpacho* to start with was reasonable but excessively thin, and the melon to follow was under-ripe. Some you win, some you lose.

The following morning, I spent so long lounging in my great big bed and washing in the enormous shower that, by the time I was ready for a public airing, the hotel had finished serving breakfast. I wandered out into the sunshine with the elation that comes from hour after luxurious hour of deep sleep and fabulous dreams, and spent yet another leisurely hour on a terrace with perfectly grilled toast, freshly brewed coffee and the newspaper. And then, without the merest hint of urgency, I began to stroll the streets of Seville. Let there be no doubt about it: I was fast perfecting the art of the Spanish saunter. If I didn't watch it, I'd catch their time-keeping habits too.

Seville is a city rich with history and folklore. It was in the city's royal dungeons that Cervantes started to pen the epic tale of Don Quixote and his sidekick Sancho Panza. (Cervantes worked for ten years as a government purchasing agent in Seville, where his unbusinesslike methods landed him in jail several times.) Bizet set the opening act of his opera *Carmen* outside the city's old tobacco factory, which today is frequented by a rather different type of young woman. It's now a part of Seville university and swarms with skinny girls in tight hipster trousers slung low beneath the knicker line, who drag deep on Camel Lights (bought with their own allowances rather than rolled from scraps of tobacco picked off the factory floor) while reciting the mantra: poison-the-fat-cells, poison-the-fat-cells, poison-the-fat-cells. For this is Spain, and they know they've only got a few years left. After the age of thirty, all Spanish girls – with the notable exception of Penelope Cruz – are doomed to explode widthways. It's called the Revenge of the Olive Oil.

Seville is also the city in which Christopher Columbus was received by Queen Isabel and, arguably, in whose cathedral the explorer's remains now lie. There is some debate, though, as to whether the tomb dedicated to him actually contains any mouldering Columbus atoms at all. Columbus himself expressed his wish to be buried on the Caribbean island of Santo Domingo and his body was accordingly interred there. Nearly three hundred years later, whatever small shards were left of him were apparently moved in their urn to Cuba, from where the Spanish reckoned they brought him home to rest in Seville at the end of the nineteenth century. The Santo Domingans, however, say that the *real* urn never went to Cuba at all. That means that the putrid remains that the Spanish brought back to Seville weren't Columbus's but the decomposed body of somebody else. In that case, Columbus himself has got lost somewhere in the Caribbean – again. Apparently the whereabouts of the voyager's remains is still an issue of some contention between Spain and Santo Domingo, which seems extraordinary when you consider that even the cats who ate the birds who ate the worms who ate Columbus must have decayed long since into a load of old rot.

The city's most famous landmark is the Giralda, the minaret of the former Great Mosque of Seville. The minaret's the only bit they kept, though – the Christians demolished the rest of the mosque at the beginning of the fifteenth century to make way for their own cathedral. It was a great time to be a cathedral builder in Spain. With the Moors driven back into their ever-diminishing kingdom, the Christians were seized with a fit of 'anything you can do we can do better'. They blasted their way through the mosques and – often on the same site – spared no expense in demonstrating the material power of the Catholic church. Seville is an extreme example: when the church authorities made plans for the new cathedral, they reputedly decided to 'build a church so large and in such style that all those who finally see it will take us for lunatics'. The result is the largest Gothic church in the world. It's certainly magnificent although – and Sevillean readers should now shield their eyes – I found it gloomy and foreboding.

After the requisite ten minutes in the cathedral, I dutifully climbed the Giralda with 1001 other tourists. It's easy to walk up as there are no steps, just a series of shallow ramps apparently designed not to ease the climb for ageing German tourists after a plate of *rösti* too many but so that guards of yesteryear could take their watch on horseback. One has to ask what good a horse can do stuck at the top of a tower, but all the guards are dead now so there's no-one to answer.

Horse or no horse, it would have been easier to get to the top in the fifteenth century than it is today. The spiralling passage that leads there is only wide enough for two lanes of human traffic – one going up, the other coming down. (It was this tower, if you remember, that inspired the Catalan architect Gaudí to consider building a 'double ramp' in his building La Pedrera in Barcelona.) We shuffled along bumper to bumper like motorway traffic in a jam: the groups of bewildered Chinese whistle-stop tourists blinking exhaustedly at their itineraries and wondering which country they were in; stout Scandinavian matrons with map books

233

and sensible shoes; their paunchy husbands with binoculars, sandals and socks; and skinny Australian backpackers looking like hairy hunger-strike victims. Together we trudged to the top. Once there we had to queue some more to get close enough to the grilles to see the view and when, at last, the great climax arrived and our turn was upon us, well, there was Seville just as we had expected. I stayed two minutes, took a couple of photographs as proof of my efforts, and made good my escape. I had a pressing errand to run, something considerably more exciting than traipsing up a tower with a bunch of sweaty tourists. I had to go shopping.

I had shrunk out of my trousers. My wardrobe, as I've said before, was limited by the little space in my panniers. Every evening for the last five weeks, apart from those few heady, wardrobe-rich days in Barcelona, I'd taken off my cycling kit, showered, stretched, and put on the same pair of grey crease-proof cargo pants and the same black vest top. Before I went to bed, I'd taken the tube of travel wash and rinsed out my cycling clothes and anything else that stood a chance of drying before the morning. This meant that my trousers and T-shirt were only washed when I stayed in more expensive hotels where the improved ventilation made for a better drying room. Sometimes, of course, it all went wrong and I ended up wearing damp clothes. At one point, I worked out a brilliant system for drying my socks by sticking them over the windy end of the hairdryer and turning it on full blast. I had to give this up, however, when I found that my socks, though beautifully dry, had holes burned into them.

By this stage in my trip, I'd cycled 1,185 kilometres and burned, according to my heart rate monitor which professes to know about such things, 21,752 calories by cycling. That's equivalent to 320 chocolate biscuits, or 207 bananas, or 149 bottles of beer that I had burned *in addition* to normal daily activities, such as breathing and walking around town and surfing between *Lois y Clark* and the weather report with the TV remote control. As a result, my body parts had redistributed themselves. Large chunks of flesh had vanished off my bottom and stomach and appeared as harder, meaner bulges on my quadriceps. I had, of course, been trying to make up for all this fat burning and muscle building by very diligently filling my face at every opportunity. I could have tried harder.

My trousers had always been functional rather than glamorous but now, with all this activity, they were positively clownish. The waist hung precariously round my hips – a couple more mountain passes and they'd slip humiliatingly round my ankles. The crotch hung six inches too low and sagged around my legs like the baggy pants of a teenage skateboarder. In this country, where even the stray dogs preen themselves, I felt a dork. It was a shame, of course, but there was nothing else for it. I had to break my no-shopping rule and buy a new pair.

El Centro, Seville's main shopping area, is a maze of narrow cobbled streets emanating out from the central artery, the glamorous Calle Sierpes. This is where Seville's plastic-toting well-to-do come in search of style, sophistication, and suitably bursting carrier bags. These streets buzz with that special energy given off only by women in retail therapy. Teenage girls in groups scuff along the street with their Camper shoes and Camel Lights. They don't buy much, but form disorderly, manically chattering queues around the changing rooms, their arms piled high with tight tees and long flared jeans. They crowd into the changing cubicle four at a time. Gasps and exclamations emanate from within:

'Man!' Giggle giggle. 'Those are just so frumpy, man! I mean, you can't even see your knickers! That is *so* unsexy!' Giggle.

'*Oye, Lidia, me hacen gorda estos pantalones?*' Hey, Lidia, does my bum look big in this?

'Sssh. SSSSHHH.' Giggle. 'It won't light.' Giggle. 'Shut *up*, Eva, someone will hear you!' Giggle giggle.

And the suspicious smell of tobacco wafts out from within before they saunter forth with very grown-up pouts.

Young professionals strut the streets alone, trotting along in their short, tight skirts and well-polished heels, glancing anxiously at the time as they desperately scour the shelves for a last-minute outfit for some special dinner – something flattering, something sexy, something that will hide the fact that they've been too busy to get to the gym this month and are due a week's sleep. The portly, middle-aged women have mastered shopping better. They stroll amicably in pairs comparing thoughts on the lampshades in El Corte Inglés before taking in a coffee and cake to work up the strength to shop some more. Over coffee, they put the world to rights.

'*Es una vergüenza*, it's a disgrace. Old Mrs Méndez wore *navy blue* to mass on Sunday! Did you see? Can you believe it? *Por Dios!* And only *fourteen years* after the death of her poor husband, may God have pity on his soul!'

Furious signs of the cross.

For an hour or so, I walked among them, queuing up for the changing rooms with the teenagers and then feeling disappointed when the hip-hugging, low-slung flares didn't look quite as alluring on me as they did on the fifteen-year-olds. I moved on to the Levi's shop.

'I'm not sure those will fit you.' The assistant peered at me down his supercilious, I-come-from-Seville-so-my-ancestors-were-Caesars nose. 'Perhaps you'd like to try a size larger?'

'I'll have you know, *señor,* that my bottom is incredibly small right now, and pert to boot,' I wanted to tell him – but I slunk humiliated out of the shop instead.

I tried on pretty much everything in Zara, scoured the

shelves in Mango, and mooched around El Corte Inglés for hours before finally, triumphantly, emerging with a tiny new pair of navy-blue trousers.

It was with a greater sense of sartorial dignity that I made my way to the Museo de Bellas Artes, Seville's fine arts museum dedicated to Sevillean Golden Age painting. During the latter half of the sixteenth century and the first part of the seventeenth, Spain was big on culture. This was the Golden Age, the era of the playwright Lope de Vega and the 'first novelist', Miguel de Cervantes. It was also an immensely prolific time for the visual arts. King Felipe IV, who ruled from 1621 to 1665, was fond of art and an avid collector, though he himself with his bulbous red nose, deep, domed forehead and sickly complexion was no oil painting if Velázquez's portraits are anything to go by. Having said that, Felipe IV had thirty illegitimate children so some people must have found him attractive.

Seville was the second most important arts centre in Spain after Madrid. It was a bustling trading post, a popular departure point for voyages to the New World, and an established intellectual centre. Religious works of art were particularly in demand: not only did all those missionaries and New World settlers need them for the churches and monasteries they would inflict on the South Americans, but even on home soil religious ostentation was doing a roaring trade. The church authorities, having run out of mosques to demolish and improve upon, now found a new cause. Following the Reformation in the sixteenth century and the subsequent split of the Protestant and Catholic churches came a Counter-Reformation of Catholicism, which felt the need to prove itself bigger and better than ever. Churches, chapels, and cathedrals sprang up – and they needed paintings, statues and carvings to decorate them and confirm their status. It was a good time to be an artist in Seville.

The best known of Seville's Golden Age prodigies was

Diego Velázquez, though he only lived in Seville up to the age of twenty-three. After that, he became court painter to Felipe IV in Madrid and painted a good number of what we must assume were kindly portraits of that unprepossessing monarch. Though much of his later work hangs in the Prado in Madrid, the Museo de Bellas Artes houses a handful of his early paintings as well as works by Murillo and Zurbarán, among others. This being a religious period, there is much celestial rapture and a good selection of austere and pissed-off-looking saints.

Sharing the formerly tranquil space of the museum with me that afternoon was a group of British teenagers. These were Kids Away From Their Parents. It must have been a sixth-form school trip – half term, perhaps – and they blasted through the museum with that teenage pack mentality that sends regular human beings running for cover. They swept through the doors and along the corridors, the girls' jeans slung unnervingly low, the boys manfully flaunting downy facial stubble. There was only a handful of other visitors; we flattened ourselves against walls and pinned ourselves slimly against doorways until the danger of the Lesser-Bearded, Greatly-Spotted Roaming Teenage Beast had passed.

Strolling home along the west bank of the River Guadalquivir towards the Torre del Oro (whose commissioner Yusuf II, incidentally, met a grisly end in 1224 when he was gored to death by a cow in Marrakesh – you want to watch out for those) I passed Seville's famous bull-ring and, seeing that they gave tours every twenty minutes, joined up with the group waiting in the foyer. We peeked through the window at the infirmary, with its one solitary bed surrounded by trolleys and trays full of pristine operating and life support equipment. We saw the tiny *traje de luces* (the tight, silk bullfighter's outfit) of a nineteenth-century torero who took up professional bullfighting at the age of nine. We peered into the chapel, just by the great door through which the bullfighter enters the ring. This is the torero's last stop before facing the dance of death (possibly his own but far more likely the bull's). He comes here to pray for success in the arena, though you have to wonder what a benevolent God would make of his art and just whose side he would be on.

We trooped round at the heels of our guide, who trotted out tales of gorings and deaths with utter detachment.

'And this is the mother of the bull that killed Manolete,' she recited, wearily raising her arm to point at the head of a brown-eyed cow who looked dolefully down on us from the wall above.

Many of the bulls' heads were short of an ear or two: if a matador is particularly heroic, the president will grant him one or two ears, which he hacks off the slumped, lifeless animal before a wildly cheering crowd. (There's even an annual Golden Ear award – yes, really – which the gloriously valiant El Juli has won for the last three years running.) The heads, glued to the museum wall, betrayed no emotion. The fear was extinguished from their eyes, the cascades of blood cleaned from their hides which, I suppose, is more sanitary but in no way realistic.

Bullfighting fans wouldn't see this as a contradiction or a cover-up. To mount a bull's head on the wall is an honour to a courageous beast. (One animal that died in the Seville ring in the mid-nineteenth century, and whose head adorns the wall, was so brave that he killed eleven horses in a single afternoon, and it took fifty-one stabs to finish him off.) The way a bull dies in the ring, an aficionado will argue, allows him much greater dignity than the fate of a burger-bound beast who is butchered in an abattoir, and the bull leads an idyllic life until his number is called. Some people will even tell you that bullfighting is an ecological movement. The bulls must be kept in the wild and need vast tracts of pasture

239

to roam in: the acreage of pasture in Spain devoted to Iberian fighting bulls is equal to all of Spain's national parks put together.

After a starlit dinner of roasted peppers with tuna and a half bottle of Valdepeñas ('Is it good?' I asked the waiter. '*Hombre!*' he replied as if only a half-wit could ask such a stupid question of a local wine), I made a second attempt to find flamenco in Andalusia. Michael from Texas had failed me; I'd have to hunt it out for myself. At about midnight, the earliest hour I could hope to find any kind of nightlife, I trekked off down a solitary, ill-lit alleyway to find a bar where good, live flamenco was said to strike up most nights of the week. It was a cavernous place, packed full of flushed female students clapping excitedly as a young man played the guitar. Nobody seemed to have a drink in their hand, and nobody spoke; all just stood gazing with rapt adoration at the guitarist. And yes, he was good – but he wasn't playing flamenco and, at the end of the day, I felt uncomfortable standing all on my own in a dingy little bar in a foreign country in the middle of the night. I can cycle 1,600 kilometres alone, I can eat on my own, I have even learnt to talk to myself quite satisfactorily – but hanging out in bars on my own seems to be beyond me. I thought of my four-poster bed with its small mountain of pillows, of cable TV, of the bathtub with the big, gold taps . . . and I retired.

Another day dawned, and I was becoming far too comfortable dividing my time between my Great Big Bed and the pavement cafés of Seville. My bicycle and my aching bottom had receded into an unpleasant but distant memory as I whiled away another morning on yet another charming patio, reading the paper and drinking coffee and juice in the sun. It couldn't go on. I didn't have one of those tiresome Catholic upbringings that requires you to feel guilt every time anything nice happens – God knows how it is that the Spanish manage to lead such cheerful lives – but even I couldn't get away from the fact that I wasn't supposed to be enjoying myself quite this much. I was meant to be suffering, sore and lost. I was also going to go bankrupt fast if I stayed much longer in this wonderful hotel. It was time to hit the road and the rubber-sheeted *pensiones* – but before that, I had one last day in Seville.

I felt obliged to visit the Alcázar. It is, after all, one of Seville's main tourist sights and I hadn't been there before. The fortress began life in 913, but its most sumptuous palace was built for the notorious Christian king Pedro I, who rose to the throne in 1350 at the tender age of just fifteen. The problem was that even at that age he wasn't very tender. After becoming king, he embarked on a campaign of blood-thirsty persecution against his father's concubine and her offspring. Historians reckon that he killed, among others, an archbishop, several cousins, quite a lot of friends and a number of his own illegitimate half-brothers. He murdered the Red King of Granada and thirty-seven of his courtiers for the simple reason that he wanted the ruby in the king's turban. Pedro later gave the ruby to the wife of England's Edward the Black Prince who sent troops to help Pedro fight his half-brother Enrique. The ruby now has pride of place in the imperial crown in the crown jewels in the Tower of London.

Despite all the blood-letting, the jury's out on Pedro. While he's generally thought of by posterity as Pedro the Cruel, those who were on his side called him Pedro the Just. The latter camp argue that his entire reign was troubled by battles with the rebellious nobles who thought his younger brother Enrique (known to history as Enrique the Bastard) should be king instead. Still, the pro-Pedro contingent wasn't great in numbers – Pedro once said, 'One loaf of bread would suffice to fill the bellies of all those loyal to me'

– so his friends' argument probably wasn't heard by many. In the end, Enrique the Bastard won, stabbing his brother to death with his own hand while a French noble held him down.

I don't know what Pedro would have made of the rebellion I came across on my way home. The main road was closed to traffic and flanked by scores of policemen standing behind barriers in full riot gear. In the street, thousands of students marched, protesting against the government's plans to monitor more closely the universities' performance. At the end of the street, police vans were lined bumper-to-bumper and hordes more helmeted men in navy overalls stood around. They needn't have bothered. Had the students exchanged their banners for floats and effigies of the Virgin, it could have been a festival parade. They swigged beer out of bottles, chanted and sang, and seemed to be having a grand old time.

It must have been a big day for demonstrations in Seville – either that, or the Sevilleans are a demonstrative lot – because later that day I came upon another one. I'd just come out of the post office, from where I'd posted my too-baggy trousers back home, when I heard more chanting, accompanied by whistle-blowing and blaring sirens. I assumed the students were back on the streets several litres of beer later, were becoming anti-social and that the sirens were accompanying their journey down the nick. Being a nosy type, I went to have a closer look, only to find that the demonstrators, this time, were the policemen themselves. It was a curious sight. Marching along the road were about a thousand men and women, out of uniform but with banners and posters proclaiming loyalty to the police union and pressing the government to 'fulfil their promises', whatever they might have been. They were blowing merrily on their policemen's whistles and making a splendid cacophony with sirens. Police? Demonstrating? I thought they were meant to

242

be the strong, silent ones who *kept* the order. Whoever said *they* were allowed to express themselves?

After my failure to find flamenco last night, I resorted to seeing a show. It was meant to be a cut above the normal tourist rabble; it took place in the open-air, cloistered terrace of a Cultural Centre dedicated to Andalusian art and, for the time being, to the promotion of the best of young flamenco performers.

Outside the Cultural Centre, a long, orderly queue of British, Germans and Scandinavians stood obediently. There was not, of course, a Spaniard to be seen – they were all busy being impassioned elsewhere. There were a couple of worthy-looking, half-starved backpackers in their early twenties, who gazed upon the show with that intent, considered expression, heads slightly askew, that is meant to express that they are appreciating 'art'. There were the usual middle-aged couples in sturdy shoes, and a French couple with two small children.

Flamenco is meant to be spontaneous, the performer surrounded by foot-stamping, hand-clapping crowds. The only spontaneous person among our prim little audience of tight-lipped tourists was the small French girl, aged about two, whose wide eyes lit up to the rhythm. A beam spread across her face and she started to clap in time to the music, until her too-Gallic mother hissed sharply to her to stop. And so we sat in our rows, not an *olé* amongst us, silently observing the show with studied yet slightly pained expressions that said, 'I've paid my eight quid and now I'm damn well going to work out what's so great about that woman's wailing.'

The *flamencos* no doubt exhibited their art perfectly well. The guitarist seemed skilful, the singer soulful, and the wildly energetic young dancer with his glorious long black hair, sideburns, and roguish demeanour stamped and

243

twirled with such vigour that he had to go off and change his sweat-drenched shirt halfway through. But to try to understand flamenco by going to see a show like this is like trying to get a grip on Irish culture by going to see *Riverdance*. It was like going to watch the water puppets in Hanoi, the gamelan in Yogyakarta, the Chinese Opera in Beijing. You dutifully traipse along, try not to wince too obviously at the clanging, discordant bongs and the high-pitched tonal wailing, try to tell yourself you're having a cultural experience – but deep down you know you'd have a better time in the pseudo Irish theme pub next door drinking imported Kilkenny and listening to The Cranberries.

'Oh, to hell with Spanish culture,' I muttered to myself as we emerged back into the warm, evening air. And on that note, I found an open-air restaurant and ordered a beer and a chicken curry.

After I'd eaten, I returned to my room and, reluctantly, spread my maps over the bed. Tomorrow I would be back on the road. I consulted my bike computer. Things were looking bad. I'd covered just 1,185 kilometres. My absolute minimum goal – the lowest acceptable mileage with which I could go home and still show my face in public – was a thousand miles, or 1,610 kilometres. I had just seven days left before I was meeting two friends in Toledo for one last, celebratory weekend. I needed to get on my bike.

20

Tigers, Togas, Etc.

I should of course have cycled from Seville to Mérida. Cycling, after all, is what you're meant to do when you go on a cycling tour, as opposed to taking the bus. But Mérida was several days away pedalling at my pace and I didn't have several days to spare after all that lolling around in town squares drinking beer in the sun. What's more, if I'd cycled, I would have run the risk of spending those days in glorious solitude, with just my own sweet thoughts and views of the rugged Extremeño countryside to amuse me. I would have missed out on the enriching experience of sharing a stuffy bus with twenty-something excessively energetic school-children, and the delights of trying to converse with a fractious bus driver.

Strangely for a direct Seville–Mérida bus that had 'Mérida' clearly marked on its destination board, the bus did not go from Seville to Mérida.

'Change at Zafra,' barked the driver when I showed him my ticket.

'But isn't this the bus for Mérida?' I queried. It was the wrong thing to say. The driver glared at me with a fierceness that made his eyeballs bulge; with an exasperated intake of breath, his chest protruded so that his already tight bus driver's uniform pinched and his face became quite pink.

'I've just told you, for Mérida, you have to change at Zafra,' he glowered.

I retreated chastened to a seat at the back of the bus. With a lurch, we clattered out of the bus station, and bade farewell to Seville. After an hour or so, I began to worry. Wouldn't it be dreadful if I failed to recognize Zafra, stayed on the bus, and found myself carried on to Badajoz? I once spent a whole weekend in Badajoz and can say with some assurance that is an ugly, dilapidated old dive. The best entertainment one could hope for in Badajoz would be a functioning TV set showing Venezuelan soap operas. Mérida, on the other hand, used to be the largest Roman city on the Iberian peninsula; while it might have little else to promote it, visitors can at least tour the old lumps of rock and console themselves with fantasies of lithe, suntanned legs in skimpy little togas. The bus driver and I had a few more exchanges regarding the exact whereabouts of Zafra ('Excuse me, is this where I have to change for Mérida?' . . . 'For heaven's sake, I told you before, you have to change at Zafra') but, after several hours' intense concentration on the road signs, I arrived unscathed.

I'm not usually a big one for bits of old pot, but the relics at Mérida are truly amazing and, better yet, free from the hordes of fellow tourists you find in the larger cities. OK, so you can buy a six-inch replica of a Roman bust if you must, or indeed a fake mosaic fridge magnet from any of the souvenir shops lining the road to the remains, but there's nothing very aggressive about it, there's no audio tour in six different languages and there are no flag-toting guides.

A visit to the old Roman theatre is most educational in the matter of old Roman bottoms: they must have had ample ones, as each behind was allotted fifty-six centimetres here. Perhaps they had eaten a roast hog or two too many; clearly they hadn't put in time on their bikes. Fat-bottomed audiences besides, the old Roman theatre is remarkably well preserved (it lay under rubble for sixteen centuries before being excavated) though slightly marred, on the occasion of my visit, by a group of primary-school children who were being encouraged by their teacher to stand up on the grand, column-backed stage and sing tuneless little ditties to their classmates.

The amphitheatre next door, however, was deserted and I had the place to myself. I sat down on a scraggy lump of stone and considered the fact that, two thousand years ago, a large betoga'd bottom would have sat on this very rock while in the arena that lay just a metre before me lions and tigers would have roared and raged and gobbled up gladiators in tinier togas for their tea. (I have to say that I don't know quite how tiny gladiators' togas used to be. I'm willing to accept, though, that they might not have been quite as tiny as Russell Crowe's in *Gladiator*, because I can see that showing off your finely honed quads might come low on your list of priorities when you're about to be eaten by a real tiger as opposed to a computer-simulated one.) Admittedly the clearing didn't really look like an arena any more; it was overgrown with tufts of grass and the stone steps had paid the price of two thousand years of erosion, but you could still see the cross-shaped pit in the middle, where they say the lions and tigers were kept starving and snarling under trap doors until it was deemed to be their dinnertime. Instead of the heckles and jibes of fourteen thousand bloodthirsty Romans, the air was now filled with nothing more barbarous than the sweet chirrups of birds. But as I sat there in silence it wasn't hard to imagine the stands packed with cheering, jeering spectators, and the arena the final battleground for doomed and desperate men whose fate hung on the whim of one man's thumb. And yes, yes, if I fantasized really, *really* hard, I could just about hear him, that virile

247

voice, oozing bravery from every testosterone-laden pore, booming in a faint echo around the ancient rocks:

'My name is Maximus Decimus Meridius, commander of the armies of the north . . .'

The most astonishing thing about Mérida, though, is its museum. Being the cynical type, I was expecting a couple of shards of old pot, the odd chipped brick at best. I arrived at the door forty minutes before it closed for the day. This didn't worry me as I was expecting to be in, out, and sitting in a pavement café with a beer in ten minutes at the most.

I could have stayed for hours. The museum was filled with vast, beautiful mosaics, whose incredible detail and subtle shading left my jaw gaping every bit as wide as those of the ravenous beasts shown on the fresco taken from the amphitheatre wall. The sections of fresco were in a remarkable state of preservation, their glorious yellows, reds, greens and blues vibrantly depicting hapless gladiators jousting to the bitter, bloody end. In addition to the mosaics and frescoes were a good number of statues and, of course, many bits of old pot. Heck, Mérida might even be worth a detour, even for those who never deemed themselves interested in dusty old relics.

Extremadura, I considered as I pedalled out of the town the following morning, is much underrated. This is the region where I once lived for a whole year, the third year of my university Spanish course, and I've been sniggered at so many times since by slick, city hipsters who consider Extremadura to be beneath them that I started to believe my happy memories must have been addled by too many litres of local Larios gin, that the fact that I had rather a good time here can have been due only to my own shamefully low standards. When I've told chic Spanish urbanites that I lived for a year in Plasencia, they have raised their perfectly plucked eyebrows and wrinkled their matt-powdered noses. (This is unkind, as the Extremeño donkeys, which some farmers still use to till the fields round here, don't smell *that* bad.) Then, rather tellingly, they've always asked the same question: 'Where exactly *is* Plasencia?' Perhaps they should go there and find out.

I'd applied to be a teaching assistant in a secondary school and asked to go to Salamanca because I'd heard the buildings were pretty and that it had a wild and exuberant nightlife. Such things were important in those years before my body had figured out the meanings of the words 'hangover' and 'fat'. Things didn't work out quite as I'd planned. Instead I was sent by the Ministry of Education to a town called Plasencia in Extremadura. It was only an hour's car ride south of Salamanca, but a whole world away. There was only one other English person living in Plasencia; his name was Stephen and he drove a hearse painted pink. Apparently it was very useful for moving furniture.

I channelled all the energy that might have been frittered away on the four-a.m. streets of Salamanca learning instead about the *fiestas* of the Extremadura region. I was something of a celebrity in this area that hadn't seen a great number of twenty-year-old English girls. Free beer and language practice both flowed easily. In Plasencia, I went to my first *matanza*, or pig slaughtering, an event still much celebrated in rural parts of Spain though not seen for some years in England other than through the pages of Thomas Hardy novels. I was well advised to snooze in bed long enough to miss the actual butchery, which can be both messy and noisily high-pitched for those who've been out practising their language skills the night before, and to turn up instead for the post-execution party. We sat around from late morning until well into the night, drinking bottle after soothing bottle of frothy Spanish beer in the warm January sun while slabs of the freshly slain pig roasted gently on the barbecue.

Then there were the carnivals – five days of non-stop drinking and dancing – and the *romerías*, marginally more sober events when each village celebrates their patron saint's day. The whole village packs a picnic, including plenty of beer and wine, and walks up to the local hermitage. At some point the saint, or Virgin, or whoever it is that watches over the villagers so kindly week after week, year after year, comes out and takes a turn, but mostly it's just a chance for a party with a countryside theme. And then, of course, each town and village has its own annual *feria*. Plasencia's takes place in June, and it was here that I saw my first bullfight – and the proud, strutting prowess of top matador Enrique Ponce. I was entranced.

At weekends I drove around in my puttering old car, and was astonished to find that it went above the speed limit without bits falling off.

'That's eighteen thousand pesetas. In cash. On the spot,' said the policeman in his tight-fitting olive-green uniform complete with powerful-looking pistol. He was wearing Oakley shades. Are they police-force standard issue in Spain? In different circumstances, well, I had to admit, he would really have been quite attractive. He was kind of like an Antonio Banderas with floppier hair.

'*Eighteen thousand?*' Had I been going *that* fast in my ten-year-old Nissan Micra with a one-litre engine? Surely not! I gasped and widened my eyes as alluringly as I knew how. I counted up all my cash, including the stray pesetas stuck in the fluff under the passenger seat. I had four thousand, three hundred and thirty-five.

'Well, in that case we'll have to immobilize your vehicle,' said the outrageously good-looking policeman rather unkindly. Things were not going well. How exactly would they 'immobilize my vehicle' anyway? Confiscate the wheels and leave me there? All on my own? Slap bang in the middle of nowhere?

Putting on my best sad face, I blushed and stuttered my apologies. I flirted shamelessly. I was just working myself up to shed a tear when the astonishingly attractive policeman took off his Oakleys, batted his lustrous lashes over his big, brown eyes, smiled to display his pearly-white teeth and said, 'Oh well, never mind.' And shaking his floppy black hair at the already written ticket, he added, 'We'll just stick this on the next guy. Drive carefully now!'

My goodness, please can they transfer him to England? Surely our shiny-new, united Europe must be good for something.

Driving only marginally more slowly, I visited tiny villages and steaming metropolises, and worked my way through as many of Spain's bars as my robust student liver and somewhat frailer student purse could bear. Being a natural glutton, I sampled everything I was offered: pigs' ears turned out to be eerily eary, and gave an unpalatable crunch between the teeth. I only tried them once. Pig's snout was more successful – fatty and tasty, it was like a particularly succulent piece of crackling. Tripe never settled well in my stomach, but *morcillas*, the Spanish version of black pudding, soon became a firm favourite. I learned to choose a good chorizo, to cook a passable tortilla, and to put together a *gazpacho* without making the kitchen look like a murder scene.

In Extremadura there are no grand towns or classy cities, but the area is littered with points of passing interest. Between them lies a wonderfully rugged countryside punctuated with evergreen oaks under whose boughs snuffles the infamous black-haired Iberian pig. As cycling terrain goes, it's near perfect, with its rolling hills providing long, spinning descents that don't kill you as you climb back up. On either side of the road stretch green pastures with the occasional covering of buttercups, rocky outcrops, dry stone walls, herds of cattle, flocks of sheep and, of course, plenty of well-stuffed pigs. And one thing I can say absolutely for certain: nowhere in Extremadura have I ever, ever heard the dulcet tones of a wannabe Frank Sinatra.

My first stop after Mérida was Trujillo, the home town of New World explorer Francisco Pizarro. Pizarro had a less-than-glamorous early life: he was illegitimate and his father rejected him, though the family changed its tune after Pizarro's marauding in South America made him rich. After eighteen years in the brave New World, Pizarro returned to Spain with breathtaking tales of the wondrous riches of the Inca empire. After winning royal backing for his project to return to Peru and pinch their gold, he came to Trujillo where he was given a hero's welcome and gathered four of his half-brothers to join him on his adventures. When they eventually arrived back in Peru they managed, through some extraordinary turn of fate, to capture the Inca emperor with just 180 men and thirty-seven horses. The imprisoned emperor offered to buy his freedom by filling with gold the room in which he was held. The noble conquistadors took the gold – and then bumped off the emperor anyway.

It was the rampages of Pizarro and his ilk that led to the backlash of the Black Legend, that body of literature which portrayed the Spaniard as evil and cruel – 'the swarthy fellow with black pointed beard and wicked Toledo blade, who is not only cruel and greedy, but treacherous and lecherous to boot' as historian Mark Williams describes the villain of this 'cape and sword fiction'. The Black Legend writings were inspired by the Spanish conquistadors' treatment of the native South Americans and the colonialists don't come out of it prettily. Take this sixteenth-century English writer's description of a Spaniard: '. . . a craftie fox, a ravenous wolfe, and a raging tygre; theyr filthy, monstrous and abominable luxurie, theyr lustfull and inhumaine deflouring of theyr wives and daughters, matchless and sodomiticall ravishings of young boys . . . a filthie heape of the most lothsome, infected and slavish people that ever yet lived on earth.'

Fortunately, the little museum in Trujillo is able to put us right, to tell us the *real* story: that the glorious, valiant Spanish nobly overthrew the unwashed, underdressed natives who were so uncivilized that they *fired poisoned arrows* at the nice invaders. The ungrateful wretches!

The great Pizarro is further honoured by an imposing bronze statue in Trujillo's Plaza Mayor, though this, like its subject, is of dubious origins. Rumourmongers have it that Charles Rumsey, the sculptor, originally intended to depict Hernán Cortés, the conqueror of the Aztec empire, and donate his work to Mexico. Unfortunately, Rumsey didn't do his homework and failed to find out that the Mexicans take a dim view of the man who so ruthlessly overthrew their indigenous forebears. When they turned down his statue, Rumsey was left with a rather large piece of bronze on his hands so he gave it to Trujillo instead and called it Pizarro. Another story tells of Rumsey's wife's insistence that the statue should depict a tall and debonair hero. The sculptor was therefore forced to bend the truth – Pizarro (or was it Cortés?) was in real life squat and ugly.

The most likely story, however, is also the most banal – that Rumsey was asked to produce the sculpture for the Panama Pacific Exposition held in San Francisco in 1915. (Charles Nichauz created the Cortés statue for the same event.) Pizarro, say the sculpture experts, is not depicted as unrealistically tall and handsome; it is the horse, in contrast, who is plain and short for strong, stocky ponies were favoured by the conquistadors. When the exposition was over, a number of versions of Rumsey's statue were made, one of which was donated to Pizarro's home town.

Whatever the statue's origins, it's certainly striking. In fact, the image of the all-conquering Pizarro on a big bronze horse was just about all I could remember of Trujillo from my last visit ten years before, when as a language assistant in nearby Plasencia I hiked around pretty much anywhere of passing interest in my own squat, stocky steed, my little Nissan Micra. It was with some anticipation, then, that I pushed my bike up the steep, bumpy cobbles that led to Trujillo's Plaza Mayor – only to find that the square had been dug up. Pretty flagstones had been overthrown by mud, rubble and piles of brand-new plastic pipes. Pizarro and his pony were still holding their line, but in doing so they stood alone among the carnage of the Battle of the Bulldozers.

Trujillo was described by my guidebook as 'one of the most perfect little towns in Spain [which] can't be much bigger than it was in 1529' (when Pizarro and his merry band set forth for Peru). I will forgive the writer for not having been there on a day when the town square was being dug up. After all, it's these very restorations that allow guide-book writers to claim that the place is virtually unchanged; if it really were virtually unchanged, it would bear rather more resemblance to Mérida's crumbling amphitheatre than to a historical town square. But bulldozers and renovations apart, this is a town that is stuck firmly in the twenty-first century. To start with, the road on which I arrived was lined with row upon row of characterless housing blocks which I'm willing to bet were built well after Pizarro's day; the outskirts of town are filled with car dealerships and electrical goods warehouses. In short, Trujillo has grown with the times. Not that I can fault it for that. After all, who wouldn't lop down a few trees to build a house with running water that allows you to bath more than once a month and wash your hair more than once a year? Who wouldn't prefer flared hipster jeans to frilly neck ruffles, powdered wigs and heavy coats of armour? And who wouldn't chuck in a little olde worlde charm for the pleasures of a mobile phone that rings to the tune of 'Evergreen'?

I checked into my hostel, which was dire. Both the proprietress and her husband had an obsession with their electricity bill.

'You must remember to turn out the lights every time you leave the room,' said the woman. 'Here is the switch. You turn it off like this. See?' And with that she flicked the little white switch on the wall up and down a few times, which in itself must have used up a few watts.

'Make sure you turn the lights off when you go out,' said her husband about three minutes later. 'You flick the switch upwards like this. See?'

'You have turned the light out, haven't you,' the woman hollered from her lair as I left the *pensión* for the relative peace of the street outside. 'You had to flick that little button on the wall, remember, I showed you how?'

Sí, señora.

Unfortunately, the light switch demonstrations had disturbed the room's resident gecko. I am frightened of geckos, though other people refer to them with such unlikely adjectives as 'cute' and 'harmless'. But then those people have probably never pulled a bag of muesli from their kitchen cupboard only to have it leap violently to life in their hand. They may never have hurled their cereal across the kitchen and watched a small pink gecko scuttle from the wreckage. Neither will they have stood rooted to the floor in fear as the same gecko ran down the length of their bare leg the following day when they disturbed it in its hiding place among the folds of their umbrella. Such things can play on one's perceptions.

Eager to escape the gecko, I left my room the moment I'd passed the light switch test and went for lunch in a café in the Plaza Mayor, still serving despite the less-than-perfect view. The service was execrable. I swiped away every last coin of change leaving no tip, which I found curiously empowering though I don't suppose the waiter even noticed, then pottered round the sights: the museum, the castle and a number of churches. Duty done, I retired back to the dusty Plaza Mayor for a beer.

Matters didn't improve with dinner, which I ate in a restaurant described by my guidebook as the best in town. I was beginning to fall out with my guidebook. Meson La Truja might have been the best restaurant in town if you happened to be a camel with two large humps for storing excess food, a camel which had had its taste buds surgically removed into the bargain, for this was a restaurant that valued quantity over quality. Light suppers weren't on the menu: you could only order the *menú del día*.

'An aperitif, on the house,' proclaimed the waiter, and slammed down half a potato omelette, a vast Pyrex bowl of salad, a plate of chorizo and an entire loaf of bread. I was then obliged to pick two courses – I went for the *gazpacho* on the basis that it was light, and the lamb – a house speciality, no less – which wasn't.

'And an extra dish, on the house,' declared the waiter, proffering a small mountain of chewy, fat-encrusted lamb and another plate brimming with unidentifiable brown stuff. Oh Christ, what was it? Shit-encrusted tail of bull? Stewed stray cat? The waiter stood a few steps away from my table and watched over me intently. Would the stupid English tourist actually eat the double-minced gecko's innards? They probably had bets on it in the kitchen. 'Ha!' Pedro the Plate Piler was laughing with Paco the Plongeur. 'That'll get them back for nicking Gibraltar.' The panic surged.

Stuffed full from the earlier courses, I chopped up the bits and pushed them round the plate for a while before asking for the bill.

'You can pay at the door,' said the waiter with a reproachful stare at the four kilos of uneaten meat beneath whose weight the table still groaned.

By the door there lay, entombed in a sagging armchair

256

whose springs had long since creaked and croaked and passed on to armchair heaven, a very large old lady dressed entirely in black. She was snoring gently. The waiter bent over so that his mouth was within a centimetre of her great, drooping earlobe.

'*Cobra!*' he bellowed. (This, in Spanish, is an instruction to cash up as opposed to a warning that you are about to be punctured by the fangs of a deadly-poisonous snake). The old woman shuddered and shook for a moment, then came to sufficiently to wipe the drool from her chin.

'That's twelve euros,' she wheezed.

'May I have a receipt?' I asked as I handed over the cash.

'*Qué?*'

'RECEIPT?'

'*Receipt?*' the old hag quavered indignantly and blinked her rheumy eyes. 'Well, well! That'll be another three euros.'

Oh forget it, you stupid old lump of lard. My belly's about to burst from all that chorizo and leaden, home-baked bread. You're as deaf as a post. I can't face an argument for fear of being drowned in your copious, flying spittle.

I gave in and made good my escape back to my drab little room, where there were no face-offs with unidentifiable food or vast, black-shrouded centenarians, and I could nurse my burgeoning belly in peace.

21

'Did You Sleep Alone?'

I tossed and turned on a crackly plastic sheet until five o'clock in the morning. My room was on ground level; the passers-by on the street were just a metre away and their every drunken, Saturday-night shriek sailed through the window and bounced around in my head. The sheets were threadbare and unsavoury. That's it, I thought, as my body staged a full-scale revolt and refused to sleep. I'm blowing the budget. I'm never staying in a grubby, cheap, gecko-plagued *pensión* again.

What really peeved me, though, was that, despite the ragged bedlinen and grimy bathroom with its crusty shower head, this *pensión* wasn't *that* cheap. It certainly wasn't worth the thirty euros the proprietress charged me the next morning. I asked for a receipt.

'No,' she said, and resolutely folded her fleshy arms across her capacious, unyielding chest.

'What? You can't give me a receipt?' I was incredulous. This woman wasn't even offering to *sell* me the paperwork.

'No.' She stared at me steadily, stubbornly. 'No,' she repeated determinedly. 'I can't.'

The landlady's failure to make my sleep-free night a tax-deductible experience wasn't the only thing that aggravated me, though. Some minutes later, as I was loading the panniers onto my bike, she reappeared.

'Did you sleep alone last night?' she asked.

'Of course,' I choked.

Who on earth was she expecting me to have slept with? A hard-hatted pipe layer from the Plaza Mayor? Her own pernickety, light-switch-obsessed husband? Or perhaps I might have had a raunchy, lesbian fling with the ponderous, dribbling woman from the restaurant – though, realistically, it's unlikely I would have made it through to the next morning without being squashed flat.

'Oh,' she said. 'Well in that case it's only twenty-five euros.' And she handed me five euros back.

I cycled off dwelling on the landlady's remarks. I was peeved by her comments and resentful about the poor facilities, not to mention her refusal to supply a receipt. Still, there was no point in raising my voice, in waving the super-strength Kryptonite bike lock threateningly over her head. I was above all that now. I could deal with my anger, and channel it into a sweeter, more calculated revenge. So here goes.

Note to the Inland Revenue Department of Spain: I don't think the old witch of Pensión Paz in Trujillo is paying her taxes. To find her, go to the Plaza Mayor and take the left hand turn by the Palacio de la Conquista. She lives a few doors down on the right.

I set off for a second day through the Extremadura country-side, past the occasional aged farmer with his donkey tilling the land and, every now and then, a posse of black-haired pigs. I followed a route down tiny back roads, with hills that rose steeply and fell away again, sending me climbing high before hurtling me down the other side. It was heady, adren-alin-pumping stuff.

'Yeeee-haaa!' I shrieked in the direction of a surprised roadside pig as I plummeted fast and furious down the hill, momentarily forgetting that I was a solitary cyclist and not a wild-west rodeo performer.

This was the countryside in which Spain's great film maker Pedro Almodóvar grew up. Almodóvar's the force behind such Spanish cult masterpieces as *Women on the Verge of a Nervous Breakdown*, *All About My Mother* and *Talk to Her*. He was born in the harsh, dry land of La Mancha but when he was eight years old his family moved to Extremadura, to a village called Madrigalejo about fifty kilometres from Trujillo. Madrigalejo is in the middle of nowhere even by Extremadura's remote standards. Young Pedro was sent to a Catholic boarding school where, he later said, the priests tried to deform his spirit with 'religious tenacity'. Luckily, there was a cinema just down the street to which Pedro used to escape and, no doubt, let his misshapen spirit run amok.

Almodóvar took flight as soon as he could. He moved to Madrid at the age of seventeen and, unable to study film because Franco had closed down the film-making school, he worked for the Spanish phone company and saved his salary to buy a Super 8 camera. The fast-moving Madrid scene suited him better than life in the wilds. He's had nothing but bad words to say about the countryside since.

'The first goal is to get out of there as soon as possible,' he writes in his essay 'Advice on How to Become an Internationally Famous Filmmaker'. 'Catch the dawn "express" to the capital and promise yourself you'll never return . . . Deep down you know that if you ever remember all that, it will be with the sole intention of making an anti-rural film in which you'll talk about food poisoning, varicose veins, obesity and halitosis. These are all characteristics of rural life that are never dealt with in rural films.'

The food did not make me sick; contrary to the vile insinuations of that poisonous proprietress in Trujillo, I didn't find myself close enough to anyone to discover whether or not they suffered from halitosis. And obesity wasn't proving to be one of the greater dangers of my cycling tour: shrivelling away and becoming a skeletal stick was far more of an immediate threat. So I put off heeding Almodóvar's advice for a few days yet. I had a couple more country curiosities to look at before the bright lights of Madrid would beckon.

Towards the end of the day there was one substantial climb to a *puerto;* from there it was all downhill. I simply had to hang on as I flew along a glorious, freewheeling descent through the jagged, rocky countryside all the way to the town of Guadalupe.

Guadalupe has just one claim to fame, and that's its Virgin. (Note the capital 'V'. Apparently there are still just about enough virgins with small 'v's left in Spain to avoid attracting day trippers.) Guadalupe's Virgin is a small, black doll. She was found by a shepherd on the banks of the River Guadalupe seven hundred and something years ago having been hidden there many centuries earlier by Christians fleeing northwards from the Moors. The shepherd named this effigy of the Virgin Mary after the river by which she was found and built a hermitage to shelter her. Not long afterwards, King Alfonso XI decreed that a monastery be built on the site. Monks moved in, pilgrims came and worshipped and Guadalupe's status was established.

The Virgin of Guadalupe's influence was not limited to this part of the world. It was from Extremadura that many of the conquistadors came. Pizarro and Cortés we've already met. Columbus himself was originally from Italy, but he commended his soul to the Virgin of Guadalupe and it was in this monastery that Fernando and Isabel signed the letters ordering Columbus be given his ships and crews. The first two Indians to be brought from America were baptized in the Guadalupe monastery's font, although the European germs didn't suit them and they soon passed on to the big brotherhood in the sky. When the conquistadors arrived in the New World, they built churches for their Virgin, named canyons, mountains and towns after her. Columbus named one of the West Indies' islands after her; there are towns called Guadalupe in Mexico, New Mexico, Texas, California and the Philippines, another Spanish ex-colony. And, of course, they taught the natives to pray to her. Perhaps in recognition of their efforts, in the sixteenth century the Virgin of Guadalupe made quite a journey herself and appeared to a Mexican peasant in a series of apparitions. Her image has been worshipped devoutly – on taxis' dashboards, on tea towels and souvenir mugs, and in thousand upon thousand of churches – ever since.

The monastery at Guadalupe goes to show what a long way a girl can come in seven hundred years. Far from being trodden underfoot in a muddy field and shat upon by sheep and goats, Our Lady of Guadalupe is now a matron of extraordinary wealth. The tour group I joined comprised maybe a hundred people. Most of them were country folk on a Sunday-afternoon outing to take a look at the region's most famous effigy, middle-aged couples who had grown up in Franco's conservative, Catholic Spain with a healthy respect for the church and its trappings. (Franco, not a man known for his tolerance, used the church as a powerful political tool and, while he didn't exactly ban non-Catholic religions outright, he forbade them to be promoted in any way. To help him on what he considered to be his divine mission, the dictator slept with the pickled hand of St Teresa by his bedside every night for nearly forty years, from the Civil War until his death.)

These men and women, then, were taking their visit to the Virgin seriously. They were dressed in their Sunday best, the men in jackets, the women in freshly set perms. We had to queue for quite some time; the anticipation was palpable.

Eventually the imposing wooden doors at the end of the entrance hall swung open. A bossy young man, aged about thirty, with black slicked-back hair and an air of extreme self-satisfaction, herded us into the hallowed cloisters and bolted the door behind us with a resounding thwack. Escape was not an option.

'*Silencio!*' Silence! boomed the bossy man, and the tour began. We shuffled obediently into the first room; the door was locked behind us – think *Prisoner Cell Block H* – and our guide began to lecture us on paintings by Goya, El Greco and Zurbarán, wringing his hands unctuously before him as he spoke. He then granted us a brisk trot round the room to examine the treasures for ourselves before drawing back the bolts and shepherding us imperiously down the cloister.

'Hurry up! Don't loiter!' he commanded as we moved into the music room to be shown glorious frescoes and several hundred vast, richly illustrated, gold-leaved music books that apparently weigh as much as a fully grown person. Two old ladies with perfectly matching orange hair whispered awestruck comments under their breath.

'Be quiet,' chastised our warden. 'Even if you're not interested in what I have to say, at least have the courtesy to allow the others to listen.'

Our next stop was the Virgin's jewellery room. Here lay astonishing quantities of diamonds, rubies, pearls, gold and silver. As recently as 1960 the Franciscan monks of Seville donated a remarkably ornate silver contraption something like a sedan chair on which the Virgin is carried when she goes on walkabout. With my scandalously cynical mind, I couldn't help but wonder whether the money might not have been better spent if it were donated to a hospital.

The climax of the tour, however, was kept for the end. This was the visit to the Virgin herself, an honour so profound that our own, clearly very important guide was not grand enough to take us. Instead we had to wait at the bottom of a staircase. There a friar would meet us and accompany us upstairs where we could 'get to know the Virgin'. We would be allowed right up close, the guide revealed in hushed, awed tones; if we wanted, we could even kiss her mantle.

The friar appeared, a short, plump man with little glasses and a long brown robe with a rope belt. We climbed the stairs behind him, the whispers of the crowd becoming increasingly excited and urgent. We arrived in the Virgin's chamber; she sits on a rotating contraption in a hole in the wall so that she can face either into the church, on the other side of the chamber's walls, or, if her stand is turned, into the room itself. When we arrived, she was facing into the church. All we could see was the back of the contraption, an ornately decorated panel. The friar stood imperially by the Virgin's controls; more people pressed into the room, flesh squeezed against flesh. We waited a little more. Finally, one member of the group could bear it no longer.

'Please,' she whispered breathlessly, 'do you think we could see the Virgin now?'

Deliciously slowly, the friar turned the handle. The contraption began to rotate. The crowd was utterly silent, every eye fixed on the spot where the Virgin would, any moment, appear before us. As she spun into view, the crowd gasped and shuddered. All hands flew in wild, repeated flurries of the sign of the cross. The women's ample bosoms heaved and juddered; one or two even wiped a tear from

265

their eye. From the silence of anticipation rose a wave of impassioned sighs. '*Ay, que preciosa,*' Ah, isn't she beautiful, they moaned as they scrambled forward to bestow frenzied kisses on the mantle.

I was way out of my depth. The Virgin, to the non-converted, was a small, plain, black doll (though, admittedly, her dress was pretty). As the feverish crowd surged towards the statue, my unease grew into fully fledged panic. I was being squeezed, pushed, carried on a wave of human emotion towards an ugly, centuries-old *object*. I had only come to observe; I had no intention whatsoever of kissing a raggedy piece of cloth that had already been touched by millions of slobbering, germ-carrying lips. I wanted out. I struggled against the flow, shoving my way through billowing bottoms and bosoms until I reached the safe, cool staircase and scuttled away.

They played Gregorian chants in the long, high-ceilinged monastery dining room that night, which felt soothing after the excitements of the day. I was staying in the Hospedería del Real Monasterio, a hotel set up around the monastery's Gothic cloister. It cost me only fractionally more than last night's abomination and was considerably more charming with its pretty arched courtyard and tables for an open-air aperitif. For certain, in such hallowed surroundings, nobody would dream of querying my sleeping arrangements. I sat and chewed my pork and chick peas and contemplated the strange events of the day.

I'd been through some stressful times in the last few years, but compared to some of *these* people I was positively laid back. Let's face it, however bad things had been, I hadn't ever drunk alcohol for breakfast. I'd never paid good money to eat pigs' ears. I hadn't permed my hair and dyed it orange, thrown myself in front of a raging bull for fun, crooned Frank Sinatra songs in public, or driven a bus round a mountain switchback hands free. I had never flown into a psychotic rage because it was raining; I hadn't declared that gunfire in the street was 'nothing'. I had never uttered the words, 'Oh yummy, Scotch and Fanta, my favourite.' And I had never, ever wept and shuddered at the sight of a small, black doll.

22

A Castle in Castile

In keeping with my new, elevated sleeping resolutions, tonight I was staying in a castle. First, of course, I had to get there, pedalling through the ups and downs and ups and downs and ups and downs of this temperamental land. At the beginning it was fun to charge helter-skelter down the short, steep hills as fast as the wheels would turn, dodging the donkeys as I went and hoping against hope that the momentum would carry me up the brutal ascent on the other side. After a couple of hours, though, I was exhausted and longing for a stretch of flat. I never did have a very long attention span.

The roads were tiny and deserted though coloured yellow on my map. That's the same grade of road as the freeway I risked life and limb on as I approached Seville. Even when the yellow roads had not treacherously transformed themselves into motorways, they had throughout my trip been main roads boasting a healthy helping of cars and lorries. But this was Extremadura and, funnily, nobody seems to want to come here so the roads are gloriously empty. I had sneakily slipped a cheese sandwich from the monastery breakfast buffet into my pannier – not a very Christian act, I know – and after an hour or two I unwrapped it on the edge of a forest. Sitting on a little mound of soft brown pine needles under the trees, I munched my sandwich amid a relentless tapping. At first, I couldn't work out where the noise was coming from; then I noticed that the tree trunks were perforated with thousands of small holes and hopping vertically up and down them were a number of tiny woodpeckers. To my side a battered old signpost was stuck in the ground: '*Coto Privado de Caza*' it declared – Private Hunting Reserve.

Do the Spanish like hunting? Were Fernando and Isabel Catholic? The Spanish propensity for killing things extends well beyond the bullring. If you thought the British were big on blood sports, stop and consider for a moment that the Spanish Hunting Federation boasts over five hundred thousand members while the biggest shooting association in the UK has only 114,000 among a considerably larger population. Hunting has also matured into a booming tourist industry in Spain, with foreigners arriving by the planeload eager to take a shot at their dinner. Drive along Spain's country roads and you'll see the forests and hillsides emblazoned with signposts declaring an area to be '*coto privado de caza*' or '*coto público de caza*', its public equivalent. It's here that the wild animals – the boar that I was so nervous about high on the mountain pass, the Pyrenean chamois, the Spanish ibex, the Hispanic goats, the partridges, the quail and the hares – roam and breed and sometimes meet a grisly demise at the end of a huntsman's gun.

After mid-October, when the hunting season begins, it's not just the larders of gun-toting folk that acquire that peculiar, hanging-game smell. In rural hunting areas, the restaurants' menus take on a gamey flavour, too. Even if you can't bag yourself a wild boar, you'll almost certainly find partridge and rabbit on the menu most places you go. The flavour of these dishes, which generally come stewed, is invariably excellent, although you may find yourself spending more time spitting out the bones than actually chewing the meat. Still, you can always console yourself with the thought that wild rabbit meat is meant to give you sweet dreams. It's supposed to be particularly effective in the case of loners and merry widows – whoever they may be.

The meat from bulls killed in the bullfight is also considered to be a type of *caza*, or game. Bulls, after all, are wild animals who live virtually free from human contact up until the fateful day of their fight. (When young bulls are moved from field to field, or speared to test whether their spirit is sufficient for the ring, they tend to be approached by men on horseback. The idea is that, if young bulls learn too much about men, they might think ill of them and make the mistake in the ring of charging the torero rather than the cape. The jury is out as to whether or not this would serve the torero right.) But back to the matter of meat. After a bull has bravely or otherwise met his maker, his meat is often sold to local restaurants as *carne de lidia* or bullfighting meat. The chef then whips up a banquet – ragout of bull's tail, sirloin of fighting bull or, if you're really lucky, the greatest delicacy of all, a fighting bull's testicles.

I soon crossed the border into Castilla-La Mancha. With the exception of Toledo, the region's capital, there isn't much in Castilla-La Mancha to attract tourists. This is the dry, desolate expanse of Spain's famous *meseta* and, contrary to Henry Higgins's elocutionary assertions, there's very little rain on the plain in Spain. The words La Mancha come from an Arabic expression meaning 'dry, waterless land'. The *meseta*'s glum stretches of dust and olive groves are punctuated by dull, dreary little towns; buses between them run only about once a day. Pedro Almodóvar was born in La Mancha. He lived in a small town called Calzada de Calatrava before his family moved to Extremadura when he was eight. He later called his native region 'a land so hard there was no understanding of colour'.

Almodóvar may have felt his creativity was stifled here (his mother has now returned to live in Calzada, where her neighbours complain that all the famous filmmaker does is say mean things about the place where he was born), but earlier artists found the harsh landscape inspirational. This was the region of Spain that the intellectuals of the Generation of '98 chose to identify with. They took their name from the year in which Spain lost the last of her colonies following the disastrous war with the USA. The proud, glorious empire was no more. While the rest of Western Europe was steaming, spinning, pumping ahead under the auspices of the Industrial Revolution, Spain creaked along behind.

'Wretched Castile, yesterday the ruler / wrapped in rags and scorning all that it does not know,' wrote the poet Antonio Machado. *Madre de Dios!* Here was a *whole country* on the verge of a nervous breakdown.

Spain lay awake at night, its collective mind racing with the agonies of failure while the country's self-esteem faltered and ground to a halt. Did these exhausted, overwrought Spaniards spike their *gazpacho* with barbiturates as Almodóvar's madcap women would do nearly a century later? They may well have done – barbiturates were popular at the turn of the century in the form of Veronal. The problem was, the chemists hadn't quite perfected the dosage yet and they had a nasty habit of sending people to sleep for a day and a half, which did nothing to improve Spain's productivity. So where, asked the Generation of '98, had Spain gone wrong?

'There is a generation or two of intelligent people. Then comes a political catastrophe, and we have to begin all over again. We are so deeply divided between Catholics and liberals, right wing and left, that one half can never profit by

272

the knowledge and achievements of the other,' wrote Francisco Giner de los Rios, the movement's forerunner.

Focusing on the contrast between Spain's turn-of-the-century demise and past glories, the writers used the landscape of Castile to symbolize the great Spanish virtues – stoicism and energy – which they hoped they could re-invoke to make Spain great again.

They were perhaps also inspired by Castile's numerous castles, themselves towering, indestructible reminders of Christian Spain's powerful past. For the castles that pepper this sparse land are La Mancha's heritage from the Re-conquest. The *meseta*, vast, central and largely flat, played an important role in the Christians' battle to regain Spain from the Moors. The *meseta* was both strategically and symbolically important – it was the central core of a country the Christians hoped to unite under their own flag. To stay in a castle, then, a fortification built to secure the heart of Spain, seemed appropriate for my first night in the region.

I arrived at Oropesa at lunchtime. The palace that adjoins the castle was the ancestral home of the Duke of Alba: it was first built in the fifteenth century by the great-great-etcetera-grandfather of the Duchess of Alba who frolicked with Goya in Sanlúcar de Barrameda and finally lost her feet. The palace is now a *parador*, one of the chain of government-run hotels that promote Spain's cultural heritage. The *paradores* were set up in the 1920s by the short-lived dictator Miguel Primo de Rivera, whose pigeon-perch statue I visited in Jerez. A handful of *paradores* are newly constructed, but most feature buildings of historic interest. The *parador* in Santiago de Compostela is in the old pilgrims' hospital; the Hondarribia *parador* on the French border is a thousand-year-old medieval castle that has played host to dignitaries from Juana la Loca (I don't know whether she had her dead husband's rotting body in tow at this point) to Carlos V and Felipe IV. The *parador* at Granada is an old convent built

273

within the grounds of the Alhambra. Its setting is so glorious that the hotel's generally fully booked six months in advance.

Luckily for me, the *parador* at Oropesa was not as desirable, and I was able to book a room at a mere two days' notice. The man on reception was about five foot tall. He was a garrulous character.

'Ah, you like to cycle,' he began, leaping to this conclusion at the sight of my Lycra-clad, oil-blackened legs. 'When I was younger – I won't say when I was small because I still am . . . ' he squawked with laughter at his own joke, which I had the feeling he had told a few times before, 'I used to cycle every day between my village and the factory in town where I worked. That was about twenty kilometres each way. But then on festival days I had to go even further, to the village where my relatives lived . . . all on my bicycle . . .'

The story continued for quite some time. I smiled and nodded and muttered polite banalities along the lines of, 'My goodness, that *is* a long way,' and wondered when I would be allowed to go to my room. I picked up my panniers.

'No, no, no,' he squeaked, 'that's my job.'

And so we tottered off, the tiny old man stumbling under the weight of my luggage while I carried nothing at all.

The fact that I was able to book a room at such short notice – and, perhaps, the reason the diminutive ex-cyclist on reception had so much spare time to chat – had nothing to do with the hotel, whose rooms are vast and exceedingly comfortable, but was due to the fact that there is not a great deal to do in Oropesa other than wallow in the bathtub or channel-surf on cable TV. Having said this, Somerset Maugham apparently liked the place so much when he came here for lunch that he ended up staying for some time. Maybe Mr Maugham was as weary as I was because that particular Monday afternoon it suited me perfectly to have nothing to do at all. I lay in the great bath until my skin was wrinkled. I then ambled over to the one, tiny shop that was open and bought an obscene quantity of chocolate, crisps, Coke and beer, and retired to a comfy armchair, being careful to position both the TV remote control and the junk food close enough for me not to have to shift so much as a centimetre to reach them whenever the mood should take me.

23

Three Men and a
Cake Shop Lady

The next morning I made an enthusiastic attempt to get my money's worth at the breakfast buffet – bread, cheese, potato omelette, bacon, magdalena cakes, fruit, juice and coffee – beneath the intricate, vaulted Gothic–Mudéjar ceiling in the ancient, imposing dining room. In this very dining room, six hundred years ago, Don Francisco Alvarez of Toledo, Duke of Alba and Count of Oropesa (they were all the same person – one man, many hats) would have eaten his very own bread, cheese and bacon and, no doubt, the odd spit-roasted boar for good measure, being careful not to drip the hot grease on his padded codpiece, for this was the time when they wore such things.

The codpiece came into fashion out of necessity rather than design. In the early fifteenth century, it became trendy for men to wear their tunics short. The problem was that men's hoses in those days had no fly. When tunic hemlines reached the top of the thigh, certain parts of the male anatomy were exposed to view that made the ladies tremble. When really racy men abandoned the tunic altogether and took to going about in just their hose and shirt, something had to be done: the codpiece was born.

Originally, a codpiece was just a fabric flap that covered the offending area. But men in the fifteenth century, just like men today, were most concerned about the size of their members. In no time, they discovered that codpieces could be used to pad out their natural endowment and so enhance their virility in the eyes of the world – or, at the very least, their own self-delusion. By the mid-sixteenth century, the Spanish court was so bursting with virile pride over its prowess in the New World that its codpieces grew quite out of hand, protruding from the noblemen's tunics so long and hard the ladies must surely have quaked in their corsets.

After he'd feasted in this long, vaulted dining room, Don Francisco would perhaps take his codpiece for a walk into the courtyard, and even wander into the adjoining fortifications that guarded the road between Extremadura and Castile during the *Reconquista,* and then during the later battles that ensued between Pedro the Cruel and his half-brother, Enrique the Bastard. The castle's architect incorporated a number of traps for the unsuspecting enemy: if you climb up the keep and try to enter the castle from the bottom door, you can't reach the floor upstairs without exposing yourself to a shower of enemy arrows from the sentry walk outside. Even if the enemy did manage to reach the walk, they'd have to cross a wooden floor, which could be removed in case of attack before they reached the stairs.

Whether the large white rabbit that was lolloping freely around the entrance hall when I arrived also constituted some kind of ancient trap, I couldn't tell. As far as I could see, there were no rabbit holes leading to long passages, tiny doors and bottles labelled 'drink me'. The man on the till – who seemed to be on exceptionally good terms with the rabbit – took note of my cycling shorts.

'Ah, you like to cycle,' he sighed wistfully.

I explained my tour to him. His eyes gleamed; this man too, then, was a closet Lycra case.

'I like to cycle myself, when I can,' he said.

And so I braced myself to listen to yet another Spanish cyclist's tale. This one had cycled last summer from Oropesa up to the Pyrenees. He waxed lyrical about the beauty of the mountains, the herds of semi-wild horses, the rugged Basque coast. He, it transpired, had had a couple of run-ins with rather ferocious dogs, but no close brushes with cantankerous mother pigs.

Eventually, I made good my escape and climbed the stairs where, perhaps, the enemies of centuries past had breathed their last as a flurry of sentries' arrows punctured their vital organs. I poked around turrets and ramparts – for this was a very traditional kind of castle – and imagined the knights of bygone times clattering around in their armour, and scanning the sierra and distant horizon for news.

Today was meant to be a gentle day as far as cycling was concerned. It didn't seem that way. To start with, I miscalculated the distance, and there were many hills. I was beginning to feel tired, and the knowledge that tomorrow I had to cycle my greatest distance yet – 117 kilometres – did nothing to make me feel fresher.

The woman presiding over the bar where I ate my midmorning sandwich was watching a chat show on daytime TV. It was hard to hear the guest clearly because she was trapped inside a vast silver contraption. It looked eerily similar to the suits of armour the knights would have worn all those centuries ago, but this, apparently, was a twenty-first century, all-disaster survival suit.

'So, *señora*, tell me about your suit. How long did it take to build?' asked the presenter, an excessively bouncy woman with unnatural-looking platinum blond hair.

'Yeah, well, it took me about three years.'

'Right . . . and can you tell us what the point is?'

279

'Yeah, well, you see, the world's full of really nasty chemicals and stuff so this suit, it filters the air and removes the poisons from the air I breathe. Also, it can withstand nuclear holocaust. At least, I think it can, but of course I've not really had the chance to test it.'

'So can you move about in your suit?'

'Well, it's quite hard to move because of all the filters and stuff. And eating was quite hard too but now I've devised this really great tube so you can get all your food fine as long as you blend it in the food processor first. It's really good for soups, though.'

'Is it machine-washable?'

'Er, no, in fact, it's best not to wash it at all because, you know, the shell and stuff shouldn't really get wet.'

'So do you think your suits are going to catch on?'

'Yeah, yeah, I think there's going to be a really big demand for them. I've been in the local paper and stuff, and now I'm on TV. I think this just goes to show that people are really concerned about all the dangers that surround us, and because of that they'll all need a suit just like this one.'

Quite, quite mad.

I arrived at Los Navalmorales at about four o'clock. Let there be no mistake: this isn't a place you'll be wanting to come for your holidays. I was staying here only because there was a bed to sleep in, and in this part of the world such luxuries aren't all that easy to come by. I made my way down the dreary, dusty, silent streets, my sense of doom burgeoning. I had to spend sixteen whole hours here, and at least six of them *awake*.

There was not a soul to be seen. Only one or two houses seemed to be inhabited at all; the rest were tightly shuttered. They looked as if they had been that way for some time. My hotel looked grimy and faded from the outside. It sat opposite a squat, characterless building with a cracked and chipped overhanging sign. The word 'Discoteca' would once have been painted in bright blues and reds; now, though, many years of filth coated it. It was beginning to look as if I had made yet another poor choice of lodging.

Things looked up a little inside. I enquired about the noise levels emitted by the *discoteca* at night. The proprietor, Don Miguel, and his waiter – for this was also the only restaurant in town – looked at each other with some confusion.

'*Discoteca?*' they asked, perplexed. And then it dawned on them. 'Oh, that. That's not a *discoteca*. That's just a room for watching TV and playing cards.' This multi-purpose entertainment hovel, it later transpired, was the most happening place in town.

The main light in my room didn't work. When I pointed this out to Don Miguel – perhaps a new bulb would do the trick, I suggested – his eyebrows shot up in surprise.

'Doesn't the little light by the bed work?' he asked.

'Well, yes.'

'Well,' he asked, astonished, 'you're only staying here for one night, aren't you? Won't one light do?'

I apologized for my ridiculously demanding nature, and spent the rest of the evening trying to read by that one dim little light. In the bathroom, the water came out brown even after extensive running of the tap. I was probably the first guest to have come to Los Navalmorales in several months, perhaps years. The lavatory flush was out of order. It looked as if it hadn't worked for some time as the porcelain top to the cistern was missing. When you wanted to flush, you had to stick your hand into the scummy, grey water inside and pull up the lever.

I went out to find a supermarket, and discovered that not only was there no such thing in Los Navalmorales, but it was extraordinarily difficult to find anything to eat at all. In the end, I had to settle for a cake shop. Most of its shelves were despondently empty. I ended up picking some unappetizing,

281

dry-looking biscuits and hoped they'd fill the horribly long gap before dinner. The streets were still deserted. An elderly priest wobbled out of the church. He didn't look very sprightly.

I imagine the priest, the cake shop girl, Don Miguel and the waiter must have been good friends, seeing as they were the only four people alive in town. There must have been considerable pressure on the cake shop girl, I should think, to keep the population of Los Navalmorales going into the next generation. Who would she choose to help her with this weighty task – the hotel proprietor, the waiter, or maybe even the priest?

Theoretically, I suppose, the priest should have been out of the running, but you can never tell. 'Ah, women,' a Spanish priest once sighed to me when I was living in Extremadura. It was about two a.m. on a Sunday and he was doing a tremendous job of integrating with his flock in the town's watering holes. 'Well, you see, the thing with women is that you're not *supposed* to have them – but you can really, because God is very good and he forgives you.'

Dinner started at nine once more. I battled through my starter, for in Spain you seem always to be obliged to eat two courses, then went for the lamb chops with potatoes. At about ten o'clock, the plate arrived: seven lamb chops and six tiny, crisp little chips. I can only assume the Spanish market is very lucrative for Rennies. Either that, or they wash it all down with a Scotch and Fanta digestif. That should be enough to dissolve most things.

As I battled with the half a dead animal on my plate, Don Miguel came over for a chat.

'My goodness, you've been about a bit, haven't you?' he said.

At last! Here was a person who understood the rigours of my trip, who appreciated my achievements.

'Well, yes,' I replied with a smug, smug smile. 'I started in the north, in San Sebastián. Then I cycled over the Pyrenees, to la Seu d'Urgell. The first day was quite hard, and then on the second day I came across this really fierce pig though the piglets were quite sweet. On day three, I cycled from Burguete – that's almost on the French border, you know! – to Ainsa . . .'

And then I trailed off because he had a vacant expression in his eyes.

'No, no,' said Don Miguel gently. 'I didn't mean this trip. I meant from your passport. You've been to Hong Kong! And Vietnam. What's that like? And Cambodia, and Thailand! I saw a programme about Thailand on the TV once. They have elephants there, don't they?'

I explained to him that I'd been living in Hong Kong for the past four years.

'My goodness,' he said again. 'Has it changed much since they took it back from the Americans?'

24

Tilting at Windmills

'You'll be leaving early in the morning, I suppose?' Don Miguel had said to me the night before. How did you guess, *señor*? I was on my bike and out of that hick little town by eight-thirty a.m. I didn't even stop for breakfast. I couldn't; nowhere was open.

This was going to be my longest – and my last – day on the bike. It was 117 kilometres to Consuegra, my destination for the evening. The next morning, I'd be taking the bus up to Toledo and then Madrid, for a final weekend with two friends who were coming out to help me celebrate having survived a thousand miles on a bike.

I cycled for an hour before stopping for breakfast in a town called Navahermosa. There was not so much as an open bar. There was, however, a man selling bananas so I stopped and asked him where I could get a coffee. He looked perplexed.

'Well, there's nowhere round here,' he said. He thought a little longer, then added, 'But if you carry on out of town, I think there might be a little bar at the petrol station.'

There was coffee but no toast. The woman had a few packet pastries; I ate two.

I stopped again at Orgaz, home to yet another impressive

castle and not much else. Sitting at the bar with my sandwich, I found myself explaining my journey to the bartender and her two elderly customers, who were enjoying their mid-morning tipple.

'Aaah. You don't want to go via Los Yébenes,' said the woman, shaking her head with a woeful expression. 'There's a tunnel. You'll never come out of the tunnel alive. Not on a bicycle.'

'Absolutely not,' concurred one of the elderly, flat-capped characters. 'It's almost a kilometre long. I'm sure you're not allowed in there on a bike.' The conversation continued in this vein for a while, the three of them becoming ever more adamant that I was doomed, that I couldn't take the tunnel, that I was damned to staying in awful Orgaz for the rest of time.

'Well, I suppose she could always take the other road,' one of them eventually piped up, after a good ten minutes of debate. 'You know, the one that doesn't go through the tunnel . . .' Which, it turned out, was the road I had been planning to take all along.

I trundled along, being good and sure to turn off the main road before being sucked into the terrible jaws of the black hole that constituted the tunnel's entrance. I climbed up and up, over the top of the hill that the tunnel cut through. As I went, I passed an unhealthy number of stone crosses. At first I imagined these must be memorials to the deceased of particularly gruesome car accidents – an awful lot, I thought, for one small road with no cars. But then I looked closer and found that these were the crosses of the Civil War dead, stones erected in the memory of Nationalist soldiers 'murdered by the reds'.

There were no memorials to the Republican troops killed by the Nationalists, but then there rarely are. Franco was not big on forgiveness. His regime continued to execute large numbers of those who had opposed him well after the Civil

286

War had ended. Many of those who were not shot were sent to labour camps following Franco's assertion that they could be 'redeemed by work'. The prisoners built dams, bridges and irrigation canals. By far the most dramatic result of these labour battalions, though, was the construction of the Valle de los Caídos, the Valley of the Fallen, Franco's monument to his glorious Civil War victory and, subsequently, his mausoleum. It took nearly twenty years and twenty thousand prisoners to dig from solid granite the 850-foot-long basilica and to build the monastery. The cross that tops it all, which can be seen for miles around, weighs 181,620 metric tonnes and is 150 metres high. Its arms are forty-six metres long, and wide enough to cover two saloon cars parked end to end. Franco opened the site on 1 April 1959, twenty years to the day after the end of the war.

'His speech, about the heroism of "our fallen" in defence of "our lines", was triumphant and vengeful. He gloated over the enemy that had been obliged "to bite the dust of defeat" and showed not the slightest trace of desire to see reconciliation between Spaniards,' writes biographer Paul Preston.

The Valle de los Caídos is still open to the public today. It's situated just northwest of Madrid, about ten kilometres from El Escorial, the brainchild of Felipe II (he's the one whose pickled body part collection included 103 heads), who saw his own vast, grey-granite palace as a metaphor for the then blossoming Spanish Empire. That Franco's architectural representation lies just down the road was no accident. The dictator saw the Valle de los Caídos as a symbol of Spain's return to glory, with himself at the helm, the divinely appointed leader of a great crusade. Today, the mausoleum and its surrounding gardens are a popular Sunday-afternoon outing for city-dwellers and their picnics. None of them seems to pay a jot of attention to the triumph and agony that the vast granite cross represents. The Spanish, after all, are a nation that have entered wholeheartedly into their post-dictatorship *pacto del olvido,* the pact of forgetfulness.

From Los Yébenes, I had just twenty-seven kilometres to go to Consuegra. My odometer read 1,600 kilometres. That's 992 miles. Another eight miles and I had achieved my goal. All being well – assuming that in the next twenty-seven kilometres I was not squashed flat by a maniacal lorry driver, spirited into a precipice by a sprightly gust of wind, or munched for lunch by an angry mother pig – I would arrive in an hour or so in Consuegra having cycled 1,627 kilometres, or 1,010 miles. I would be tired but happy; I would drink a celebratory beer before climbing the hill to see the windmills of La Mancha that so fooled Don Quixote, that most quintessentially Spanish of figures. And then, bliss, I would take the bus all the way to the blessed comfort of Toledo's luxurious *parador.*

The last stretch of road was a tiny white line on the map, marked alongside with the green coding reserved only for the most scenic of routes. I had high hopes that those last twenty-seven kilometres would make a fitting close to my journey. They would take me, I reckoned, along a straight, panoramic, traffic-free, perfectly flat road, right into the heart of Spain.

At Los Yébenes, the signs to Consuegra disappeared. After several minutes of wily detective work, I found them again, disguised under shrouds of white plastic. Somebody, it seemed, didn't want me to complete my mission. I pressed on, following the polythene veils regardless. I'd come almost a thousand miles; I wasn't about to allow a mere conspiracy of signposts to beat me now. About a kilometre further on, the plot thickened. The road was barricaded: 'Road closed for construction works. Diversion via Urda,' read the sign.

I debated the matter for about five seconds. This was the

last hour of my cycling odyssey. I'd come a long way in six weeks; I'd been transformed from a flabby nervous wreck to a taut, lean woman in total control. I had picked my way across boulders and fields, I'd scuttled terrified along highway hard shoulders. I'd escaped untidy demise in the jaws of countless fearsome dogs, I'd sprinted in my clippy-clop shoes into the path of motorway traffic. I'd climbed to the top of twenty-five mountain passes and an infinite number of smaller hills; I'd sat in the saddle and pedalled for 105 hours. I had one more to go. I was not going to be distracted from my undertaking by the measly matter of a dug-up road.

I skirted round the barrier. My wishes had, to a certain extent, come true: the road was traffic free, if you discount the JCBs lying silent in their sandpits. It was panoramic as long as I looked only out of the very corner of my eye so as to see the sweeping plains of the *meseta,* and not the heaps of reddish, half-constructed dirt. And, other than the pebbles and carefully landscaped hills of sand, it was relatively flat. For the most part, it was even passable on two wheels, though I did occasionally have to get off and carry the bike over the particularly loose, sinking sand piles. I waved cheerily to the workmen; they looked on with astonishment. And, eventually, there in the distance loomed the windmills, high on the hill above Consuegra. I had made it.

I checked into my hotel, another drab dive in another drab town. I was beginning to grasp why tourists don't come to La Mancha. It wasn't a great spot for celebration: what was I meant to do? Get drunk in my room all alone? Call my mother?

I visited the castle and windmills instead. The windmills, after all, were the reason I'd come here, for La Mancha's greatest claim to fame is its most enchanting eccentric: Don Quixote. The nutty knight-errant has inspired paintings, an

289

opera, cartoons and computer games in the five hundred years since Cervantes penned his adventures. And his most famous mistake was to tilt at the windmills of La Mancha.

' "Look there, friend Sancho Panza, where thirty or more monstrous giants rise up, all of whom I mean to engage in battle and slay," ' proclaimed Don Quixote, spurring his ragged nag Rocinante into battle. ' "Fly not, cowards and vile beings," he shouted, "for a single knight attacks you." A slight breeze at this moment sprang up, and the great vanes began to move . . .'

Cervantes wrote *Don Quixote* in the early seventeenth century, a time of angst and moral decline in Spain (one of many such times, it has to be said). The glories of the sixteenth century, the exploits of the fearless explorers who forged the empire and returned to Spain in ships laden with gold coins and chocolate, were already beginning to fade. 'Unlike the burgeoning middle classes of other countries, here the young dandies were disinterested in commerce, industry, technology and science – all the things that were propelling Europe into a new age. Instead, a sense of fatalism and decadence began to creep over the land,' writes historian Mark Williams.

Enter Don Quixote and cohorts. Quixote is an impoverished nobleman who sets out on a journey to revive the glory of knighthood. Quixote has a perfect conception of courage, honour, pride and goodness – but this ideal world exists entirely inside his head. Of the realities of life, Quixote understands nothing. His uneducated sidekick, Sancho Panza, is Quixote's opposite. He has no lofty ideals; he can't even read. He is cynical and cunning – and able to survive in the world. The novel is a comic satire against the chivalric romance novels that were fashionable at the time, but also reads as a dig at society itself with its overblown self-delusion. 'It was a brilliant parable for a crusading nation that had found itself tilting at windmills, just like the lovable but pathetic knight-errant,' writes Williams. Put the deluded Don Quixote and the earthy Sancho Panza together, and there you have Spain. And so I went to see the windmills, those popular symbols of Spain's glory, of its delusions of grandeur and its painful return to reality, of the proud nobility of its people and the corruption that has eaten them, not just in the seventeenth century, but time and again across the ages.

Consuegra's seven windmills stand high above the town in a line that undulates with the hilltop. They are no longer working, but have been immaculately whitewashed, renovated for the tourists. I arrived as a group of Japanese were parting eagerly with their euros to go inside one of the mills; I followed behind them. We climbed the windmill's perfectly renovated stairs, then stood around and stared at each other in disappointment. We had paid our money for nothing. The windmill was an empty shell.

25

And a Plain,
Black Coffee to Finish

It was *yet another* public holiday. The bus service was skeletal; the first bus to Toledo didn't leave till twenty past one. I seriously debated ditching the bus and riding my bike – Toledo was only sixty-five kilometres away, after all – but I'd promised myself that all that nasty, painful cycling was over. The road to Toledo was a national highway, a dull, monotonous route popular with thundering lorries whose fumes would make me choke, and whose bulk might blast me from the road for good. My bottom was as sore as it ever had been; my legs ached. I just didn't *want* to cycle today.

The man in the hotel bar, where I ate breakfast among the cigarette butts, reckoned there might be a bus at ten o'clock. Deep down, I knew he was wrong. I had checked the timetable, after all. But so eager was I to leave town and hit the city, I decided to chance it. I checked out, loaded the bike and, delusionally optimistic, set off for the bus station. Perhaps there's a little of Quixote in all of us.

The bus station was emphatically closed. It was dark inside; the doors were bolted. The station café had iron grids

293

pulled over the doors; inside, the chairs were upended on the tables. There was not a soul to be seen.

'The next bus leaves at twenty past one,' called the woman in the *churros* kiosk next door when she saw me.

It was now ten past ten. That meant I had three hours and ten minutes to kill in Nowheresville.

I went for a walk, pushing my bike as I went, just to make sure there was no tiny corner, no nook or cranny of town I had missed in my previous forays. There was nothing, just one grey, characterless street after the next. Today, everything was closed for All Saint's Day, but on a working day things wouldn't have been much better. In Consuegra there was little to be seen. There was only a handful of shops – an ironmonger's and, most excitingly, a shop selling balls of wool in *different colours*. (My, what would Pedro Almodóvar have had to say?) Eventually, I happened upon a newsagent that was actually open and, in my panic about how to fill the next three, long hours, I bought enough newspapers and magazines to last many months of internment in a nuclear bunker.

Sitting in a café some minutes later with my small forest's worth of reading matter, a momentous fact dawned on me: nobody else in Consuegra – or any other of these small towns I had been travelling through – had anything to do either. The old couple working in the *churros* kiosk stood there *all day*, even on public holidays, *doing nothing*. The old men in the town squares and bus stations, and sitting motionless on pavement benches, had nothing to do. That was why they were in the bars drinking spirits at eight o'clock in the morning. It probably deadened the pain. The young girl behind the counter in the café where I was sitting was an attractive and cheerful character – what on earth did she make of her life behind a bar in this blot on the face of Planet Earth? Most of the time, she did nothing at all. Occasionally, one of the old men would finish his glass of cheap liqueur

294

and order another, or ask for change for the slot machine, which allowed him a second or two of excitement in his otherwise humdrum life. And these people were going to spend the *rest of their lives* in this leaden, arid town, holding out for a marriage proposal, for a lottery win, for the angel of death.

Even with the inhabitants of the café to entertain me, I was back at the bus station an hour before the bus was due to arrive. I was concerned not to miss it – the next one didn't leave till six-fifteen. The place was now populated by two extraordinarily filthy, smelly men who had passed out on adjoining concrete benches. Every now and then, an unwelcome gust of wind carried their odour towards me – stale alcohol, too many days with no sight of a shower, a week or two without a change of clothes. One of them opened a bloodshot eye as I leaned my bike up against the wall.

'Where you going, *chica*?'

'Toledo. And you?'

'Back to our village.' He paused to let out a loud, rancid burp. 'Been down in Cádiz for a few days. Bit of a party. But, *qué coño*, there are no bloody buses. *Hijos de puta* are all on holiday. *Hostia*, I feel like shit.' And then he put his head back on his rucksack and passed out once more.

The bus eventually appeared at 1:35. Instead of nipping swiftly up the highway, it perversely toured every village I had cycled through yesterday – Urda (the bus driver clearly preferred the conventional, surfaced road), Los Yébenes, Orgaz... We eventually crawled into Toledo some time after three p.m. Before too long, I had a table in a delightful, shady courtyard, and was eating homemade paté and suckling pig. It was a pleasant meal, if you overlook the fact that a bird on one of the leafy boughs overhead shat on my leg midway through the first course.

*   *   *

If Madrid is the modern capital of Spain, a vibrant, vigorous rush of a place, the backdrop of the ultra-colourful films of Almodóvar and a crazy character in itself, Toledo is the country's stony, sombre, historic core. Lying just seventy kilometres to the south of Madrid, Toledo was the capital city for the Romans; the Visigoth king Atanagild followed suit, making Toledo the capital of his kingdom in the sixth century. (The Visigoth kings, incidentally, were fond of funny names. Others were called Witteric, Wamba, Wittiza and Erwig. There was even a King Sisebut.) Toledo was the most important city of central Spain for the Muslims; it was the Christian capital too for nearly five hundred years until Felipe II decided in 1561 that Madrid was a better spot. The city sits loftily on a hill, surrounded on three sides by the natural moat of the winding River Tajo. Above the flowing water, man-made defences tower – the vast, square fortifications of the Alcázar, the hefty turrets of the city walls – barricading the city against modernity.

Toledo, with its Christian, Muslim and Jewish heritage, encapsulates Spain's past just as Madrid's skyscrapers and pulsating streets represent the future. Here in Toledo, they say, Christians, Jews and Moors lived in relative harmony, even after the Christians took the city in 1085. There were eleven synagogues before the Jews were expelled from Toledo, as from the rest of Spain, by the Catholic Monarchs in 1492. The synagogue of Santa María la Blanca blends unmistakably Arab decoration – white horseshoe arches and intricate plasterwork – with the Star of David; it was later converted into a Christian church. A couple of mosques still stand as testament to the Moors who once lived here, their Moorish architecture shaping the Christian frescoes that followed.

It was from Toledo, legend has it, that the Visigoth king Roderick let in the Moors and inflicted – or perhaps bestowed – upon Spain eight hundred years of Muslim rule.

Roderick was besotted by a girl at the royal court named Florinda. One day, as he hid in the bushes and watched the object of his affections bathe in the river, Roderick found himself unable to contain his lust any longer. He leapt out of the bushes and seduced her. Florinda's father, Count Julian, was the governor of Ceuta in North Africa. When he heard about the king's less than majestic behaviour, Count Julian went to the Moors and plotted with them the invasion of Spain. The Visigothic state by this time was so weakened by internal feuds that the Moors had little trouble marching through the country. In no time, they arrived at Toledo, took the capital, and killed the philandering king.

But the Sisebuts and Erwigs, synagogues and fortress were going to have to wait. I had another sartorial emergency. The friends who were coming to meet me in Toledo are a stylish pair. They are tall and skinny and glamorous; when they emerge from fashionable London restaurants, the paparazzi have been known to leap to their feet and whirr, click and flash in their direction for several reels of film before realizing, sheepishly, that Tazim and Peter are not famous and their photos won't help sell copies of *Hello!* magazine. They would arrive in Toledo looking beautiful, of that there was no doubt.

I, on the other hand, had just one set of clothing and, although my new tight trousers still thankfully fitted, my one functional sweatshirt was covered in black oil smears. In my current state, Tazim and Peter would be embarrassed to be seen with me. They would have to saunter elegantly on the opposite side of the road; they would be ashamed to speak to me in public. It was time for another visit to Zara.

Several bulging carrier bags later, I was feeling rather more confident, and I met up with the dashing duo in the *parador* just as I was trying to negotiate express return of my laundry with the chambermaid. We strolled about the historic city with all the elegance we could muster, fighting our own small and bloodless battles with the crowds of holiday-weekend tourists. We visited the cathedral, the mosques and the synagogues, studiously attempting to absorb the unique blend of cultures that our guidebooks assured us was the lifeblood of the city. We studied the guns at the Alcázar, transformed by Franco into a military museum, and listened to the tape of an imitation of Colonel Moscardó on the phone, in many different languages.

Moscardó was a Nationalist commander in the Civil War; he and his men were holding the Alcázar. The Republicans, having failed even to dynamite them out, captured the colonel's son. They then telephoned Moscardó, so the story goes, and told him he had ten minutes to surrender the fortress or his son would be shot. The indomitable Moscardó asked to speak to his son, and then told him unflinchingly: 'My son, commend your soul to God, shout *Viva España*, and die like a hero!' (The historians, always ones to let niggling little facts get in the way of a darn good story, say the tale can't possibly be true as by then all contact with the Alcázar had been cut. Still, the Nationalists liked it because it made them look very brave, and the tourists think it's top.)

We strolled the streets, played swashbuckling games with Toledo swords until the terrified sales assistant begged us to stop, and wondered how we'd smuggle them past the airport security without being battered by a nightstick. We debated the aesthetic benefits of buying a full suit of armour to decorate the patio back home. We guzzled marzipan made by barefoot nuns cloistered in convents as, very peculiarly, marzipan seems to be made all over the Hispanic world. We ate tapas, we drank beer, we ate dinner, we drank wine; we lolled about on the *parador*'s elegant terrace with several bottles of celebratory *cava* and took photos of the panoramic view of the city. At breakfast I astonished everyone by eating five full plates of food.

298

We queued at the Iglesia de Santo Tomé and gazed in appropriate rapture at the great El Greco's *The Burial of the Count of Orgaz*. El Greco lived in Toledo though, as one might surmise from his name, he was born in Greece. He came to Toledo in 1577, shortly after Felipe II had moved the capital to Madrid, in the hope of finding work painting the king's new palace, El Escorial. But El Greco was a little too large for his knickerbockers and the bigwigs didn't like him much. Felipe II rejected his kind offer, but the painter stayed on in Toledo anyway, and passed his time perfecting the point of his spiky little beard and taking on private commissions. Toledo, though, was already sliding into provincial disrepair. The capital had gone, in more senses than one. By the beginning of the seventeenth century, both Toledo and its most famous artist saw their grandeur starting to crumble. Now, nearly five hundred years later, the tourists rule the roost while Toledo's real population dwindles little bit by little bit more. The suburbs are cheaper and more comfortable; the lure of Madrid, with its commerce and higher wages, is just up the road.

And so we went there.

'No,' said the bus driver. '*That* won't fit.'

He glared at my oily bike and its six weeks of encrusted grime. But by now I was an expert. I knew all the tricks. In a trice I had spirited the bike around the other side of the bus and found a whole free luggage compartment. The bus driver glowered, his moustache bristling with indignation.

We arrived in Madrid.

'No,' said the first taxi driver.

'No way,' said the next.

And so we stood and we waited and we smiled in a relaxed, controlled, unruffled way. And in time, when the traffic was sufficiently blocked and we'd been in the way for a minute or two longer than anyone could bear, one of them gave in.

A stout, beaming character came forward and shook my hand.

'Hello,' he said. 'My name is José María. You are in the way. You are blocking all the traffic. You must come in my cab before one of these mad Madrileños becomes any more enraged and beats you round the head with a gigantic chorizo sausage.' Or something like that. And off we shot, through the manic streets of Madrid once more.

The busy, urban world buzzed by. For in the hurly-burly of modern Madrid, there are no toothless old men in flat caps with nothing to do. There are no unlikely wildlife encounters, no dead hours to kill before dinner is served. The landladies of Madrid don't ask you if you slept alone; the hotel proprietors don't gawp in astonishment at your passport visa stamps. This is a twenty-first-century city, a hip cosmopolitan capital. It's busy, it's ebullient, and sometimes it's rude. There are skyscrapers and suburbs, there's noise and hustle. Even at three in the morning, the streets of Madrid are manic, lively, living, for this is a hotbed of hyper-activity, a city that never sleeps. Just as Toledo quietly, stonily, blends the many elements of Spain's past, Madrid brings together the present. In Madrid there are Basque-style *tascas* and flamenco from the south; there's Iberian ham from the west and *cava* from the east. There are reggae concerts and bullfights, pickpockets and prostitutes, bankers and buskers, cycling fanatics and football fans, towering department stores and offbeat boutiques.

Peter announced rather casually that he knew a great place for breakfast. My goodness, we hadn't even been planning to come here so early in the day! How many other cities in the world can he just turn up in unexpectedly, mutter that he knows a fabulous spot for breakfast, and amble off there as if he were on his home stretch in south London? How cosmopolitan can a person be? Where would one go for a great breakfast in Lagos? St Petersburg? Cincinnati? I've no doubt he'd know.

And so we breakfasted standing up in the whirl of a Madrileño breakfast bar. We elbowed our way to the counter, where the busy city folk bellowed their orders to intimidating men in white coats. I tried my best to holler over the chaos.

'Er, *un café sólo, un café con leche, un café* . . .' How do you say skinny decaf latte in Spanish anyway?

'*Qué?*' The man in the white coat looked a tiny bit cross. '*Venga, señorita, de prisa!*' Come on, woman, hurry up.

We mooched round the Rastro street market, lunched in La Latina and watched the crazy people of Madrid livin' their *vida loca*. But we had to leave them to it, it was time for us to go.

Tazim and Peter hopped – beautifully – into a cab. Their plane left a few hours before mine. I wandered into the Retiro, Madrid's glorious, glamorous park, sat with a plain black coffee and watched the world go by – the elegant ladies, the sandalled tourists, the smooching students.

I'd come a long way in the last few weeks, I thought, and it wasn't just a matter of miles. I could now unclip my cleated shoes from my pedals without falling off my bike, even if I did have a few scars to show for the learning process. I had survived countless face-offs with four-legged beasts and several more with accusatory landladies and lecherous men. I had eaten my way through several pigs, a river's worth of trout and a few fields of potatoes. I'd consumed stews, omelettes, sausages and many, many litres of olive oil. At the end of all that, my waist was three inches smaller.

This cycling business may hurt from time to time, I decided, but it does have its advantages. Admittedly, some of the uphill bits were rather arduous, and carrying the bike over fields and boulders had tried my patience. But, to look on the bright side, I had been able to eat and eat and eat and I hadn't gained a pound. On that note, I realized a whole hour had passed since I'd had lunch.

'*Hay tapas?*' I asked the waiter.

He nodded and smiled and sauntered off to fetch some.

Sources

Spain's Wildlife/Eric Robins, Lookout Publications

The Basque History of the World/Mark Kurlansky, Vintage

Tour de France, Tour de Souffrance/Albert Londres, Le Serpent à Plumes

The Pyrenees/Hilaire Belloc

Homage to Catalonia/George Orwell, Penguin

Barcelona/Robert Hughes, Harvill

The Letters of Private Wheeler/ed. B H Liddell Hart, Windrush Press

Guernica! Guernica! A Study of Journalism, Propaganda and History/Herbert R Southworth, The Regents of the University of California

Franco/Paul Preston, HarperCollins

The Shameful Life of Salvador Dalí/Ian Gibson, Faber & Faber

Life with Picasso/Françoise Gilot and Carlton Lake, Virago

Tales of the Alhambra/Washington Irving, Editorial Everest

South from Granada/Gerald Brenan, Penguin

Lorca: A Dream of Life/Leslie Stainton, Bloomsbury

The Patty Diphusa Stories and Other Writings/Pedro Almodóvar, Faber & Faber

Don Quixote/Miguel de Cervantes

The Story of Spain/Mark Williams, Santana